Life After Divorce

BY TANYA STEWART, ESQ.

The Smart Guide To Life After Divorce - Second Edition

Published by

Smart Guide Publications, Inc.
2517 Deer Chase Drive
Norman, OK 73071
www.smartguidepublications.com

For information, address: Smart Guide Publications, Inc. 2517 Deer Creek Drive, Norman, OK 73071

SMART GUIDE and Design are registered trademarks licensed to Smart Guide Publications, Inc.

International Standard Book Number: 978-1-937636-61-6

Library of Congress Catalog Card Number:
11 12 13 14 15 10 9 8 7 6 5 4 3 2 1

Printed in the United States of America

Cover design: Lorna Llewellyn
Copy Editor: Ruth Strother
Back cover design: Joel Friedlander, Eric Gelb, Deon Seifert
Back cover copy: Eric Gelb, Deon Seifert
Illustrations: James Balkovek
Production: Zoë Lonergan
Indexer: Cory Emberson
Executive Director: Cathy Barker

ACKNOWLEDGMENTS

I would like to thank Ruth Strother, my tireless editor, who worked ceaselessly to ensure the book was accessible to the everyday reader.

And Mary Sue Seymour, my agent, who offered me this wonderful opportunity.

I would like to thank David, my ex-husband (no, really), who helped me demonstrate that divorce can indeed be different from the stress-filled drama that most experience.

I would like to thank the staff at Smart Guides who believed in me while I got this done. And the illustrator, James Balkovek, who did such a marvelous job of bringing the different sections to life with his creations.

I'm grateful for my parents, Evelyn Wade and Raymond Stewart, and my stepmother Yvonne Allen-Stewart, for being such great cheerleaders in my life.

I would like to thank all of the clients who have shared their lives, struggles, and hopes with me. I also would like to thank my mentor in business, Dan Kennedy.

This book was made possible by my beliefs in love and God and choice. Finally, I dedicate this book to the readers who are brave enough to seek help to improve their lives. Find my gift to you in the back of the book! Thank you.

Tanya Stewart

TABLE OF CONTENTS

INTRODUCTION

Was your divorce awful? Did it seem to drag out forever? Did you spend too much money—do you still owe money? Were your days filled with witnesses, depositions, police reports, therapists, and custody battles? Did you have to deal with your ex lying and cheating? And to top it all off, did you have to stand before a judge who didn't like your case? Welcome! *The Smart Guide to Life after Divorce* is written for and dedicated to those whose divorces would be great fodder for a reality show.

Divorce is rampant in the United States. Nearly 50 percent of first marriages end in divorce, with the rate rising for each subsequent marriage. The process of divorce can turn your life upside down. It is exhausting and expensive, and it can be more stressful than grieving the death of a loved one. But if you're reading this book, you're nearing the end of your nightmare; the magic day has arrived, the papers have been signed, and your divorce is final.

So now what? Can you really just go on with life like normal? Can you just skip through your days, whistling a tune, and move on with your life without a care in the world? Not likely. You probably have to start over and rebuild your life, but this time you have less money, less time, little motivation, and a pretty bent and broken spirit.

Now there is a book to help you find your way back to a happy, healthy life. *The Smart Guide to Life after Divorce* gives you advice on such hurdles as raising wounded kids, juggling higher bills, and handling visitations. Read this book and you'll feel better about your newly single life, whether you chose it or not. You will be able to look back at your divorce as the moment you turned the corner toward a brighter future.

The Smart Guide to Life after Divorce offers you practical legal advice fused with support to direct your life and control your stress. Attorney Tanya Stewart shares over a dozen years of legal experience, consulting, and life coaching to guide you to your new life. She uses easy-to-follow instructions, checklists, templates, and much-needed humor to show you how to reduce fear and prevent problems. Relying on her solid planning and stress coaching, you will learn to manage your postdivorce life and move toward new happiness.

PART ONE

Assessing Your Divorce

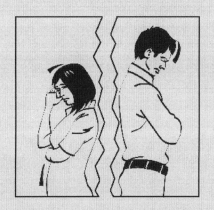

CHAPTER 1

Taking Stock

> ## In This Chapter
>
> ➤ Your financial threat level
> ➤ Emotional stress checklist
> ➤ Health checklist

Your divorce is final. Now you can breathe easy, right? Actually, you will be facing some trying challenges in this new life of yours. A good way to know how to approach these challenges is to sit down and take stock of where you're at right now. This chapter will give you some tools to do just that. It starts with helping you get a clearer picture of your financial status and threat level, and then continues by helping you assess your emotional stress and physical health.

Rating Your Financial Threat Level

Your answers to the Financial Threat Survey (below) will give you a better understanding of the financial challenges you're facing right now. Your answers will give clear indications of just how you're doing financially and how aggressively you need to handle the issue (or crisis!) of your finances.

Financial Threat Survey

1. If you have recently reviewed your credit report, please select the best description of your current credit rating.

a) Terrible
b) Ok
c) Pretty Good

2. In the event of an emergency, like the loss of your job, how long can your current savings maintain necessities in your household?

a) Less than three weeks
b) One to three months
c) Four months or more

3. What best describes your ability to pay basic home utilities each month?

a) I'm unable to pay; utilities have been disconnected
b) I'm able to pay before the cutoff date
c) I'm able to pay on time or slightly before the cutoff date

4. When do you buy groceries for your home?

a) Just when I have the money
b) Every one to three weeks, but I can't buy premium/health foods
c) Whenever I need to; quantity and quality are not an issue

5. What best describes your ability to pay your rent or mortgage each month?

a) I struggle with making the payments; I'm often behind and fear legal consequences
b) I can barely afford the payments, but I make them every month
c) I comfortably afford my payments each month

6. How do you describe your ability to manage and correct your finances?

a) I'm not good with money and need help
b) I am pretty good with finances but have to sit down and figure out how best to start over
c) I am very good with money, but the divorce set me back

7. What best describes your ability to handle the payments for your car?

a) I struggle with making the payments; I'm often behind and fear legal consequences
b) I can barely afford the payments, but I make them every month
c) I comfortably afford my payments each month

8. What best describes your ability to handle the payments for your credit obligations?

a) I struggle with making the payments; I'm often behind and fear legal consequences
b) I can barely afford the payments, but I make them every month
c) I comfortably afford my payments each month

9. In general, I feel _____ about my financial future since my divorce.

a) Alarmed, hopeless
b) Okay, concerned
c) Confident

Tally the items you consider to be a luxury in each of the following groups:

Group A

Your Score: ___/9 total

> ➤ Kids' extracurricular activities
>
> ➤ Internet connection
>
> ➤ Movie rentals
>
> ➤ Dinners out
>
> ➤ Necessary book purchases
>
> ➤ Pets
>
> ➤ Furniture replacement (lost from the divorce)
>
> ➤ A cozy, warm house in winter
>
> ➤ Childcare

Group B

Your Score ___/13 total

> ➤ Basic cable
>
> ➤ Cell phones for children
>
> ➤ Pleasure reading
>
> ➤ Video game system
>
> ➤ Home decorations
>
> ➤ Updated computer/laptop
>
> ➤ Home phone line
>
> ➤ Car insurance for driving teen
>
> ➤ Gourmet coffee by the cup
>
> ➤ Nonessential clothing
>
> ➤ Updated cell phone
>
> ➤ Organic/health foods
>
> ➤ Fast-food meals

Group C

Your Score ____/12 total

➤ Premium cable

➤ Cool house in the summer

➤ Theater tickets

➤ Name brand clothing

➤ Salon/spa services

➤ Annual vacation

➤ Concert tickets

➤ Home entertainment (movies and music)

➤ Housekeeping services

➤ Car washes

➤ Bottled water

➤ Car payments

If your score is highest in Group C, your financial threat level is low. If your score is highest in Group B, your financial threat level is medium. If your score is highest in Group A, your financial threat level is high.

High Financial Threat Level

Your financial threat level is high, which means your divorce has left you in dire financial straits. But don't panic! Take some comfort in knowing that the most likely move for you is up and out of this financial mire. But you're going to need assistance and discipline to get yourself on solid financial ground, and you will need to attack this problem aggressively. I've placed a number of resources to help you learn to manage your money in the Appendix.

Medium Financial Threat Level

Your divorce left you reeling, but it didn't knock you out! Oddly enough, your stress level can be as high as or higher than those with a high threat level. Why? You probably didn't have extreme financial problems before your divorce, so having constant money worries now, without an additional income provided by a spouse for you to fall back on, is a brand-new stressor for you. Most of your problems are not at true emergency level, though, so careful attention to your divorce decree and management of your future financial plans should get you some peace. Don't skip easy sources of help to put a money plan together, especially if you're on the thin edge of okay. The problem with being right on an edge is that it doesn't take much to knock you off.

Handy Tip

You can get help putting a money plan together from banks and other financial planning institutions, but don't overlook the wealth of information you can find free on the Internet. Type key words like "postdivorce financial planning" in the search box and take your pick of the myriad sites offering help and advice.

Low Financial Threat Level

Congratulations! You're sitting pretty: you've survived divorce with a sound financial future intact. Chances are you already have a financial plan in place, and hopefully you can comfortably afford not just the necessities, but some creature comforts too. All the time and energy you don't need to spend worrying about money can be directed to ensure the other parts of your life are stable and growing.

Take Heed

Don't rely on monies you get from your ex as child support, alimony, or property division payments for your financial stability. If your threat level goes up when you remove all of these support payments, then you need to proceed as if you're at a higher threat level.

Determining your financial threat level is important because money issues are one of the biggest obstacles the newly divorced have to get past to rebuild a new life. Pat yourself on the back. Just doing the exercise to know where you are is a great start to getting money to work for you. Your threat level will impact other decisions you'll make as you work through this book.

Taking Inventory

After going through a divorce, it's important to take inventory of what to expect from your ex and where you stand emotionally and physically.

Ex Inventory

Knowing your ex's character is important when it comes to how you interact after your divorce. The following list will help establish your ex's characteristics and make it easier for you to know what to expect from him. Just choose which statements best describe your ex, and his profile will come to light.

> ➤ Must have control no matter what the consequences are; verbally abusive—can get pretty scary

> ➤ Wants to win at any cost; threatened to take the kids just to hurt me and maybe to avoid child support

> ➤ No one will believe me when I explain all the crazy things he has done; he acts so charming in public but is dangerous and capable of anything

> ➤ Is violent—has already hit me or others; damaged property

> ➤ Blows lots of hot air; will keep it up until the bill for bluffing hits, then calms down

> ➤ Will agree to anything

> ➤ Lies continually and is good at it

> ➤ Lies continually and is not good at it

> ➤ Hides money; is self-employed and made the finances a nightmare; will never cooperate on finances

> ➤ Had total control of all the assets so I wouldn't know where to start; kept me in the dark on purpose

> ➤ Is passive-aggressive; acted out to make me file for divorce so it'd be my fault; wanted everybody's sympathy for my "bad" behavior

> ➤ Is very religious

> ➤ Abuses religion to manipulate me and others

> ➤ Money is critical; will do anything to keep costs down

> ➤ Pride is critical; will do anything to avoid the shame or embarrassment of the court system

➤ Isn't bad but is under the control of a third party (family, church, friend) with an agenda

➤ Is a physical danger to the child(ren)

➤ Is a mental danger to the child(ren)

➤ Isn't bad; will fuss some but then will be reasonable

➤ Absolutely refused to agree to the divorce

➤ Needs to be handled gently

➤ Has diagnosed mental health issues

➤ Abuses drugs and/or alcohol or seriously abused them in the past

➤ Acts the martyr or victim

➤ Needed to punish me whether it's for something real or imagined

➤ Used me to fulfill his needs; doesn't like or want to work or handle things fairly

Emotional Stress Inventory

Below is a list of the most common states of mind people find themselves in after their divorce. Circle all the descriptions that describe you and note your personal recommendations.

Which sounds most like you when you're on the phone with your best friend or your lawyer discussing problems after the divorce?

➤ You are relieved that the divorce proceedings are over, confident that it came out well enough, and can laugh at jokes.

Personal recommendation: You are ready to deal with the fallout from your divorce.

➤ You whisper that you needed the divorce, but you're fearful about what to do now that you have it.

Personal recommendation: Build a support system and learn how to handle those who attack your decisions (see Chapter 23).

➤ You're crying because it feels like the beginning of the end; you feel that you betrayed your religion or family and are unsure if the divorce was worth it.

Personal recommendation: Build a support system and learn how to handle those who attack your decisions (see Chapter 23); seek counseling or speak to your clergyperson.

➤ You feel guilty about your mistakes and think you took the easy way out.

Personal recommendation: You were honest with yourself and your ex about your marriage, and being honest is not the easy way out, it's the only way out. It's likely that your ex was unhappy in the marriage too.

➤ You're still shell-shocked; you had no idea your ex wanted a divorce, and you don't have a plan or reaction beyond the hurt.

Personal recommendation: Build a support system and learn how to handle those who attack your decisions (see Chapter 23).

➤ Everyone else was convinced you needed a divorce, but you still aren't sure.

Personal recommendation: When you go through the process of divorce and survive the aftermath without being committed to your decision, the road is so much harder. Figure out your feelings right now and look to the future regardless of whether your divorce was needed or wanted (there is a difference!).

➤ You knew you needed or wanted a divorce but feel let down by the lack of support from others.

Personal recommendation: Build a support system and learn how to handle those who attack your decisions (see Chapter 23).

➤ You didn't want the divorce, you were pressured into it.

Personal recommendation: Most likely your divorce did not require your consent; if one party seeks a divorce, it will eventually be granted. Focus on moving forward and build a support system (see Chapter 23).

➤ You have personal safety issues and don't think the divorce will solve them; you have no more money for legal fees.

Personal recommendation: You must act to protect yourself. Your children must be protected from direct and indirect violence (see Chapters 9 and 20).

➤ You worry you gave up too soon and about the potential spiritual consequences.

Personal recommendation: Seek counseling or speak to your clergyperson; build a support system (see Chapter 23).

➤ You'd feel better to have an expert tell you this will all be worth it.

Personal Recommendation: You will need support to go through this process (see Chapter 23).

➤ You are emotionally exhausted; you gave up everything to get away from your marriage.

Personal recommendation: You will need support to go through this process (see Chapter 23).

➤ Your marriage was long dead; no one was hurt by the divorce but discussions need policing.

Personal recommendation: You are ready to deal with the fallout from your divorce. Work on starting over so you can feel, grow, and love again.

➤ You are still angry over what your ex did or refused to do.

Personal recommendation: You need to sort out your emotions and get your darker feelings under control (see Chapters 3, 7, and 21).

➤ You are completely overwhelmed.

Personal recommendation: You will need support to go through this process (see Chapter 23).

➤ You call lawyers every so often to get advice but get talked out of enforcing the decree.

Personal recommendation: You need to sort out your emotions and get your darker feelings under control (see Chapters 3, 7, and 21).

➤ You want your ex to pay for what he did; it's not right and it's not OK.

Personal recommendation: You need to sort out your emotions and get your darker feelings under control (see Chapters 3, 7, and 21).

➤ You go back and forth between happy and wrecked, it just depends on the day.

Personal recommendation: This is pretty common. You need a good support system (see chapter 23). If you need to go back to court, you need a focused lawyer who will not be swayed by your momentary weaknesses (see Chapter 16).

➤ You are fine, but your kids need help with the fallout of the divorce.

Personal recommendation: Be certain you really are fine, otherwise you cannot give your kids what they need (see Chapters 21 and 22), and build a support group (see Chapter 23).

➤ You were entirely dependent on your ex, and now you have to start all over—it's like a punishment.

Personal recommendation: To help you feel more stable, get yourself on the right emotional track and build a support group (see Chapters 3 and 23).

> ➤ You want a quiet life without fighting or drama.

Personal recommendation: This sounds very reasonable, but taken to an extreme can cause a person to run when she needs to stand her ground. Select a trusted legal advisor for your future; if he advocates fighting, you will know there was no other way (see Chapters 13 and 14).

> ➤ You are scared to go back to court for any reason, even if your ex is wrong.

Personal recommendation: Confront your fears; there are some legal advantages to filing necessary litigation first. Select a trusted legal advisor for your future; if he advocates fighting, you will know there was no other way (see Chapters 13 and 14).

> ➤ You think counseling may help you and your ex get back together.

Personal recommendation: Some relationships are like cars, bananas, and potato salad: once they go bad, there is very little you can do. Figure out how you're feeling right now and look to the future regardless of whether your divorce was needed or wanted.

> ➤ You are worried about your ex's connections, money, or power.

Personal recommendation: See Chapter 14 to learn how to protect yourself.

> ➤ You can't eat, sleep, or work; you're losing weight and blaming yourself, but you know your relationship with your ex can't be fixed.

Personal recommendation: The truest crime is to betray yourself so as not to betray someone else. You are abusing yourself, hurting your body, and weakening your spirit. You need to sort out your emotions and get your darker feelings under control (see Chapters 3, 7, and 21).

For more information on stress and how to overcome it, go to the American Psychological Association web page, www.apa.org/helpcenter/stress.aspx.

Your Physical Health

What is your most valuable possession, one that can never be taken away by your divorce? Your health. Unfortunately, many people take their health for granted when distracted by their failing marriage and the divorce process. Whether you have high blood pressure, are overweight, or suffer from a debilitating disease, you can always improve your health to some extent.

Complete the following health survey as honestly as you can. Choose from these responses for each question.

0 Never or almost never
1 Seldom
2 Occasionally
3 Regularly
4 Often
5 Always

➤ You eat nutritious meals

➤ You get seven to nine hours of sleep each night

➤ You wake up feeling rested

➤ You eat a sufficient breakfast every day

➤ Your snacks are a mix of fruits and packaged snacks

➤ You avoid processed foods

➤ You have one or more bowel movements daily

➤ Your skin is firm, moist, and healthy looking

➤ You exercise at least three times a week

➤ You exercise for at least 30 minutes at a time

➤ You use stress relievers to keep you from getting stressed to your breaking point

➤ You are careful to avoid people who you know stress you unnecessarily

➤ You drink five to ten glasses of water a day

➤ You resist drinking alcohol to excess

➤ When you feel depressed, you talk to someone to help you get over it

➤ You try to solve a physical problem at its source before taking medications

➤ Your immune system works well and fights off illnesses

➤ Your weight and BMI (body mass index) are in the normal range

Divorce Vocab

Body mass index (BMI) is a number that is calculated from a person's weight and height. It's used as an indication of the amount of body fat in a person and can be an alarm for possible weight problems.

➤ If you gain weight, you make changes in your diet and life right away to lose it

➤ If you set out to lose weight, you hit your target weight

➤ You can breathe normally after walking one mile

➤ You make and keep regular dental appointments

➤ You see a dentist if you develop tooth pain or other dental concern

➤ You get your eyes checked regularly

➤ You have infrequent headaches that go away easily with over-the-counter medicine

➤ Your blood pressure is within the normal range for your age and weight

➤ You see your doctor annually for a checkup

➤ You have an annual pap smear and breast exam

➤ You eat one to two pieces of fruit each day

➤ You eat one to three servings of vegetables each day

➤ You consider yourself to have a positive attitude toward your personal health

➤ You share your full family health history with any medical professional who needs it

➤ You avoid smoking and second-hand smoke

➤ Your energy level is sufficient for you to accomplish all you need to do each day

➤ You make efforts to maintain a healthy environment in your home

➤ You consider the atmosphere at work to be healthy

➤ You set health goals for yourself, reach them, and then set new ones

➤ You set aside time each day to unwind

➤ You set aside time for reflection or pursuit of spiritual activities

➤ You surround yourself with other people who are healthy

Tally your score and use the following key to determine your health level:

➤ 0 to 90: Your health level may be poor.

➤ 91 to 140: Your health level is likely average.

➤ 141 and above: Your health level is probably high.

Poor Health Level

A person in poor health has difficulty focusing on or accomplishing anything in day-to-day life. If the survey indicates that your health level is poor, it is important for you to seek the assistance of a doctor or other person in the medical field.

One of the difficulties that results from many divorces is the loss of health insurance. Do not let the challenge of nonexistent or inadequate health coverage keep you from trying to obtain the best quality care and advice you can receive. Do what you can to correct and improve your health as soon as possible.

Average Health Level

Your health level as average, which means you're doing OK. But even though your general state of health is good, you shouldn't dismiss health concerns that may come up now and again. This is the perfect time to increase your level of preventive care so your health doesn't have a chance to reach a critical state. Even without deep pockets or great health insurance you can keep yourself in tip-top shape (see Chapter 8).

Good Health Level

You've been making some good choices. If you come through divorce and your health is in good shape, it's because you've taken the time to make it a priority. Make sure you continue to do so while you deal with the unique problems a newly single person with an ex must face. Being in good health enhances decision-making abilities and emotional flexibility, so you can better enjoy this new life you've fought so hard for.

CHAPTER 2

Challenges of the Newly Divorced

In This Chapter

➤ How to make it on little or no money

➤ Disarming your ex's threats

➤ Five worries regarding children

In most cases, people who have been through a divorce find themselves with a whole new set of fears. If your divorce was rife with conflict, it is likely that your finances are strained and your ex has already begun feeding your fears in an effort to retain control. Even worse, the children's interaction with your ex is likely causing them problems. In this chapter, you will learn how to find money when things are tight, how to disarm your ex's threats, and how to handle five tough kid problems.

Money Matters of the Newly Divorced

The divorce process drains money from most people's accounts, but some find themselves more cleaned out than others. No matter where you are on this continuum, the checklist below will help you identify sources of support you can still tap. You can check more than one box for each source.

Possible Sources of Support	One time	Re-occurring	Check in 3 mo.	Check in 6 mo.	Already declined	Need to investigate
Salary from income						
Child or spousal support						
Loan from bank						
Loan from credit card(s)						
Loan from family/friends						
Sale of house/ land						
Sale of personal items						
Government-funded aid like food stamps						
Shelter aid*						
Religious organizations**						

*May be available only to victims of domestic violence, but check to be sure

**It is not always necessary to be a member of an organization to seek assistance

Monthly Expenses

Before developing a financial game plan, you need to determine whether you're able to pay unexpected out-of-the-ordinary expenses as well as your monthly bills, or whether you're barely able to keep up with your cost-of-living expenses. If you fall into the former category, you'll have an easier time getting financial assistance. The thinking is that you were handling your finances just fine until your divorce derailed you, and it won't take much to get you back on track.

If you struggle to pay cost-of-living expenses like rent, car payment, car and health insurance, school fees, utilities, and groceries, your situation is more serious—you have an ongoing struggle that needs addressing every month. Lenders are more reluctant to help people in this situation because more than money is needed; an adjustment in how they handle money is required.

If you fall into this latter category, you need to get organized. Here's one way to get started. First, gather these items:

➤ A cleared-off table, desk, counter, or floor space

➤ A notepad or scratch paper and pencil

➤ A calendar

➤ A calculator

➤ A checkbook

➤ Last two months' bank statements

➤ At least two recent pay stubs

➤ All the bills you can lay your hands on (old or not—try to have at least one bill from every creditor you owe money to)

➤ Three shoeboxes, bins, or folders

Now follow these steps for each month:

1. Separate all the month's bills into individual stacks by creditor so each has its own pile. Arrange the bills in date order with the most recent bill on the top.

2. Take your pencil and start filling in Table 2.1 Money Owed. Make additional photocopies of the template if you need more room.

Table 2.1 Money Owed

Name of creditor	Monthly payment	Interest rate	Total amount due	Status: due now	Status: past due	Status: in negotiations	First priority	Second priority	Third priority
Rent/ Mortgage									
Phone									
Electricity									
Gas									
Car payment									
Car insurance									
Health insurance									
Tuition									

3. Use a calculator to add up the numbers so you can clearly see how much you owe.

4. Use your pay stubs to figure out how much money you bring home each month. Be sure to check your most recent stub for any unnecessary deductions, and then cancel them the first chance you get.

Handy Tip

Ideally, you should have a 401(k) contribution automatically deducted from your paycheck, but if canceling that monthly deduction will keep you from losing your utilities, remove it. You can reintroduce the deduction later when you're back on your feet.

5. Subtract the total you owe from your income for the month. If the number is negative, you have to deal with the shortfall. The larger the shortfall, the more radically you will have to act to reverse the problem.

Divorce Vocab

A shortfall is a failure to meet a requirement, goal, or expectation: a shortage. This term is often used in financial contexts and can also refer to the amount of the shortage. When you don't have enough money to pay your bills, your income is not meeting your needs. You're dealing with a shortfall.

6. Now subtract the total of your first-priority bills from the income you brought home that month. Hopefully, you are still in the positive or at least come out even. If you've been able to pay your first-priority bills or even have a little left over, you can hold your own. If you have some money left over after your first-priority bills have been paid, start tackling your second-priority bills.

If, for example, you run out of money halfway through paying your second-priority bills, you may want to consider alternating payments to your second-priority creditors by paying half of the creditors one month and the other half the following month. Or you could pay 50 percent of each second-priority creditor's bills each month. It won't be the right amount, but it will show that you are trying to pay.

Take Heed

Many creditors charge an interest rate if a bill isn't paid in full each month, which can make your financial responsibilities more than expected. To avoid any unpleasant surprises, be sure you figure in interest charges for each month. Keep in mind that depending on the creditor you may be able to shop around for a lower interest rate.

If your income does not cover your first-priority bills, you must seek out a financial wiz to help you figure out a way to meet your obligations. This wiz could be a friend or family member, or a professional financial planner.

Becoming more financially savvy yourself is a good step in the right direction. Look into the slew of free financial advice and planning software that can be found on the Internet. Just search for "free financial planning" or some other combination of key words, and you'll have your pick. Keep your eyes and ears open for free seminars and clinics put on by the government or a nonprofit organization as well.

When first-priority bills can't be paid, something radical usually has to be done along the lines of getting a new job with higher pay, taking on a second job, moving to a less-expensive home, surrendering a car with high car payments (where there are high car payments, there is usually high car insurance!), filing for a modification of your support order (if legally permissible), or getting a roommate. None of those solutions make anyone happy, but continuing to live under the shadow of being unable to pay the most necessary bills each month is even less appealing.

This is often when panic and resistance sets in. It may be hard to imagine, but the stress of trying (and failing) to maintain a large house in a great neighborhood is worse than the "shame" of moving to a smaller house or an apartment that you can afford.

Ending the monthly struggle, however you have to do it, to cover your first- and second-priority bills is essential. If you have to consider a radical change, be certain that the change will ensure your top two categories of debt are completely covered.

Handy Tip

Do you know any other single parents who are struggling financially? Getting a roommate to share expenses and possibly provide child care assistance is a great financial move.

There are myriad resources available to help you out of crushing debt. Some are better than others, but getting some third-party help is essential. See "Chapter 1: Resources for Learning to Manage Money" in the Appendix for some resources that will help you get on the right path.

What Your Ex Wants You to Fear

These are the most popular threats and accusations that exes have held over the heads of my clients throughout the years:

➤ If you are poor: "I'll take custody of the kids!"

➤ If you don't cooperate enough: "I'll take you to court!"

➤ If you date: "You're a bad parent!"

➤ If the kids aren't always happy: "You're a bad parent!"

➤ If you don't allow visitation beyond the court decree: "You're harming the kids!"

➤ If you have a present or past mental health issue: "I'll take custody of the kids!"

➤ If you can't account for every penny of child support: "You're committing fraud!"

➤ If the ex remarries and you haven't: "I can take custody of the kids!"

➤ If the children are having problems at school: "It's your fault!"

➤ If you can't buy the children what they need: "You're harming the kids!"

➤ If you remarry: "I'll fight you every step of the way!"

➤ If you move: "I'll take custody of the kids!"

➤ If you lose your job: "I'll take custody of the kids!"

➤ If you cause problems: "I'll reduce my support payments!"

➤ If you need extra money for the children: "You can't handle money!"

➤ If your family gets too involved with the children: "I'll take you to court!"

These threats play on your fears and, unfortunately, work rather effectively. The quickest way to determine if these threats can be carried out is to ask a local divorce attorney. You won't have to make too many calls before an attorney will answer the question. Here is a brief look at the threat or accusation, the misunderstanding that can cause you to panic, and an appropriate next step.

Poverty Will Cause You to Lose Custody

No court in the United States will take custody of a child just because a parent is poor. Custody of children has been taken away for failure to feed, groom, obtain and administer medicines, seek necessary medical treatment, maintain utilities, ensure school attendance, and supervise adequately, for instance.

If you are poor, you need to ask yourself how you would handle a court representative showing up at your home unannounced and examining all of those areas listed above as well as your refrigerator and pantry. The state and federal governments offer assistance to those who are extremely poor. It is the worst form of pride to ignore these opportunities and have your children go without. If you are one of the working poor, struggling from check to check but not poor enough to receive aid, make sure you seek financial coaching to help you get out of the situation. It is also a good defense to be able to show the court the plan you are using to address and correct your shortfalls, and the time frame for its completion.

Not Cooperating Will Land You in Court

Whether your ex can take you to court for being uncooperative depends on his wallet. As a practical matter, you can find an attorney to file any kind of case, even if it has no merit. So don't rely on the truth to protect you from lawsuits from angry people. There are easy things you can do to protect yourself here. One of them is to document everything.

I have a client who has to record every call and save every e-mail. Every two years it saves her. If your state does not allow recording someone without direct permission, at least take good notes and keep them. It doesn't require much more than a pen and a new notebook every few months. Try your best to create a trail that identifies when you are

Handy Tip

Be prepared and protect yourself from the financial fallout of going to court by opening a savings account, preferably one that earns interest, earmarked specifically for lawsuits in case one ever comes up. You don't need a lot of money for this; regular deposits of $10 or $20 add up.

cooperating, and list the absurd demands that you refused and why. If you get called into court, your meticulous documentation can turn the tide.

Dating Makes You a Bad Parent

Accusing someone of being a bad parent due to dating is common among the angry exes of the world. These exes are either not dating or have already remarried (Funny how their memory of dating before their remarriages is oddly fuzzy.). However, how frequently you date, the character of your dates, and the manner in which you involve your children can indicate good or bad parenting. I've seen single parents who haven't dated in years in an effort to stay away from any of these possible problems and to appease the angry ex. Read Chapter 4 for advice on dating.

Setting Limits Makes You a Bad Parent

There's a term for children who get everything they want so they'll be happy all the time: *spoiled*. Children who always get what they want or are allowed to do anything they want to do grow up to be narcissistic, antisocial adults with a strong sense of self-entitlement. They will have difficulty interacting with family members, friends, and coworkers. Not setting limits and giving children everything they want isn't doing them any favors.

This accusation is often used by a parent to manipulate the children. The ex tells the little darlings that they should have everything, but they aren't going to because the other parent is selfish. The ex can manipulate the kids to say they want to live with the deep-pocketed parent so they can be happy. If this tactic works, children often realize that the grass isn't greener with the other parent and return to their original home in less than two years.

Handy Tip

No matter how stressed or frustrated you are, seek counseling or intervention by an uninvolved adult whom your child respects before making statements like these to your children:

➤ "If you don't like it you can go live with your father." Many teen custody changes start with those words, usually from mother to daughter.

➤ "Your father doesn't really love you and only wants custody so he can stop paying child support." This is a direct attack on the child's greatest need and personal self-esteem,

Denying Unlimited Visitation Harms the Kids

The ex who likes to show up whenever it's convenient and return the children whenever he gets bored or busy is fond of accusing the other parent of harming the kids by sticking to the legal visitation schedule. The ex's tendency to ignore the schedule results in cancelled plans, the need for emergency child care arrangements, and just plain stress and uncertainty for your whole family.

An ex who is threatening to spend time with the kids only if he can do so willy-nilly is probably looking for an excuse not to show up at all. This kind of ex is inherently unstable and will likely do something to disrupt the children's lives on a major scale. Your best option is to find a counselor for the kids (use the school's counselor if you don't have funds or insurance) before the full storm hits.

If your ex continually violates the visitation decree, you can seek a reduction in his visitation time. You may even get more child support to cover the additional expenses of living with the children most, if not all, of the time.

Mental Health Issues Affect Custody

Many primary parents with depression, ADHD, bipolar disorder, and anxiety are awarded and retain custody. The key factor is whether the mental health issue is being properly addressed and currently controlled. You can be at risk if you've been diagnosed with a mental health disorder and aren't doing what your clinicians have recommended.

Many people have had suicidal thoughts and have even attempted suicide during their marriage, but they retain custody of their children. If your mental health issue predates the divorce, you're in a stronger position. Generally, courts do not want to hear about incidents that happened before they issued the most recent custody order. So your angry ex will have a hard time bringing up your hospitalization in 2005 if you were divorced in 2009, let's say, unless you do something new after the decree or last court order. Then, the ex can try to link the old to the new incidents.

Your best option, then, is to stay mentally healthy or follow your doctor's orders.

Handy Tip

If you have a history of mental health issues, it's a good idea to proactively check in with a mental health worker every so often so that if challenged, you can immediately produce proof of your health-improving activities.

Not Accounting for Child Support Expenditures is Fraud

Many people who pay child support don't know what expenses it covers. Most jurisdictions would consider all of the following to be covered by child support:

➤ Groceries

➤ Car payments

➤ Car insurance

➤ Utilities

➤ Rent or mortgage

➤ Daycare

➤ Child's clothing

➤ Child's activities

➤ Child's gifts

➤ Child's travel

➤ Furniture

Not accounting for all your child support spending is not considered to be fraud. In case you are challenged, it's a good idea to be prepared by keeping records of your expenditures. It doesn't have to be hard or time-consuming. All you need to do is throw the receipts for everything you buy that is even remotely child related into a grocery bag. Change bags every three months, use a marker to label them with the date, and store them in a closet. Now you have a detailed record to back you up in case you're called out on your spending.

Handy Tip

Courts usually don't rule in favor of a stepparent over a biological parent just because the stepparent's schedule is more flexible and available.

The Remarried Ex Can Take Custody from the Single Ex

Courts do not keep changing a child's custody arrangement based on which house looks the prettiest or has a married pair in it. If this were true, custody of children would likely shift every two to three years. Unless the primary parent is doing something to harm the kids, changes are not likely to be made to the custody agreement, no matter how perfect the other parent's home life appears to be.

It's Your Fault the Children Are Having Problems at School

Be careful with this one. It's easy for the more absent parent to blame the children's academic troubles on the primary parent. This argument can succeed, especially if the primary parent is not involved with the school or available when problems arise.

Make sure that you keep appointments with teachers and administrators, and contact your children's teachers individually so they get to know you. Most teachers are e-mail friendly, so even a busy parent can reach out and communicate. These e-mails will also help document your involvement and how you proactively sought for and implemented solutions. Your solutions are not required to work, but you are required to try.

Don't keep using the same discipline when it is obviously not working. Instead, involve your ex, even if you would rather not. This is better for the children and makes it harder for your ex to hold you 100 percent responsible for the children's school problems.

A lot of school problems are caused by the interaction or lack of interaction the children have with the absent parent. The school counselor is an important resource for helping your children, and you will have documentation to protect yourself if you ever need it.

You're Harming the Kids by Not Buying Them What They Need

The assumption is that the word *need* does not apply to health and welfare staples. This taunt is most commonly voiced by the parent who has a significant financial advantage over the other parent.

Don't launch into the stereotypical "I don't make as much money as you do" defense. Instead, send your ex a polite letter asking for additional funds to cover any of the items he believes the children ought to have. By the second letter, the complaints are often put to rest.

It is also good practice to sit down with your children and go over your budget for necessities and discretionary items. If you let the children pick what they want to get with your discretionary budget for them, they are likely to accept the choices and be happy with what they do get.

Your Ex Will Fight Your Plans to Remarry

Your ex is trying to make you fearful of moving on. There are several steps you can take to help this situation.

➤ Have a frank talk with your fiancé. After all it's not just you who will be under attack!

➤ Presuming you have already told them you are going to remarry and they approve, enlist your children's help. There is nothing wrong with telling them (in an age-appropriate manner) that their other parent is feeling sad or lonely or hurt about you remarrying and may not handle it well.

➤ Attempt a frank, businesslike talk with your ex. Make it clear that you're going forward with the marriage and that you would appreciate it if he could be neutral for the sake of the children. Then address some of your ex's fears, which may include concerns about the kids calling your new spouse Dad (they won't), or your new spouse spanking the kids (he won't). Promise to update your ex on wedding details as they happen (like ceremony dates and times—be careful of visitation and holiday rights here; never set your ceremony during your ex's time with the kids.

Your Ex Will Take Custody if You Move

Under the laws of most jurisdictions, your ex won't be allowed to take the children if you move. But your ex can file suit to take the children. This is an important concern to bring up with a local divorce lawyer.

Generally, it is considered unconstitutional for a court to refuse to let a parent move. The question is whether the children can come with you. Tons of factors will be in play in this situation: distance of the move, increased costs of visitation, loss of time and connection with the other parent, reason for the move, wishes of the children. The very first moment you think you want to or have to move, consult a strong family lawyer to get the local details so that you can minimize the legal maneuvering.

Your Ex Gets Custody if You Lose Your Job

This threat is similar to that of losing custody due to poverty. Immediately come up with a one-month, three-month, and six-month plan in case you remain unemployed. Try to explain to your ex that you are working out a plan that will ensure the children's school and necessities will not be interrupted.

If your job loss immediately threatens the safety of your children, you have to make a hard decision. Handing your children over to your ex may be the lesser of all evils. This temporary exchange of custody is best documented by an attorney. At least find the money for that legal work so when the time comes you'll be able to get your children back.

Your Ex Will Reduce Support if You Cause Problems

As a legal matter, the grounds for reducing child support are predominantly financial. The best advice is to look at your support and finances. If your support needs are clearly provable and your "problem causing" is basically not violating the court order, you are likely on solid ground.

Take Heed

It is important to note that the amount of time that children spend with the non-primary parent may be a reason to alter support payments.

You Can't Handle Money if You Need More

No matter how fair a judge tries to be, determining the amount of child support is far from an exact science, and it rarely stretches as far as it is needed. One way you may be able to get your ex to stop complaining is to compile a list of your income and expenses. A lucky few find the other parent steps up aid to the children (usually directly) based on the new knowledge.

Family Over-Involvement with the Children Will Land You in Court

The involvement of your family with your children is not grounds for court action, with a few notable exceptions:

> ➤ If a family member has a known and relatively recent criminal past, especially one that involves crimes against children

> ➤ You are away so much that your children are being raised by a family member

> ➤ You are taking your ex's visitation time and giving it to your family

> ➤ You have a family member who aggressively, verbally or physically, attacks your ex, especially if done in front of the children, and does not respond to requests or orders to stop.

If none of these scenarios describe your situation, you are less likely to get in trouble with a court over your family's love for and time with your children. If you are even close to one of the mentioned exceptions, you need to seek local family lawyer advice.

Kid Conundrums

As we all know, divorce doesn't just affect the ex-spouses; it affects the children as well. And sometimes the children are the biggest casualties. Many factors determine how a child will react to divorce, but there are some common issues that arise among most children of divorce. Here, we give you some useful advice on the five most common conundrums.

Children Don't Want to Visit Your Ex

Many families of divorce struggle with getting the children to visit the other parent. Under most circumstances, the children still have to go. A court order remains in place until it is changed by another court order. The fact that the kids don't want to go does not make any difference. The fact that the kids are teenagers and should have a vote on whether they go does not make a difference. If you have a serious reason to keep your children from going on either a single visitation or a continued visitation, you must obtain an attorney and move to modify your ex's visitation privileges and access.

The Ex Buys Your Children's Love

There's nothing to stop your ex from spending money in an effort to increase favor with your children. Will it work? It may in the short term. But in the long term, children may resent the manipulation.

Usually the best action to take if this is going on with your family is to seek counseling for the children and yourself. It is unlikely you'll be able to get your ex into family counseling unless your order requires him to cooperate in the children's counseling. You should also sit your children down and have an age-appropriate discussion with them about how you love them, how you show your love, and ask them ways in which they feel love from the both of you. Kids are smarter than we want to believe, and they can often put it together when you are not being direct.

Your Ex Moves and the Children are Angry at You

You are the only one around to be mad at and your children trust your love enough to show you anger and defiance. They aren't afraid that you'll leave, so they can take out their pain on you. The other upside to being the emotional punching bag is that your children are not turning to drugs, sex, or violence to release their hurt and frustration. That said, you and your kids will have to learn to redirect that hurt.

If you can't afford counseling for your children, consider checking out www.rainbows.org for help and advice. You can also see a counselor a couple of times to learn how best to handle the matter with your kids. Ask the counselor to recommend a few books on the subject.

Your Ex is Violent with Your Children

You can act to protect your children, but that puts you in danger too, so you need to be careful. If you believe visitations are an outright danger to your children, you can keep them away from your ex. One of the risks of taking this action is that you are liable if the court does not agree with your judgment call, and you can be found in contempt of court.

Take Heed

It is difficult to get a court to react to threats from an ex-spouse. Unfortunately, the ex-spouse has to harm the children, often repeatedly, before the court will be moved to protect them.

The sanctions for contempt can include a mild rebuke, being required to pay your ex's attorney's fees and make up all his missed visitations, and forming the grounds for a petition to modify custody away from you based on your contempt violation. This is a very serious situation, and you must seek experienced legal counsel to help you make the right choice.

Your Ex Dates Openly Around Your Children

A parent can expose their children to people they're dating if their divorce decree does not specifically prohibit it. A morality clause, which you see more frequently in the southern United States, can be added to a decree. This clause excludes either party from having their children in the presence of a party of the opposite sex unrelated by blood or marriage at any time or, more commonly, overnight. Morality clauses are almost always created by negotiation, not judicial decree.

What do you do if your divorce has been finalized without a morality clause? Document all of the incidents you find objectionable. Once you have a list of three to five solid examples, write a letter to your ex explaining your concerns and request your ex to do one of the following:

➤ Talk to the children, if they are mature enough, to find out how they feel about their parent dating

➤ Talk to the children's counselor if they have one, or consult the school counselor to get feedback and advice

➤ Set a date and time with you to discuss what can be done to reduce the impact on the kids

Note I did not say send your ex a letter requesting that he stop dating. Your ex is not likely to honor requests coming from you, and he may even increase the behavior to spite you.

As a last resort and if your ex is in an established relationship, you can try talking to the significant other. If the significant other has children, you stand a better chance of getting some relief by direct communication.

CHAPTER 3

The Emotional Fallout

In This Chapter

➤ Dealing with losses

➤ Controlling your worries

➤ Drug and alcohol abuse

➤ Negative emotions

Divorce is rife with feelings of grief, loss, and anger. These emotions can be overwhelming at times, but they are not insurmountable. It's important to stay in control and keep your losses and worries in perspective. The first step is to recognize your emotional turmoil. Then you can address ways to overcome it.

Coming to Terms with Material Loss

People experience two kinds of losses after a divorce: loss of items with monetary value, and loss of those with sentimental value. We'll start with the material losses because it's easier to get your arms around.

Fill out template 3.1 below. Be sure to note both the purchase value and the fair market value (fmv) of the items lost in the divorce.

Template 3.1 Material Loss

Expensive Items Lost	What It Cost (Purchase Price)	What It's Worth Now (FMV)	Total

Divorce Vocab

Fair market value is what the item is currently worth in its used condition. Refer to books or websites such as www.usedprice.com to help you determine the fair market value of used items.

When you are done, subtract the fair market value of the items you were able to keep, if any. You should now have a number that represents the amount you lost through items that are no longer yours as a result of your divorce. Write this number in all the blanks below and then read the paragraph out loud.

He took $_____ from me by taking things that I liked, loved, needed, and wanted. It was not fair. I am hurt that I have to start over without these things and the value they represent. However, my life is worth more than $_____. If someone came to my door and offered to return the $_____ to me with the condition that I remain miserable, I would say no thank you. If someone offered to return the $_____ and all I had to do was spend _____(how many months you have already spent angry) more months being miserable, I would say no thank you. Each one of the days that I am alive is worth more than this money. I am more than my possessions. If a fire hit my home tomorrow and I had all my pre-divorce possessions, I would not grab them to save them. I am strong enough to recover. People all over the world have recovered from losing everything (Hurricane Katrina, Tsunami in Asia, Tsunami in Japan, Refugees from every conflict great or small). I have more than they do. I have more resources. I have more support. I do not want the $_____ more than I want to go on with my life. I do not want the $_____ more than I want to be happy. I do not want the $_____ more than I want to prove to myself that I can overcome this obstacle. My happiness and well-being are more important than $_____.

Repeat this once a day for the next thirty days and by the end of the month you will find that you view the loss of your possessions differently. Just remind yourself who you are, what is important, and why.

Dealing with the Loss of Sentimental Items

Losing sentimental items is often more difficult than losing those with value. After all, you can replace a favorite trinket, but you can't replace the family heirloom that has been passed down for generations. To help you get over the sadness and disappointment of losing treasured items as a result of your divorce, fill out template 3.2 below. Be sure to write in what each item means to you and why. Then read the following paragraph out loud daily for the next thirty days.

Template 3.2 Treasures Lost

Treasures Lost	Favorite Memory	What I Feared I Lost	Can I Move On?

I lost treasures that were beloved and irreplaceable. They were precious to me because they symbolized my love for others and their love for me. They meant hope and safety to me. These treasures are gone and I cannot get them back, but I will go on. I will find a way to memorialize what they meant to me. I will plant a tree or write a letter or help someone in need. Most importantly, I will let myself heal from this attack. I will stop fighting the closing of this wound. I will smile when I think of my lost treasures because I know that they can never, ever be taken from my heart.

In the end, no matter what you lost or why, you have a choice: do you want to stay mired in your anger and grief, or do you want to use that energy to improve your life from this point on? Strong negative emotions can make you feel as though you have no options, but life is filled with myriad choices and nearly endless possibilities.

Handy Tip

To help you accept the loss of your important possessions you can refer to the many books and websites that can help you rid your life of clutter (see the Appendix). Clutter often builds when we attach emotions to our belongings and have a hard time letting go of them for fear of losing the emotion.

Learn to Control Your Worries

If I had just one nickel for every time I've come up with a solution only to have a panicked client immediately ask, "but what if …," oh the places I could go! Here are the most common what-if fears lawyers, friends, and family hear from divorced folks:

➤ "But what if my ex suddenly quits his job?"

➤ "But what if my ex marries that goofball he's dating?"

➤ "But what if my ex moves?"

➤ "But what if my ex gets fired?"

➤ "But what if my ex takes the kids and runs away?"

➤ "But what if the kids hate visiting my ex?"

➤ "But what if my ex is late with support payments?"

➤ "But what if my ex is lying?"

➤ "But what if my ex is telling the kids to hate me?"

These questions are all pretty serious concerns that seem perfectly valid for a person to focus on. The challenge is limiting these questions to the right time and place.

Many what-if questions are asked before there is even a hint of trouble on the horizon. Worrying before there is anything to worry about is a waste of time and keeps you from moving forward in your life; it saps your energy and can make you seem crazy; it can aggravate and exhaust people within your support system; and, worst of all, it tends to make what you are worrying about actually come true.

What? How does worrying about something make it actually happen? We have all heard the phrase *self-fulfilling prophecy*, which means if you keep focusing on a potential experience, it will occur. This concept is so ingrained in humanity that scholars throughout the centuries have come to the very same conclusion, if by different means. Here are some examples:

➤ Marcus Aurelius (121–180 CE) Roman emperor: "A man's life is what his thoughts make of it."

➤ William James (1842–1910) pragmatist, philosopher: "The greatest discovery of my generation is that human beings can alter their lives by altering their attitudes of mind."

➤ Dr. Norman Vincent Peale (1898–1993) author of *The Power of Positive Thinking*: "If you think in negative terms, you will get negative results. If you think in positive terms, you will achieve positive results."

➤ George Bernard Shaw (1856–1950) author: "People are always blaming their circumstances for what they are. I don't believe in circumstances. The people who get on in this world are the people who get up and look for the circumstances they want, and, if they can't find them, make them."

Self-Fulfilling Prophecy in Action

Let's look at children as a way to better understand how self-fulfilling prophecy works.

You have two children. One you think of as being wonderful, loving, perfect, and a model for all childhood; the other you think of as being the most terrible Dennis-the-Menace kind of child. Both children will respond to your expectations of them.

The child you think of as being all sugar and honey understands your expectations and makes an all-out effort to do more and do better. On top of that, you think so highly of this child that you act with a preconceived bias. For instance, you find your sweetheart has made a mess with paints. Rather than thinking your child purposely "forgot" to clean up, you might imagine that your artist is so creative (a plus) and focused (another plus) on finishing the masterpiece that he simply overlooked putting away the tools and wiping up the spilled paint.

Your little menace also understands your expectations and is almost always in trouble because, after all, there is nothing he can do to please you. You think so poorly of this child that you act with a preconceived bias—you expect trouble from your little monster. Going back to our painting example, rather than seeing your child as acting out of creativity and focus, you see irresponsibility and defiance in this child's mess.

It's not a big leap to understand that your outlook plays a fairly large role in how your future will unfold. Worrying about your ex getting fired, for instance, sends the message that you think your ex is incompetent and likely to lose his job. Even if you don't say this outright, you're communicating the sentiment nonverbally.

Some concerns are so serious that you need to do more than sit back and, well, worry; you need to take action. The concern that your ex might flee with your children is very serious. If this is a real worry, you can't just wring your hands and fret; you need to put some safeguards in place to protect your children. This should alleviate your worries, but you still want to be on guard for any telltale signs.

Handy Tip

Some safeguards to have in place to prepare for the possibility of your ex fleeing with your children include having current photos and fingerprints of your children; teaching the older children how to seek help from police, firefighters, and teachers; and keeping possession of the children's passports. Be sure you know where your ex's out-of-state and out-of-country family live.

Take Heed

The deeper you've buried the pain and the longer you've put off getting help, the harder recovery will be. Don't put it off; get help as soon as you realize you have a problem.

If you're unsure how much your children are at risk from your ex, seek help from an experienced family lawyer, one who has been in practice for at least ten years.

Substance Abuse

Taking a mind-altering substance to feel better psychologically, deal with pain, or otherwise cope or function is a form of self-medication. Instead of seeking medical help, you find ways to mask the problem. All this does is prolong the pain and keep the source of the pain from being treated properly. This is done all the time and doesn't always involve substance abuse.

A toothache is a good example. An infection in the root of your tooth hurts. The gum becomes red and swollen and tender. So you take some pain relievers and apply numbing agents to your gum. You get momentary relief, but you have to keep medicating yourself. As the underlying problem gets worse, the pain gets worse, and you need to increase your home remedy. Eventually, nothing gives you relief, and you are forced to seek immediate surgical intervention to get to the underlying problem, in this case have a root canal.

All of us have endured painful moments in our lives. Those pains are not always right at the surface where we can easily see and address them. They are often down deep, like the root of a tooth. A typical reaction is to avoid and bury pain as a method of pain control. This acts like our home remedies and if it helps, it is often only temporary. When the pain comes back it is stronger. This is when people turn to other outside methods of pain control. Drugs, alcohol, food, sex, exercise, work, and even religion have all been used and abused as an escape no matter how brief.

Sometimes the line between substance use and substance abuse is a fine one. Ask yourself the following questions. If you answer yes to any of them, it may be time for you to seek help.

➤ Do you feel like you can't stop using drugs or alcohol even if you wanted to?

➤ Do you ever feel bad or guilty about your substance use?

➤ Do you need to use drugs or alcohol to relax or feel better?

➤ Do your friends or family members complain or worry about your substance use?

➤ Do you hide or lie about your substance use?

➤ Have you ever done anything illegal to obtain drugs or alcohol?

➤ Do you spend money on drugs or alcohol that you really can't afford?

➤ Do you ever use more than one recreational drug at a time?

You're not alone if you are self-medicating to try to dull your heartache, misery, or anxiety. The fact that you're seeking help by reading this book means you are strong enough to take the proper steps to address your pain. The first challenge is to admit that you are abusing a substance. If you can do this, you are halfway home. Now you can ask for help. There is no point in trying to deal with an addiction on your own.

Handy Tip

Many excellent organizations and health care facilities are available to help treat all sorts of addictions. You can go either to the Substance Abuse and Mental Health Services Administration's (SAMHSA) website, www.samhsa.gov/index.aspx, or to www.addicted.com to get started.

Custody Fears

Many people are very concerned about seeking help with addiction and what it will do to their custody rights. First, you must and should find a very experienced family lawyer to consult. You'll be protected by attorney-client privilege and don't have to worry about your lawyer turning you in to the police. But also keep in mind that lawyers are bound by law to protect children. If your use is actually endangering your children, the attorney may be required to report you.

In the end, though, it is better for you to get the advice. If you are at all concerned, contact the attorney's office from a blocked number and ask if you may pay for a confidential phone meeting. You would need to send a money order in advance of your appointment.

Seeking Treatment

You are better off seeking treatment, even if your issues get exposed, than waiting for the inevitable: your ex finding out you are not clean and possibly losing your children. The truth is that a lot of people who have had addiction in their past have custody of their children. Everyone respects a person who has faced down her demons. You will need to seek local legal advice, but without exception you have to address the addiction and battle your way back to minimize the impact on custody.

Your Ex's Substance Abuse

Being separated from your ex doesn't put an end to all of the problems you had in your marriage, especially if one of those problems was substance abuse. You have watched your ex's addiction progress, so you know that getting and using his drug of choice has become more and more important to him. What began with a choice turns into a physical and psychological need.

The good news is that drug addiction is treatable; the bad news is if you couldn't get your ex into treatment while married, your odds of doing so are much lower now after the divorce.

With treatment and support, you can counteract the disruptive effects of addiction and regain control of your life. Seriously consider having the family join Alcoholics Anonymous or another 12-step program such as Narcotics Anonymous. These programs hold meetings at various times during the day so there is always one available, and the sponsors have lived the program and can encourage and help you.

Your children can benefit from the programs available for teens, like Alateen, which encourage and help family members to deal with an addict. Just because you are divorced does not mean the drama of dealing with your ex's addiction is over. Without you around, your ex may just spiral out of control faster.

A common reason angry exes end up using drugs is to self-medicate their other mental health issues that have likely gone undiagnosed. It makes them feel better in the short run, but it eventually backfires. The drug only hides the symptoms of their real problems, which come out with a vengeance whenever they are not using.

You can attempt in your next go around in court to have your ex tested. Just as with mental health issues, there is no gold standard test to detect chemical abuse or addiction. If your ex is forced by the court to take a drug test, he may manage to get clean before he gets tested.

If you are wondering if your ex has started using drugs since your breakup, look for some of these warning signs of drug abuse:

➤ Bloodshot eyes or pupils that are larger or smaller than usual

➤ Sudden weight loss or weight gain

➤ Deterioration of physical appearance and personal grooming habits

➤ Unusual smells on breath, body, or clothing

➤ Tremors, slurred speech, or impaired coordination

➤ Drop in attendance at children's activities

➤ Financial problems or unexplained need for money

➤ Secretive or suspicious behaviors

➤ Sudden change in friends, favorite hangouts, and hobbies

➤ Frequent bouts of getting into trouble (fights, accidents, illegal activities)

➤ Unexplained change in personality or attitude

➤ Sudden mood swings, irritability, or angry outbursts

➤ Periods of unusual hyperactivity, agitation, or giddiness

➤ Lack of motivation; appears lethargic or spaced-out

➤ Appears fearful, anxious, or paranoid for no reason

Keep in mind that overcoming advanced addiction is not simply a matter of willpower. Addicts can't stop just because they want to. With long-term use, drugs and alcohol changes the brain and makes quitting cold turkey difficult. Support is essential to the addict's recovery. So if on a rare day, your ex calls to ask for support, be sure you take a deep breath and do what you can. It can make all the difference between failure and recovery.

The Dangers of Negative Emotions

You have grown accustomed to the sadness, the crying, the despair, and the anger. Because it is comfortable you don't want to change it; you don't want to improve it. Changes, even if they're improvements, are uncomfortable. Most people want to take the most comfortable, least stressful path through life. In most cases, this path will accomplish little and will be the slowest path to your goals.

A trait of successful people is their adaptability and acceptance of change. Most people, though, are creatures of comfort and only want things to remain the same. They follow their habits without question or introspection. That's what you're doing if you stay on the roller coaster created by your negative emotions. Do you know what happens if you ride a roller coaster long enough? Either you get sick and get off, or you grow used to it, even comfortable with it, in which case you just keep on riding.

Take Heed

Wallowing in negativity stunts your emotional growth and doesn't allow for change. It's not just you who's affected; you're hurting those who are most important to you: family and friends.

I have practiced long enough to see the effects of a parent mired in the negative emotions surrounding her marriage, divorce, or ex. It's gut-wrenching to witness. It's so hard to change because it has become a bad habit that has been interwoven into the person's life.

The Security of Negativity

Bad habits are hard to break, especially ones we lean on to get through a day. Lingering on negative thoughts is a bad habit that is much like a child's fixation on a toy or security blanket. Examining a different yet similar scenario may bring some of your own actions to light and make it easier to change. Here are the correlations between a child's security blanket and an adult's bad habits:

➤ Child: The child gets so much comfort from the security blanket that it's easier to let the child keep it.

Adult: Being angry at your lot in life, your crazy ex, and anyone silly enough to take your ex's side gets you through the day.

➤ Child: You know a time will come to force the issue, but you put off getting rid of the security blanket once and for all to make today easier.

Adult: When you are honest, you know that you will have to let go of your negativity at some point, but today just never seems to be the day.

> ➤ Child: The security object doesn't seem harmful, but it has negative effects that you don't like to think about.

Adult: At the time it doesn't seem so bad to fall back on your anger and bitterness, but you know that all this dwelling on the past and even on the nastiness of the present can't be good for you.

> ➤ Child: It's kind of scary how the child can go from being just fine to going into a riotous meltdown over the security blanket.

Adult: It's scary how quickly you can just crumple up or explode when something happens to trigger your mood.

> ➤ Child: People around a child in total meltdown over a security blanket become uncomfortable and frustrated that the "crutch" was ever first allowed.

Adult: People around you during one of your meltdowns are uncomfortable. If your divorce isn't recent, your friends are likely to wish they had encouraged you to start moving on sooner.

> ➤ Child: You know the child will be stronger in the future after giving up the security blanket.

Adult: You know that you will be a stronger, better person when you learn to keep you negative emotions in check.

> ➤ Child: You can't make the child calm down, think, or see reason when the security object is threatened.

Adult: You become irrational when your negativity takes over.

> ➤ Child: The child's whole perspective is colored by the presence (good) or absence (bad) of the security blanket.

Adult: Your whole life is colored by your out-of-control emotions, and anyone who tries to loosen your grip on those emotions is bad.

> ➤ Child: The child will become handicapped by holding on to the security blanket while playing a game one-handed.

Adult: You're handicapped by your grudges. You drift away from friends who want you to move on, and you cling to those who let you wallow in unhappiness. You turn down challenges because of the heaviness of your spirit.

> ➤ Child: It can be embarrassing to others to be with a child who has to drag along a security object everywhere.

Adult: Your friends and family are sometimes embarrassed by you because you can't get a grip on yourself. They feel like they are enabling you (they likely are) to stay in a small and frightened place filled with a roller coaster of emotions.

Staying angry is easier in the short run. But your life, your finances, your relationships, your heart will never improve. In fact, the opposite is true.

Everything around you will change and grow, but you will resist. Your children will grow older and their strong negative emotions will fade. Your friends' lives will go on, moving further away from that horrible day, the moment of your betrayal. But you will keep going back over what was, what shouldn't be, and what will never be. You will keep feeding your dark feelings; you have to or they will fade like everyone else's did. To keep feeding them, you will divert your time, your money, your love, your energy, and your very future to their care.

If you are mired in negativity, ask for help. Keep in mind that those who have been slogged down by hatred for a long time can have difficulty finding their way to fresh air without continuous outside support.

Handy Tip

Games aren't won by the defense; they are won by offensive moves. The defense, if it is good, simply holds ground. Be sure your ex doesn't have you on the defensive.

Justified Anger

Some of you are dealing with strong negative emotions because your ex is currently up to no good. You aren't living in the past; your bitterness and anger are directed at the current state of affairs. Aren't you justified in your anger? Don't you have to focus on the "enemy" to protect yourself? Not necessarily.

There are people who live in other countries run by crazy and evil governments, where the oppression is constant. Do you think there are no happy people in these countries? Do you think there are no friendships, no marriages, no birthday celebrations, no pride in a job well done? On the contrary, the people in places like these put more energy into the good things in life. Your ex may still be wreaking havoc, but that doesn't mean you need to put your life on hold and pass up any opportunities for enjoyment.

There is no easy fix, but before anything can get better, you must realize that your life is broken, living in misery hurts you and everyone who loves you, and your evil ex is overjoyed he has such a big effect on you. Don't give in to your ex this way. Consider that the biggest threat to you right now is not your ex; it's the old you stuck in a reaction loop that can be broken.

CHAPTER 4

Dating During and After Your Divorce

In This Chapter

➤ Handling fallout from affairs

➤ Dating dos and don'ts

➤ Healthy dating after your divorce

People who date before their divorce is finalized are considered to be having an affair. And although states do not openly endorse dating among separated parties, it is almost common. Knowing the consequences of your dating decisions is important to your divorce and your future. This chapter covers these hot topics and shows you how to begin a healthy dating life even if you've been out of the dating scene for years.

Types of Affairs

What exactly is an affair? It depends on who you ask. What exactly constitutes an affair is subject to different interpretations in different jurisdictions.

The most common interpretation of the word *affair* is a married person having intercourse with someone other than his spouse. But an affair doesn't necessarily have to involve intercourse. An affair can involve oral sex or even no sex at all. It's definitely going to be important to find out what the court and lawyers in your jurisdiction believe constitutes an affair.

Fantasies

I have observed different levels of affair. The least harmful are fantasies. So, let's assume that you were in a bad or a debilitated marriage and you were having fantasies about someone else. Well, thankfully, you are not going to get into trouble for this one as long as nobody knows you're having these fantasies.

Handy Tip

Do not make the mistake of telling all sorts of people that you are having fantasies about so-and-so. Keep this tidbit to yourself and stay out of trouble.

Emotional Affairs

Emotional affairs are affairs of the heart and mind, not the body. People who enter into emotional affairs are looking for support and understanding, and someone who will listen to them. Often these affairs start out as innocent friendships then escalate to sharing fantasies, fears, hopes, and aspirations. Having an emotional affair during your divorce is just plain dangerous. No matter what you are not doing (being physically intimate), everyone will presume that you are.

Dating During Separation

Dating during a separation is just not a good idea. Most people think they can date if they have separated from their spouse, but in the eyes of the court, this is still considered to be an affair and has consequences.

Be wary of the person you're dating while separated. Given your situation, you're attracting somebody who doesn't mind getting into unfinished messes. Then you have two people whose lives are up in the air creating a lot of drama.

You're also inviting people to mess with your new honey. He can be dragged into divorce proceedings, deposed, subpoenaed throughout the hearings, and investigated by private investigators.

Dating while you're separated gives an especially mean or angry spouse free ammunition to use against you as well. You're throwing a red herring into the process; instead of moving forward toward the resolution of your divorce, your affair has sidetracked the proceedings and put you on the defensive. All this will raise your legal fees as well as delay the conclusion of your divorce. Not fun.

Dating during a separation is somewhat like eating dessert before dinner; I don't recommend it.

Dating During Divorce

Dating during a divorce is messy and considered legally to be cheating as well. Generally, people who cheat also lie, and all sorts of problems go hand-in-hand with lying. A lie is an artificial construct that requires energy to create and maintain. When you lie, you're scheming and you're plotting and you're covering your tracks. The focus and energy that you should be using to get yourself through your divorce is being diverted to keeping up the lie.

Divorce Vocab

To lie is to make an untrue statement with the intent to deceive. People who lie know they are doing wrong and often heap lie upon lie until they've painted themselves into a corner they can't get out of without creating a big mess.

Lying to yourself can be even more harmful than lying to others. For instance, everyone knows you're having an affair, and you know deep down that you're having an affair, but you won't admit it to yourself. Any hope this relationship has in the future is doomed because it started with a lie.

There is a great principle penned by a woman named Leah Arendt: "Do not do what you would undo if caught." You don't want to be in the position of thinking that if you had realized others knew you were having an affair, you wouldn't have acted that way. If you would be alarmed for the judge to know and ashamed to have your kids find out about your affair from their classmates, then you shouldn't stray in the first place.

Take Heed

The divorce rate for people who marry the person they had their affair with is quite high probably because a person who was willing to cheat with you is willing to cheat on you!

Now, most of you are really most concerned about the legal consequences of having an affair. So, we'll dive into those.

The Effect Affairs Have on Custody

The biggest legal consequences of a person dating before or during a divorce revolve around custody. The golden rule if you are going to fight for custody of the children is do not cheat on your spouse.

Cheating on a spouse is a moral decision, and your ability to raise children actually requires some level of morality. Judges take affairs seriously when deciding on who gets custody of the children.

Divorce Vocab

The default when it comes to child custody is for the parents to have joint and equal guardianship over the children. Beyond that, most all the decisions made about custody are done so in the best interest of the children by a judge.

When your ex discovers that you're cheating, he will have a very strong weapon to use against you during custody negotiations. Questions of appropriateness arise such as whether the children are being exposed to the affair and if so to what degree.

Take Heed

If you are already dating someone and going through a custody battle, stop dating immediately! Even if you've been dating somebody but nobody knows about it, stop dating immediately.

It is an absolutely horrible idea to expose your children to the person that you're dating while you are still married. How do you expect a child to figure out right from wrong? You would be unfairly treating your children like adults if you expect them to understand and apply some kind of exception of morals to you. Later, when they are teenagers and start having premarital sex, you'll be wondering where they got that idea from, and all fingers will be pointing at you—especially your ex's.

It's the kiss of death for you to be having an affair during an active custody case.

It doesn't matter what the consequences are of putting an end to your affair. If this person that you're dating is really a valid, strong, upright person, he will wait out your divorce. If your beau is not willing to wait for you to finalize your divorce, then you really shouldn't be dating that person anyway—you're the one who has everything to lose.

The Effect Affairs Have on Alimony

Your affair may impact the amount of alimony you receive from your ex, depending on your jurisdiction. In the state of Georgia, for instance, an affair is an absolute bar to alimony. Even if having affairs isn't taboo in your jurisdiction, I guarantee you it is not going to help your case.

Property division also depends on the jurisdiction. The state of Georgia has what's called equitable property division, which is based on fairness. But what is fair does not necessarily mean a fifty-fifty division of property, which is how community property states like California operate.

The courts can and do consider affairs as a factor in awarding property division in equitable division jurisdictions. So once again, dating is not a good idea when it comes to money division in a divorce.

The Cost of Affairs

The amount of money spent on an affair can also be called into question during a divorce. Some people are smart and don't spend a lot of money on their affairs. But there's always the high roller buying cars and jewelry and cell phones, and paying for apartments, trips, and other goodies. If discovered in the divorce, this expenditure can be awarded back to the divorce pot for division.

Dating during your divorce can also anger or damage your relationship with people in your support group, the people who are standing by you. These supporters may include your parents, brother, and sister; they may include people from your church or other religious organization. Some of these people are likely to turn their backs on you when they find out you've been having an affair.

Hiding an affair can tarnish your credibility legally. People have a tendency to lie about having an affair until there is incontrovertible proof, and then they finally confess. How does the court know you weren't lying about other things?

Once you're caught in a lie, it's hard to prove that you've ever told the truth. Even under oath in a courtroom, saying "Oh, yeah, I lied all day about cheating. But I'm being absolutely 100 percent truthful about my salary" is hard to swallow.

The Proof

What kind of proof would be needed to catch you smack in the middle of an affair? The most common evidence of an affair can be found in e-mails, text messages, and in the old standby, photos. But more exotic evidence pops up from time to time, including such items as underwear, love notes, Valentine's Day cards, Christmas cards, anniversary cards, and pornography and sex toys.

Phone bills are commonly used as evidence these days. People just can't seem to stay off their cell phone with their lover. The number is right there for the whole world to see and it is very easy to figure out whose number goes to whom.

Eyewitnesses can provide proof of an affair when they happen upon you and your lover eating at the IHOP at two o'clock in the morning when you told everyone that you were out of town on business. One of my favorites is a man who took his mistress to church with the children during his Sunday visitation time. Right in the family pew! I don't even know how the service actually proceeded. Everybody in the entire congregation knew what was going on. I never had so many people volunteering to testify!

Handy Tip

A money trail can be a dead giveaway to an affair. Receipts for gifts and trips and from ATMs in the parts of town that you normally never step foot in can be gathered as proof of an affair.

Take Heed

Be aware that your attorney is not going to want proof of infidelity that was acquired by illegal means. Using ill-begotten proof would turn a lawyer into a criminal coconspirator.

Nearly any kind of proof can be used to ferret out an affair and be used against you, but I do tell people to be careful; there is some proof that attorneys cannot receive. We cannot receive proof that was gained by criminal means, which is to say setting a wiretap and giving a lawyer illegally recorded phone conversations is taboo, as are hacked e-mails. A person's privacy can't be illegally invaded to get proof of an affair.

Dating After Divorce

Your divorce is finalized. The papers are signed. You're legally not married anymore. So now you're free and clear to date—or are you? Let's take a look at some important steps you need to take so that you can date successfully.

> ➤ Take your time

> ➤ Maintain your space

> ➤ Train

> ➤ Get a coach

> ➤ Have faith and hope

> ➤ Expect a challenge

> ➤ Establish a review process

Let's take a look at these steps one at a time.

Take Your Time

Anyone who has ever played a sport knows a recovery period is needed after a match or game or competition, no matter what the sport.

People who run a marathon on a Saturday do not run another marathon on the following Sunday.

A divorce is an endurance event. It probably took from several months to over a year for your divorce to be finalized. Take your time; you don't need to jump for every Johnny-come-lately who crooks a finger at you.

Just as with running two races back to back, you can get hurt dating someone right after you've signed the divorce papers. Take your time.

Maintain Your Space

It's important to maintain your space—your physical space—after the divorce. Divorce by its very nature leaves people hurt, sometimes confused, sometimes lonely, and sometimes at loose ends. You need to heal and regain your equilibrium before you settle in with somebody new. The worse your divorce, the longer you may need to maintain that space. Don't move in with someone right away. You need to recover, get back on your feet.

Take the time to get back to your interests. While you were married, your interests likely blended with your spouse's. You had to compromise now and again, and you may have lost sight of who you really are and what you really like to do.

Think about the time before you were married. Did you belong to any groups? Did you have hobbies? You may still be interested in those activities or you may have developed new interests. Get back to what you love to do. If you're feeling lonely or at loose ends, rekindling your interests will give you something to look forward to, a fun way to spend your free time, and maybe even opportunities to meet new people.

Train

After you've regained your sense of self, then you can begin to think about dating again. You'll be strong, confident, relaxed, fun to be with—someone who has a lot to offer a relationship.

When getting back into dating, you need to train. Some people who have just come out of their divorce look for someone who is exactly the opposite of their ex-spouse. That's probably just a knee-jerk reaction. Don't start dating with the goal of finding Mr. Right, and don't hang your hat on the first man you date. Have some fun, meet new people, and don't expect every date to be successful.

Take Heed

Dating a number of people can be fun and exciting. But you need to be prepared for those men who don't keep their word, who aren't truthful or trustworthy, who are only looking for sex, and who see you as easy prey fresh from a divorce. Always be ready to say no. The more you date, the easier that will be.

Think of dating as being like test-driving a car before you buy one. You don't buy the first car you test drive; you shop around to find the car that best suits your needs. When you're dating, you're finding out who suits you best.

The more you train—or date—the better you'll be at discerning who is sincere, who is compatible, and who you really enjoy spending time with.

Get a Coach

A coach is someone who can help you through the postdivorce process. The ideal coach is someone who has been through it all—divorce, dating, and remarriage—and is now in a loving, stable marriage. Second-best is someone who is divorced and dating successfully.

Don't confuse coaching with cheerleading. Cheerleaders are encouraging and keep your spirits up; coaches strategize and advise. A coach helps you learn how to feel comfortable and master some techniques that will help you through the ups and downs of dating. If you can't find someone to fill the role of coach, you can get books on dating after divorce. You can use them to get some tips and tricks.

Take Heed

Don't start dating after your divorce because someone's forcing you to do it. And don't date because you're lonely and you just can't stand it. Don't date if you believe that you will never find a companion—why bother? Wait until you have had more time to recover from your divorce and build up your self-confidence.

Have Faith and Hope

You will be more successful if you approach dating with faith and hope. Going into dating with a negative attitude, feeling as though there is no one out there for you or no one will want you, will sabotage your efforts. People pick up on this aura of negative energy and will either respond in like or move on. People like being around others who are happy, upbeat, and positive people. The Eeyores of this world do not date well.

Handy Tip

Keep in mind that most men are not like your ex. Don't let that fear keep you from dating. You'll be meeting a variety of people through dating, and you'll have both good and bad experiences. You'll learn from these experiences and make some good friends in the process.

Expect a Challenge

Getting back into the dating scene isn't going to be easy. As with anything that's worth achieving, it's going to be challenging. But no one accomplishes anything without making an effort. Those people who take the challenge, swallow their fears, and follow their dreams, are the ones who accomplish what they set out to do.

Sometimes the challenge in dating is getting over disappointments. You will have good experiences and bad experiences; that's part of what makes dating challenging. But if you're prepared for the ups and downs of dating, you'll be better equipped to handle them.

Establish a Review Process

The first thing you need to review before you move on is your marriage. What happened? What went wrong? When did it go off track or was it doomed from the beginning? This deconstruction of your marriage will give you insight, and keep you from repeating your mistakes.

Some questions you need to ask yourself are how did you go from blissful happiness to shameful name calling? What caused the threats and distrust? What drove you crazy? What did your marriage lack? But you also want to look at what you liked about the marriage, what worked.

Now you need to review your dating process. How is it going? Are you meeting interesting people who are also interested in you? Are your dates wanting to spend more time with you, or is the first date generally the last? Are you making the same mistakes over and over again?

Take Heed

Part of your review process is recognizing what you're doing wrong. You could be choosing the wrong type of person to date or you could be accepting disrespectful behavior from people in general. You may not even realize what it is that you want or need. For greatest dating success, include yourself in your review process.

Many women highlight an attribute that really isn't an indication of who they really are. They may really push their sexuality, for instance, and downplay their intellectualism. If you're a bookworm, wearing stiletto heels and a miniskirt may not be the best way to draw your guy. Rather than meeting someone you can discuss books with over coffee, you'll be meeting someone who's interested in the more physical aspects of a relationship.

The same light can be shown on those you choose to date. Do you keep dating the same type of person, but it never works out? If you keep going after the jock, and you're that bookworm, you're probably targeting the wrong type of man for you.

Take a moment to consider whether you're choosing compatible qualities in your mate. If you're not, ask your coach to help you figure out what type of qualities a date should have to make the process more successful.

Process of Elimination

Dating is a process of elimination. Expect that you are going to meet more people who are not right for you than who are. When you need to turn someone down, do it kindly and don't feel bad; instead look at it as being one person closer to finding a man who is right for you.

Keep in mind that the person you're dating is assessing you as well. A date who turns you down or doesn't call you back just feels you're not the right match for him. Now you can go on and get closer to finding that person who is a better match. Experiencing rejecting and rejection without conflict is amazing for your self-esteem.

Handy Tip

Don't get discouraged. There is more than one way to find happiness and more than one person who is right for you.

PART TWO

Recovering from Violence

 Overcoming Violence in Divorces

> ## In This Chapter
>
> ➤ Staying safe
>
> ➤ Teaching your children to stay safe
>
> ➤ Other considerations surrounding domestic violence
>
> ➤ How to identify abuse

If your ex was violent during your divorce, don't expect you'll be safe now simply because the divorce was finalized. In this chapter you'll get advice on how to stay safe and ensure your continued protection and that of your children and pets—yes, pets, too, can be victims of domestic violence. You'll learn how to stay strong against peer pressure from well-intentioned family, friends, and colleagues who may think that you're overacting. And not to be overlooked for its apparent obviousness, you learn ways to identify abuse.

Your Physical Safety

Most important to your physical safety is to be prepared. I can't stress this enough. The moment there is any inkling of potential violence from your ex-spouse put a safety plan into effect. Yes—before any violence occurs. Search the Internet for domestic violence programs and shelters to contact for help with developing this plan. Teach your children what they should do in case of violence, and rehearse your plan until you can put it into action without even thinking. Never tell your ex-spouse about this safety plan, and make sure your children know to keep mum as well.

Take Heed

Keep in mind that most significant injuries and homicides occur when people leave or attempt to leave abusive or violent relationships. Be aware of any changes in your ex-spouse's behavior that could indicate a buildup to a violent incident.

This is a scary time for you. Taking a self-defense course can give you the tools to fight back, if needed, and will build your confidence. As a precaution, keep your car fueled at all times and have an extra set of car keys hidden but easily available for a quick getaway, in case you're pushed to that point. Remember that you're not alone. Reach out to the various organizations that help victims of violence. Search the Internet and compile a list of safe houses, and contact Victim Services in the Solicitor's office to find out about laws and other resources available to you.

Do all of this prior to a crisis, so you will be prepared.

Secure Your Home

One of the first steps in taking action to ensure your safety is to secure your home. Change door and window locks and install safety devices such as extra locks, window bars, outdoor lights, motion detectors, and a security system. Trim all trees and bushes surrounding your house as an additional layer of safety, have a phone in as many rooms as possible, and carry a cell phone with you at all times.

Get the Word Out

It's an old and tired adage, but there is safety in numbers. Let trusted friends and neighbors know of your situation and develop a plan with them for when you need help. Tell neighbors to call the police if they hear any suspicious noises coming from your home.

You can't hide the potential danger of your ex from your children, so teach them how to help. Instruct them not to get involved in the violence, but instead to quickly get away from it and call 911. Let your children as well as their schools and camps know who is authorized to pick them up.

Don't be afraid to talk to the police. If officers come to your house, tell them everything about what just happened and the ongoing troubles you've been having with your ex. Get the officers' names and badge numbers for future reference.

Face to Face with Your Violent Ex-Spouse

What do you do if your ex gains access to your house despite all your preparations and precautions? If you can, get to a room with a door or window so you can escape. Second best is to hole up in a room that locks from the inside and call 911. If neither of these options works for you, turn yourself into a small target. Dive into a corner, curl up into a ball face down, and cover your head with your arms.

What you shouldn't do is flee to a bathroom, closet, or any other small space, where you can be trapped. And try to stay out of rooms that have no windows from which you can escape. Never run to your children, which would put them at greater risk of getting injured.

If you get injured by your ex, get medical attention and be honest about the true cause of your injury. Be sure to take pictures of any injuries and keep a log of every incident so you have accurate documentation.

If your ex approaches you in public, yell fire. More people respond to this alarm than to any other.

Handy Tip

Call 911 or another local emergency number for help as soon as possible. It's a good idea to get the dispatcher's name as well as the names of the officers who respond to your call.

Get a Restraining Order

You may reach a point where it will make sense to get a temporary protective order (TPO), also called a restraining order, to further protect yourself and your children. It's not that difficult. You just go in front of a court and explain the circumstances of your abuse. Usually the court issues a restraining order right at that moment. Later on you'll need to go back to court for the hearing against your ex, and then you'll ask for an extension of your TPO. The most common length of time is six months or one year.

What you need to understand is that a TPO is just a piece of paper, and that piece of paper does not protect you. Yes, you're told to keep it with you and you're given multiple copies, but crazy people are crazy. They don't care about the law. They don't care about a court order. They don't care about the judge. They don't think that they can go to jail. They think that they are above it all and nothing applies to them. They are positive that they can get around any requirement. They just know that somehow they'll always get their way. So even with a TPO, you should always have your guard up.

Take Heed

How does a person get to the point where he feels he can get away with anything? Chances are that throughout his life, people have been coddling him and shielding him from the consequences of his actions. Chances are that you are one of those people. When the abuse started, did you try to explain away his actions, rationalizing them into oblivion? If so, that doesn't mean you're at fault; it means that you need to be aware of this trait, especially when you're in a new relationship, so history isn't repeated.

TPOs are most effective in cases of isolated instances. Why? Because an isolated incident is usually played out by a rational person who finds himself under such tremendous stress that he momentarily loses his mind and does something crazy. After that, his rationality returns. Rational people follow court orders. Rational people follow the law. Rational people don't want to go to jail, so restraining orders work very well for rational people.

TPOs and crazy people are not a great combination. Does that mean that you shouldn't get a TPO? Absolutely not; you should absolutely have one. But the burden is still on you to keep yourself and your children safe. That means you need to be vigilant, making sure that you are not being stalked. Don't go to places where you are particularly vulnerable: it's probably not a good idea for you to go jogging at ten o'clock at night like you normally do. You need to take proactive steps.

Divorce Vocab

A temporary protective order goes by many names. Restraining order, of course, is one pseudonym; others are injunction for protection against domestic violence, and personal protection order (PPO). The personal protection order comes in two flavors: a restraining PPO for victims of domestic violence and a stalking PPO for victims of stalking.

You must also be ruthlessly intolerant of violations of your TPO. I instruct my clients who have a TPO to call the police even if they just see their ex. Chances are your ex is not looking for pleasant conversation with you. You must assume his intentions are bad. There are a lot of people who worry about bothering the police. Don't worry about that. The police work for you; it's their job to protect. It's better to err on the side of safety.

Keep in mind that a TPO is just a warning of the potential for punishment if it's violated. It in itself can't protect you from a crazy person. It's up to you to enforce the order and to keep you and your children safe.

Preparedness

Hopefully you will never need to take advantage of this, but you should always have a getaway bag at the ready filled with important necessities. It's a good idea to make copies of all your necessary documentation to keep with a friend or at a bank for later retrieval. Here is a list of what you will need:

> ➤ Identification for yourself and your children (driver's license, passports, green cards, immigration documents, birth certificates, Social Security cards)

> ➤ Important documents (school and medical records, insurance policies, car titles, mortgage papers, welfare papers and documents, lease or mortgage documents)

> ➤ Court documents (protective orders, divorce decree, custody papers)

> ➤ Supply of prescription medications or a list of the medications and dosages

> ➤ Medical equipment (hearing aids, glasses, contact lenses, dentures)

> ➤ Clothing, toys, and other comfort items for both you and your children

> ➤ Extra set of car, house, and safety deposit box keys

> ➤ Phone numbers and addresses of family, friends, and community resources

> ➤ Money, checkbook, credit cards, jewelry, irreplaceable photos

As you can see there are a lot of important items you will not have time or the presence of mind to grab.

Safety in the Workplace

What's to stop an angry ex from barging into your office with ill-conceived intentions? Not much, and in fact it's not unusual for domestic violence to invade the workplace.

Handy Tip

It's a good idea to vary your schedule to throw off your ex. Use different routes to get to and from work, and vary the time of day when you normally commute.

If you don't think it will affect your job, talk to your manager or employer about your situation. Try to come up with some changes you can make to improve your safety while you're at work. Some of these changes can include:

➤ Transferring to a different desk, department, shift, or work site

➤ Asking your employer to get a restraining order against your ex (this would supplement your restraining order)

➤ Changing your work phone number or extension

➤ Having all your calls go through the receptionist

➤ Keep your home address and telephone number confidential

➤ Keeping the door locked to your office or department

Don't overlook the company's security department, if it has one. Whether or not your employer acquired a restraining order against your ex, register your protective order with the company's security department. Ask if you can post a picture of your ex at the security gate and instruct the guards not to let him into the building. And always have a security guard (or other coworker if a guard isn't available) escort you to your car or to the nearest public transportation stop.

Safety Outside the Home

Your diligence can't take a break just because you're not at home or at work. You need to stay alert to any signs of trouble even as you run errands and just go about your business around town. Don't be predictable. If you have a routine and tend to shop, bank, or go to the dry cleaners on the same day of the week, change your routine. For extra safety, shop at different stores, use a different bank, and find a different dry cleaner to patronize. Try to find other people to give you rides and accompany you while you're running these errands.

Speaking of banks, you have cancelled any bank accounts and credit cards you shared with your ex, right? If not, do so as soon as possible.

Always keep your restraining order and emergency numbers with you, and never leave the house without your cell phone.

Safety at the Courthouse

The courthouse is one place you're sure to run into your ex. Although security guards and law enforcement personnel provide some safety, ultimately you will need to take responsibility for staying safe. If you take the proper precautions, your court appearance will go off without a hitch.

Ask someone to go with you to the hearing so that you won't be alone in the courthouse at any time. If you can, meet your lawyer at the courthouse. Have your court order with you and stand next to the security guard or bailiff until you're called into court.

Do not talk to or even look at your ex or anyone else he has brought for support, including his family. Find a seat in the courtroom that is as far away from your ex as possible. When you're ready to leave, ask an official to keep your ex in the courtroom long enough for you leave safely. And never leave alone. If you think you are being followed, call law enforcement right away.

Keeping Your Children Safe

Children are not always the target of abuse, but they are witnesses and the prospect of abuse looms. It's important that your children know what to do during and between attacks. Sit down with your children during a quiet time and teach them the following:

➤ Never get into the middle of a fight, no matter how much you want to help

➤ Run to safety and call 911; be sure your children know your address and phone number

➤ Stay out of the kitchen

➤ Who to tell at school if they see the abuser

Handy Tip

Give the school administrators and your children a password to use when they are on the phone with you. They should always ask for the password at the beginning of the conversation to verify your identity.

To help ensure your children's safety in school, give the principal or the daycare director a copy of your court order and a photo of your ex. Give them a list of people who are authorized to pick up the children, and make it clear that no one else should take your children without your permission. Stress that they must not give your address or phone number to anyone.

After the Violence

We want to protect our children, but in cases of domestic violence, that may not be entirely possible. It's important for you to talk to your children and help them through this frightening ordeal. Here are some steps you can take:

➤ Stress that abusive behavior is wrong under any circumstance

➤ Show them peaceful ways to manage their anger and solve problems

➤ Reassure them that they are not responsible for the abuse in any way

➤ Tell them over and over again how much you love them and cuddle with them often

➤ Encourage them to talk openly about their feelings with you and any other trusted adult

➤ Seek counseling for your children if they seem to need more help than you can provide

Important Food for Thought

Keep in mind that even if your children are never in the same room when you and your ex are fighting, they know what's going on. They can pick up on the negative energy in the house, they can hear the arguments, they see the lack of respect your ex has toward you.

You are your children's role models. Think of what they're learning about families and relationships. There's a good chance that children of domestic violence grow up to be abusers themselves. But if you handle your situation with self-respect and protect yourself and your children from the abuse, you're teaching your children how to be independent and how to deal with very difficult situations. You're teaching them self-respect as well.

Take Heed

It's not a stretch for someone who abuses his wife and children to abuse his pets. This type of violence is often used as a way to wield power and prove who's in control. It's also used as a way to punish the victim after she's left. That's why it's so important to include your pets in your safety plan.

Domestic Abuse and Pets

Pets aren't immune to domestic violence, and many women won't leave their abusers because they don't want to leave their pets behind. It's imperative that you include your pets in your safety plan. Don't worry about finding housing; many organizations that help victims of domestic violence can refer people to safe housing that will allow pets.

Recognizing Abuse and Your Role

For those of you in the mire of abuse, take a step back and think about this: If it's not okay for your best friend, it's not okay for you. Think about sitting in a coffee shop with your best friend and listening to her telling you about her life of abuse. You'd be horrified—there would be no question. So why aren't you just as horrified by your own story? Abuse is abuse.

And for those of you who have finally extricated yourself from an abusive relationship, don't beat yourself up for all the times that you tried to get away but failed. Focus on your current success and move on from there.

It takes two to tango. By this I mean you, as well as your ex, had a part in this violent relationship. The victim mentality "Oh, woe is me. I was just minding my own business and these horrible things kept happening to me" just doesn't cut it. On some level you bear some responsibility. Those of you who've been enabling your abuser by hiding the abuse, making excuses for the abuse, and allowing the abuse to continue, need to examine the reasons behind your actions. This is not something you can do alone. Get a referral for a counselor from your doctor, a shelter, or other trusted source.

Recognizing the role you played in your violent marriage will help you avoid making the same mistakes in the future.

Men Who are Abused

Women aren't the only ones who suffer abuse at the hands of their spouse; men also can be abused by their spouse. The male ego makes it difficult for a man to admit that his wife is beating him and seek help through support organizations or counseling. But ego should not keep a man from hiring a strong attorney.

I usually recommend female attorneys for men who are abused by their wives. A lot of female abusers are amazing actresses, and female attorneys are better able to see through this ruse than males are. So make sure the guy you know who is suffering abuse gets connected with an experienced female divorce lawyer who has handled cases like this before. She'll be able to guide him and give him the right advice.

The other roadblock that abused men face is that many people don't believe these big, strong men are being abused by their wives. So men need to gather a lot of proof.

If state laws allow you to record conversations, carry a voice-activated digital recorder at all times, even when you're in the bathroom. If you leave the recorder somewhere, it's likely your abuser will steal it, and then you will have lost your evidence.

For a man who's being abused, having recorded evidence can be the difference between going to jail and freedom. It's hard for a judge to dismiss a recording of the wife laughing mockingly, threatening to call the police to tell them that he hit her so he'll go to jail and she'll get the money and the house and the car and the kids.

CHAPTER 6

Healing from Domestic Violence

In This Chapter

➤ Handling your memories and fears

➤ Choosing people you can talk to

➤ Becoming happy

➤ How to open up in new relationships

After going through the turmoil of domestic violence, you're going to have to go through a period of healing. In this chapter, you will learn how to leave your memories and fears behind so you can move forward into the future that you deserve. You will see the importance of surrounding yourself with caring, respectful people who can support and encourage you as you build your new life and learn to live without fear and anxiety. Finally, you will learn how to regain your self-confidence and self-esteem and be ready to embrace healthy new relationships.

Memories and Fears

I am a survivor of domestic violence from a relationship before my marriage. So I know that as long as your memories elicit anger, humiliation, anxiety, and feelings of hopelessness and despair, you haven't yet healed and you're not ready to move on.

In my law firm there is a giant quote on the wall: "Courage is not the absence of fear or despair, but the strength to overcome them." You will need to be courageous during this time so you can face down your fears and expunge your memories. Learn to be kind to yourself and surround yourself with people who will encourage and help you regain your footing. A qualified counselor can help you along this path.

Who You Can Talk To

In some cases, people who have experienced hardships can move on to a successful life. That's not likely to be the case for survivors of domestic violence, who need help rebuilding their confidence and relearning how to get back into the rhythm of everyday life.

You, as a survivor, need to be especially kind and patient with yourself, and you need to find confidants who are kind and patient as well. These sympathetic ears should know the facts and not judge you because of them. They should be proud of you for getting away from the abuse, be on the lookout for other similar abuses you might fall into, and know when to wean you from your self-pity. Above all, they should be available any time you need to talk.

Handy Tip

One of the first healing steps domestic abuse victims need to take is to gain a sense of empowerment. Relearning how to be independent and reconnecting with the support network that existed before the abuse is a good way to start.

There are a number of people you should try to stay away from:

➤ People who don't believe domestic violence is real

➤ People who criticize you

➤ People who make you feel bad

Relearning How to be Happy

Living in violence touches every aspect of daily life. Add going through a divorce to the mix and you don't have much left over to devote to everyday living. Now that the abuse is over and the divorce is finalized, you need to relearn how to live a happy life.

Right now you're probably not the most fun to be with. You probably have a grim outlook and your conversations are probably depressing and bleak. This is only natural. But to get yourself out of this mire of misery, you need to surround yourself with people who have a generally positive outlook, otherwise known as happy people.

The challenge is that positive people do not like spending their time with negative people. You may have already learned this the hard way as your friends withdrew from you over the years of your abuse. Try not to judge anyone who couldn't stand by and watch you get hurt. Sticking by an abused friend can be very frustrating and often makes people feel helpless.

This first step you need to take is to identify some happy people with a positive outlook who you can spend time with. If you can't identify more than one positive person, ask the one you know to help you find others. Then keep your conversations to positive topics and away from your experiences with abuse. Being negative is a habit you're going to have to learn to break.

Putting on a happy face may be difficult at first, and you probably won't be able to keep it up for long periods. So while you're forcing yourself to be happy and carefree, keep your get-togethers short. Meet a friend for a cup of coffee at the neighborhood café rather than plan an evening of cocktails, dinner, and a movie. The more you experience these short bursts of positivity, the easier it will become and the longer you'll be able to sustain this happy state of mind.

Handy Tip

Try to rekindle those friendships you lost during your marriage. When you make that first phone call, explain that you're now divorced and acknowledge that you were difficult to be around when you were married. Let your friends know that you're doing much better now and that you would like to reconnect. If you are comfortable enough with your friends, you can ask them to let you know if you start falling back into negativity. Your friends will like being helpful and they'll feel safe from being pulled back into your gloom and doom.

There will likely be many times that you don't feel happy. Do you hole yourself up in the house? No. You spend time with your positive friends and pretend you're happy. Eventually, the pretense of happiness will become reality. Remember that you are out of practice when it comes to socializing and enjoying yourself. The more you practice being positive, the easier it will become to look on the bright side.

Opening Up to New Relationships

Being reticent about starting new relationships is common among people who have been hurt by others. But not everyone is like the person who hurt you. In fact, most people aren't. Before opening yourself to a new relationship, make sure you've given yourself enough time to work your way back to a functioning level. If you haven't recovered enough from your ordeal, you won't have the upbeat attitude and sensibilities needed to embark on a search for a new partner.

You've determined that you've worked your way through the toughest part of recovery and are ready to stick your neck out and begin dating. Your first step is to form a brand-new friendship with a woman, someone who knows nothing of your past. Seeking a new friendship offers you several benefits:

➤ You get practice meeting new people

➤ You gain confidence that you can meet new people

➤ You see that people want to be around you

➤ You have opportunities to get out of the house

➤ You have something new and positive to focus on

➤ You get a different person's perspectives on life

Divorce Vocab

A platonic relationship is one that does not include romance or sex. You can have a platonic relationship with someone of the same gender as well as of the opposite gender.

Now that you've developed one or two new female friendships, it's time to seek a platonic relationship with a man. Do not seek a friendship with a married man—that's just asking for trouble, something you absolutely do not need. You are not looking for Mr. Right or judging whether this could be the person who can get you over any physical phobias you have. You are not looking for physical attraction. What you are looking for are shared interests, kindness, and availability to having a friendship with you. Opposite sex friendships are trickier than same sex friendships even if you aren't healing from abuse. This opposite sex friendship will give you some of the following benefits:

➤ A level of comfort with being with someone of the opposite sex

➤ Confidence that all relationships are not sexual

➤ Security of being with a nonaggressive man

➤ Practice talking to men again

➤ Fun times

You are looking for only good experiences with a male friend. If your new friend consistently flakes out on you, hit the next button. If he is nice to you but you see him being mean to his family, move on. Use these experiences to learn how to say no and to accept nothing less than the kind, upright person you want invited into your life. There is less pressure in male friendships than in romantic relationships, where you may still be somewhat conditioned to follow your partner's lead, even if it is unhealthy.

Handy Tip

One advantage of having a platonic friendship with a man is that he may have a friend who you may be interested in dating at some point in the future. But don't try your hand at a romantic relationship until you feel a level of mastery with platonic friendships. If you have been dating and it has been a disaster, consider backing up and spending time with platonic friends.

Rebuilding Your Self-Esteem

Right now your self-esteem is probably pretty low. No one can tell you how to believe in yourself again, it just takes time and a build up of positive experiences. Keeping company with positive-minded people, staying in touch with your support group, and continuing work with your counselor will give you the confidence and positive feedback to find your way back to being someone you can be proud of.

Here are some steps using the word *belief* that can help you regain your self-esteem:

Belief

➤ Become skilled

➤ Equip others to reach their goals

➤ Love someone else

➤ Imagine a positive future for yourself

➤ Expand your education

➤ Find a cause

Become Skilled

Consider what you like to do and the skills you already have and determine what activity you'd like to focus on. Do you enjoy working in the kitchen? You could become an amazing baker. If you like football, you could become a fantasy football guru. It doesn't much matter what activity you choose to focus on. What's important is that you choose an activity you're interested in and that requires effort, discipline, and acquiring new skills.

I chose to train for a half marathon (13.1 miles!) after not running for twenty years and having bad knees. I became a great runner! The progression toward my goal empowered me and gave me confidence and renewed belief in myself.

Equip Others to Reach their Goals

Zig Ziglar, an absolute giant in the motivation field, was famous for saying, "You can have everything in life that you want if you will just help enough other people get what they want." This is true! Helping someone who is struggling more than you are will go a long way to making you feel capable and worthwhile. Volunteering at a homeless shelter can renew your sense of purpose and motivate you to accomplish your goals and improve your lot in life.

Love Someone Else

Love is a powerful emotion. Feeling that your attention and affection mean a lot to someone in the world helps you feel better about yourself. Knowing that your love would be missed if it were not there reinforces how important you are.

Handy Tip

It's important to love yourself too. Show how much you care about yourself by living a healthy lifestyle and treating yourself lovingly rather than judgmentally. If you're the type of person who will go out of her way to please others, take the time to go out of your way to please yourself once in a while.

Imagine a Positive Future for Yourself

Imagination is very powerful. All accomplishments begin as ideas, and an idea is nothing more than a creation of the mind, an imagination. Often once something is imagined, it's a short step more to make it a reality. Practice daydreaming about the type of future you would like to have. Once you imagine your future, you can take steps to make it a reality.

A great time to let your imagination loose is right before going to sleep. If you're tense from your day, your imaginings should help you relax, and maybe even make you smile and laugh a little.

Expand Your Education

Learning is growing, and knowledge makes you more flexible to change and new ideas. Expanding your education will give you more confidence and open up doors to new and exciting experiences. Philosopher Sir Francis Bacon coined the phrase "Knowledge is power," and nothing could be truer. Gaining knowledge will help you become more independent, make you a better decision maker, and give you more trust in yourself.

Find a Cause

Finding a cause to get involved with is a good way to boost your confidence and recognize your self-worth. So many wonderful organizations need help promoting their message and accomplishing their goals. With your help, these organizations can make real changes to better our world.

Get involved with a cause you feel passionate about. It can be a political campaign, a human rights group, or animal welfare group—there are thousands to choose from. Throw yourself into your cause. Find out what the organization needs and how best you can contribute to it. It's not necessary for you to help financially; you can address envelopes or man a booth.

Aligning yourself and your efforts with a cause that you believe in is a great way to nurture good feelings for yourself and regain some self-respect as well. Helping your cause succeed is a great way to increase your belief in you.

 # Emotional Abuse During Divorce

> ## In This Chapter
>
> ➤ What is emotional abuse
> ➤ Why you couldn't leave sooner
> ➤ Being blamed by others
> ➤ How to forgive yourself

In this chapter, you'll learn to recognize the signs of emotional abuse and understand why you didn't (or couldn't) leave your ex sooner. The chapter touches upon why others might blame you and think you're nuts when you report the emotional abuse. It then concludes with ways you can forgive yourself.

What Is Emotional Abuse?

A person who verbally controls and dominates his significant other is guilty of emotional abuse. The abuse results in a sort of brainwashing, stripping the victim of confidence, trust in herself, and sense of worth. Constant criticism, verbal berating, manipulation, intimidation, and even never being pleased are all a type of emotional abuse.

Many people who're being emotionally abused feel ashamed, worthless, and that they deserve to be mistreated. An emotional abuse victim believes what her abuser says about her and may defend him to her friends, explaining how hard he works to take care of her. You can see the brainwashing at work here.

Emotional abuse almost always accompanies physical abuse, but it can occur separately. Like physical abuse, emotional abuse is cyclical and follows a pattern:

➤ Buildup of tension

➤ The incident

➤ Apologies and the shifting of blame

➤ A period of quiet and calm

Take Heed

Emotional abuse doesn't only occur with those who are in a romantic relationship. Children can suffer from emotional abuse as well. In children, emotional abuse can impair psychological development, including intelligence, memory, recognition, perception, attention, imagination, and moral development. It can also damage their ability to process, receive, and express their emotions. It can lead to depression, anxiety, withdrawal, sleep disturbances, age-inappropriate behavior, fearfulness, passivity, and aggression. If you have children, be alert to these signs of emotional abuse.

Many times victims don't recognize or even realize the extent of the abuse until they are so mired in it that they feel trapped, unable to get out from under the thumb of their abuser.

Common Signs of Emotional Abuse

It's important to recognize the signs of emotional abuse. Even if you're not being abused right now, you should be able to recognize it so you can avoid it in the future. Be on guard for these common signs of emotional abuse:

➤ Your partner insults you and swears at you

➤ You don't feel comfortable talking to your partner about your concerns

➤ Your partner often criticizes you and undermines your self-esteem

➤ Your partner destroys things that are meaningful to you

➤ Your partner teases you when you express yourself

➤ Your partner does something just to spite you

➤ Your partner makes you feel guilty for things you didn't do

➤ Your partner isolates you from family and friends

➤ Your partner calls you names

➤ Your concerns or worries are always dismissed as unimportant or an overreaction

➤ You experience swings in your relationship from being close to being emotionally distant

➤ You have sex with your partner just to avoid an argument

➤ Your partner has threatened the safety of your children and pets

➤ Your partner makes you do things that degrade you

➤ You walk on eggshells to keep your partner from getting angry

➤ You're afraid of your partner

Divorce Vocab

The Conflicts Tactics Scale 2 (CTS-2) is a questionnaire that was originally developed in the 1970s by University of New Hampshire sociologist Murray Straus. It is a controversial measure of domestic violence, the results of which are written up in papers and published in scholarly journals.

People who emotionally abuse others often have certain traits in common. Many times abuse is used to cover insecurities. Here are some traits shared by many abusers:

➤ They avoid responsibility for any wrongdoing

➤ They blame everyone and everything else for anything bad that happens to them

➤ They see themselves as victims

➤ They must always be treated better than everyone else

➤ Their needs always come first

If emotional abuse is still going on in your life, you are not alone! It is not your fault and there are ways to get help for you and your children. You can contact any domestic violence organization or hotline, or ask your doctor or clergyperson to recommend a counselor.

Why You Couldn't Leave Sooner

Many victims of emotional abuse can't believe how long it took for them to finally escape their abuser. Many have even said that if the abuse had reached a physical level, it would have been easier to leave. Thankfully, they didn't get a chance to test that theory.

Women have many reasons for staying in an abusive relationship. On the surface, some of them may even look justified. But dig a little deeper and you see where the thinking went wrong. Here are ten common reasons victims have for staying with their abuser:

1. They hoped things would improve

2. They didn't want to destroy the children's home

3. They were embarrassed by the abuse in their marriage

4. They rationalized their reasons for staying

5. They've become numb to the abuse

6. They grew up with abuse and didn't know it was wrong

7. They felt their spiritual obligations conflicted with leaving

8. Their partner promised the abuse would stop

9. They were too ashamed to tell anyone

10. Their partner said they wouldn't make it on their own

Hoped Things Would Improve

It is natural to hope for the best. The amount of pain and disruption that comes even with a friendly divorce is enough to stop a person who is unsure about taking that step. The victim's fear is that she acted too soon—maybe the abuse would have stopped the following week. That would mean she threw everything away for no reason.

This is just a continuation of the delusional thinking that kept the victim in the abusive situation in the first place. She can't be throwing everything away because she never had everything. At best, she had the illusion of everything.

Didn't Want to Destroy the Children's Home

A great deal of guilt surrounds staying in a bad marriage. How will witnessing your abuse affect your children? Will they become abusers? Will they think it's okay to be abused? Children raised in an abusive household tend to have difficulty forming healthy, loving relationships of their own. But the fact remains: no one wants to uproot their children.

Before taking such an extreme step, you would have to feel confident that the short-term disruption would be justified in the long run.

Embarrassed by the Abuse in the Marriage

No one likes to think of themselves as the star of their own soap opera. Victims of abuse are more vulnerable to embarrassment because their self-esteem has been destroyed. That makes it even more likely you won't speak out. See the vicious cycle? If you know someone in this loop, get them help.

Take Heed

Although not as prevalent as with women, men are victims of emotional abuse too. To what extent is not clear because men are especially hesitant to admit being the victim of abuse. One reason for this is that they are embarrassed that they have lost control of their lives. Another reason is that they fear no one will believe them. If a male friend or relative comes to you asking for help because he's being abused by his partner, take him seriously and help him as best you can.

Rationalized the Reasons for Staying

Some victims of abuse rationalize staying with their partner by convincing themselves that the abuse isn't so bad and they deserve it anyway. In some cases, these victims believe that the reasons to stay, for the children's sake, for example, or for appearances or to stay in step with their religion outweigh the potential pain and hurt of leaving.

Became Numb to the Abuse

Experiencing the same put-downs and insults over a long period of time can have a numbing effect. Some victims don't reawaken to the abuse until someone else reacts to what they're going through and points out how horrendously they are being treated. Just keep in mind that if you've become numb to your abuse, you are not just blocking the pain, you're blocking the joys you could be experiencing as well.

Grew Up with Abuse and Didn't Know it was Wrong

The biggest reason I urge parents to get out of abusive relationships is so their children don't become immune to its horrors. Early exposure to abuse as a child leads to a higher tolerance of it as an adult. This leaves victims who are already conditioned to a life of abuse vulnerable to abusers. If you find yourself or your children in this situation, it is especially important that you get help with extricating yourself from this cycle of abuse.

Felt Spiritual Obligations Conflicted with Leaving

Almost all organized religions discourage divorce and some out-and-out ban it. Usually, religions take the motives for divorce into account before expressing a decree. Emotional abuse can be subjective and difficult to prove. It is also the easiest form of abuse to dismiss.

The victim can be advised to pray more and work harder on the marriage. If you're faced with this attitude from your place of worship, you may feel as though your marriage cost you your relationship with God. Nothing is further from the truth. Seek out and find a spiritual support group or religion that welcomes you, and reestablish your connection with God.

Partner Promised the Abuse Would Stop

If you collected a dollar for each of those promises, you would easily have a retainer for a top-notch divorce attorney! When the victim finally jumps off the merry-go-round of promises and abuse, her ability to trust others has been eroded. If you've been a victim of this sort of abuse, take a step back and consider whether your experiences with your ex are causing you to mistrust the perfectly trustworthy people who are in your life today.

Felt Too Ashamed to Tell Anyone

Shame is a deeper, more judgmental form of embarrassment. It encompasses feelings of guilt, disgrace, and unworthiness and can lead to secrecy and deceit. The deceit isn't malicious; the victim is just too ashamed to be truthful. The result can be that people close to the victim feel helpless and upset that they weren't told about the abuse earlier. If you find yourself in this situation, humbly apologize to your loved ones and ask them to forgive you and move on.

Handy Tip

It's pretty common for a victim to lie about the state of her marriage; she's ashamed of her situation. The problem is that lies tend to snowball out of control. Eventually they come to light and people feel duped and betrayed. If this sounds familiar, take the time to write a note of apology to those who've been hurt by your silence throughout your years of abuse.

Believed You Wouldn't Make It on Your Own

Making the victim feel inadequate is a typical way for an abuser to exert his control. If your ex told you that you couldn't live without him and you're now divorced and living on your own, you can thumb your nose at him because you've proved him wrong. Now you just need to defeat the lingering doubts of your abilities that pop up in your mind during difficult times. Never tell yourself that you can't do something; recognize the difficulties, then move on doing the best you can.

Why People May Think You're Crazy

Your friends, family, spiritual group, and your work colleagues may have all thought you were crazy when you announced that you had to get out of your marriage. Emotional abuse is difficult to explain to people who have never experienced it. Sometimes, victims wish for physical evidence like a bruise to show everyone their pain.

Probably you hadn't told people of your abuse until recently, so try to understand their initial confusion and disbelief. How often have you thought a baby was just being cranky only to discover that he had a wet diaper? He had a reason to cry unbeknownst to you. Being unaware of the wet diaper, you judged the complaint harshly. Your friends and family did the same thing.

Now that your divorce is over, your naysayers either understand what you've been through and are sorry they weren't more supportive at the time, or they still don't get it. If they have grown to understand your nightmare, thank them! It's not easy to admit being wrong. If they still don't get it, take some more time to explain it to them.

Forgive Yourself

You'll have a difficult time moving forward with your life unless you forgive yourself for the role you played in your abuse, whether it is guilt over taking so long to leave or failure to speak up to protect yourself. If you choose to keep beating yourself up for what happened in your marriage even though you're now divorced, part of you is still back there living in the past. Part of you is still taking in the nastiness, even if it is now coming from you.

I've discovered two approaches to self-forgiveness. I call them Start Now and the Bad and the Good.

Start Now

You are going to pretend, starting right now, that you aren't angry at yourself for the role you played in your abuse. Don't try to believe this, just pretend. Sit down with pen and paper and take a look at your life. Write down what would be different in your life if you were to spend all your energy doing what you want to do and accomplishing what you want to accomplish.

What if your worrying, crying, and distress were to vanish? What would you do with all that freed time and energy? If your fairy godmother showed up and sprinkled happily ever after dust all around you, what would your life look and feel like? Write that down.

Starting right now, pretend that this miracle has occurred. Take as much time as you can, but no less than forty-five minutes, just considering this altered life. It's a pretty nice life, isn't it? Keep imagining this life until you can place the past well behind you, where it belongs.

This may take a week or two, but you will get the hang of it. Eventually, you will see improvements in your life that will motivate you to put more energy and focus into your world of make believe until it slips into being your reality.

A percentage of people never have to look back and face the details of their past, but most do. If you must do this, try to put it off until you've become very good at staying in the present, where you've chosen happiness over strife.

The Bad and the Good

Sit down with pen and paper and make a list of the worst things that could happen if you didn't forgive yourself. Make yourself experience these bad scenarios while you're compiling your list. To get you started, here are some negative things that are likely to happen if you don't find the motivation to forgive yourself:

> ➤ You become depressed, which could cost you your job and friends and wear down your family

> ➤ You become lonely, because you don't feel good enough to be with anyone

> ➤ You don't get help to strengthen yourself and end up being abused again

> ➤ Your life gets stuck and doesn't improves

> ➤ Your ex laughs at you and makes fun of your inability to do better

Now make a list of the best things that could happen if you were to forgive yourself for the choices you made in the past. Make yourself experience these good scenarios while you're compiling your list. To get you started, here are some good things that are likely to happen if you take the leap and forgive yourself:

> ➤ You feel better about yourself, which makes you a better employee, which gets you a raise and protects your job

> ➤ You can be a better friend to those who stuck by you during the bad times

➤ You can help your family move on from those darker times

➤ Your improved mood will help you meet new people so you are not alone

➤ Your life continues to improve so that eventually you are doing well

➤ Your ex hates that you are doing well and wonders why you're so happy

Once you see and feel how much better living by the good list is, you'll never want to go back. But if you are having difficulty with this exercise, you may need some extra help. Check in with a counselor or clergyperson for that extra push in the right direction.

CHAPTER 8

Taking Care of Your Body

In This Chapter

➤ How to eat to reduce stress and improve health

➤ Stress busting the easy way

➤ Why exercise

➤ Fast motivation to exercise regularly

One of the biggest side effects of a difficult divorce is stress. You can do a lot to reduce and control your stress without spending a fortune. This chapter starts with diets that reduce stress and goes on to cover specialized advice for the stressed divorcée. Finally, you'll get a discussion of the all-important and most groan-producing aspect of stress reduction, exercise.

Eating: The Divorce Diet

One of the reasons diets fail is because people don't incorporate them into a daily habit. Chances are that you ate poorly during your divorce; most of us do when we're under duress. But now that your divorce is over, there is no excuse for you to keep up that habit.

Changing the way you eat will take motivation, effort, and a certain amount of retraining. Is it worth it? Of course! The quality of your diet affects your ability to fight off illness, handle stress, and maintain energy levels to tackle whatever other challenges might arise.

Handy Tip

Ditch the phrase *going on a diet*! It just has too many negative connotations and implies a short-term change in lifestyle. You want to adopt a new, healthier way to eat that you can incorporate into your permanent everyday routine, not just change your eating habits for a few weeks so you can fit into your old jeans.

Feeding Yourself

Eating has become more of an emotional activity for many people rather than a life-sustaining necessity. You need the proper nutrition so that your bones and muscles and circulatory system and all other aspects of your body have the right amount of such foodstuffs as vitamins, minerals, protein, and fat to keep it in good working order. The body's systems, its inner workings, take place mostly backstage, so it's easy for us to forget the real reason we eat.

When you're under duress and not eating with nutrition in mind, you're likely getting too much of some things, fat and sugar for instance, and not enough of others, vitamins and minerals for instance. Some people overeat and some don't eat enough when they're stressed. Both can be problematic as far as overall health is concerned. Eating the right portions of a balanced diet is your goal.

Handy Tip

The traditional advice to eat three square meals a day has been challenged in recent years. Many believe that the body does a better job of processing and utilizing smaller meals served five or six times a day.

There's a physical response to stress that taxes the body's resources, so it's especially important to eat a balanced diet while you're going through stressful situations such as divorce and its fallout. Hormones are released in response to stress and some can cause trouble for the body. This is where water comes in. Besides keeping us hydrated, water also flushes toxins from our body. It's important to drink enough water every day to stay healthy. The general guideline is to drink eight glasses of water a day.

Supplements

It's best to get all the vitamins and minerals you need from the food you eat, but many of us don't. So a daily dose of vitamin and mineral supplements are called for. Targeting stress are the B complex vitamins.

A great guide to supplements is the *Prescription for Nutritional Healing, Fifth Edition: A Practical A-to-Z Reference to Drug-Free Remedies Using Vitamins, Minerals, Herbs & Food Supplements* by Phyllis A. Balch. It is a staple at most good health food stores. According to the book, the USDA recommended daily allowances were calculated back in the 1940s and were set based on the level of nutrients needed to prevent disease (like scurvy!). That is very different from the level of nutrients needed for optimum health and to deal with the effects of stress.

Divorce Vocab

A naturopath is someone who opts to use natural remedies for treating disease. Natural remedies can include massage and electrotherapy as well as treating with supplements and herbs.

Since supplements can interfere with certain medications or can be contraindicated for whatever reason, it's best to talk to your physician or naturopath to help you select the products that are right for you.

Changing Your Nutritional Habits

It's time for a nutrition inventory. Open your pantry and cupboard doors, peek into your refrigerator and freezer—are they full of prepackaged processed foods and meals? Is most of the food you have junk food and snacks? My guess is that your answer is yes and that you need to change your eating habits.

Handy Tip

Choose one day to prepare meals for the week. You can freeze what you plan to eat later in the week if what you're making is that perishable. Prepare salad mixings for the week so all you have to do each day is add dressing. And if you find yourself needing to pick up a quick bite, most stores offer salad bars and healthy prepackaged meals for people on the go.

A gradual way to change the way you eat is to choose one healthy food a week to add to your regimen. Below is a list of healthy foods that you can add to your diet incrementally:

➤ Garlic: A member of the onion family, garlic has powerful antibiotic and antifungal benefits and is most potent raw. It also reduces stress, blood pressure, and acne; prevents aging, boosts the immune system, and improves eyesight.

➤ Whole grain wheat, oats, oatmeal, and quinoa: Whole grains give you a bigger nutritional punch than processed grains. They boost energy levels and are great for the heart and waistline. They reduce stress, blood pressure, and acne, and they slow aging.

➤ Avocados and bananas: The monounsaturated fats and potassium in avocados and bananas help lower blood pressure. Bananas are considered a superfood for their nutritional benefits toward anger, high blood pressure, and low blood sugar. Avocados are effective at reducing stress and slowing the aging process.

Divorce Vocab

Superfoods have additional health benefits besides nutrition. They may be low in calories and high in fiber, they may contain omega-3 fatty acids or monounsaturated fatty acids, and they may be rich in vitamins and minerals.

➤ Salmon and tuna: Salmon contains Omega-3 fatty acids and B vitamins that help the brain. Omega-3 also keeps the stress hormones cortisol and adrenaline from peaking and protects against heart disease. Both salmon and tuna reduce stress, boost the immune system, and improve eyesight. Salmon also helps acne, and tuna also reduces blood pressure.

➤ Blackberries, raspberries, strawberries, and blueberries: These fruits are high in antioxidants. They reduce stress, slow aging, boost the immune system, and improve eyesight.

➤ Oranges: Oranges help blood pressure and cortisol return to normal levels after they have been elevated by stress. And, of course, the vitamin C helps boost your immune system.

➤ Soy beans: Soy beans, as well as soy products like tofu, reduce feelings of anger and are just generally healthy. They are used to reduce stress, blood pressure, and acne, and improve eyesight.

➤ Beans (black, kidney, lima, navy, pinto, white): Beans are high in fiber and can help digestion and lower your cholesterol. They reduce stress, blood pressure, and acne.

➤ Spinach, broccoli, and other leafy greens: Dark green leafy vegetables help replenish the body with critical vitamins and nutrients in times of stress. They are high in fiber and antioxidants. They reduce stress and blood pressure, slow aging, and improve eyesight.

➤ Tomatoes: Tomatoes are a source of lycopene, which can reduce the risk of heart disease and fight free radicals. They reduce stress and blood pressure, and slow aging.

➤ Carrots: Carrots are famous for eye health, but did you know that if you eat enough of them, your skin will temporarily become orangish? They reduce stress and acne, and, of course, improve eyesight.

➤ Apricots: Apricots are rich in magnesium, which is a stress buster and a natural muscle relaxant. They can be eaten fresh or dried.

➤ Green tea: Green tea is an herb that cleanses the body. It's high in antioxidents and has powerful cancer-fighting properties. It reduces stress, blood pressure, and acne, boosts the immune system, and slows aging.

➤ Eggs: Eggs are high in protein. They reduce stress, boost the immune system, and improve eyesight.

➤ Almonds, pistachios, and walnuts: Full of vitamins B and E, which help lower blood pressure elevated by your ex. They reduce stress, slow aging, and improve eyesight.

Take Heed

Stay away from food that can cause stress. Alcohol, as most everyone knows, can cause all sorts of stress and strife. Caffeine stimulates the central nervous system and can cause stress. Sugar raises the energy level rapidly, but the insulin released to counterbalance the intake of sugar can cause energy levels to drop, resulting in irritability and stress.

So, to change your nutritional habit, your plan might look like this:

> ➤ Week one: Drink a glass of water when you wake up and before you go to bed every day

> ➤ Week two: Remove one unhealthy food or drink that's part of your everyday diet

> ➤ Week three: Add one fruit to your daily diet

> ➤ Week four: Add one vegetable to your daily diet

> ➤ Week five: Add two cups of water, one mid-morning and one late afternoon when you're craving a snack

> ➤ Week six: Remove one unhealthy food or drink that's part of your everyday diet

> ➤ Week seven: Add one grain or cereal to your daily diet

> ➤ Week eight: Add two cups of water at lunch

Plan your grocery list before you go shopping so you're sure to have the food you need. Buy two weeks' worth of food so you don't have to make several additional trips to the store (stressful!).

There are a lot of reputable online diet communities that can provide more customized advice to suit your situation. Take control of your own health!

Stress

There are countless studies that document the connection between stress and poor health. To take proper care of yourself you must break the habit of automatically reacting to those around you and learn how to handle the myriad demands on your time and attention. We've already addressed the importance of a well-balanced diet, but there is more that you can do to alleviate stress in your life.

Prioritize

Like most newly divorced women, you're not just tackling your emotions; you're facing new demands on your time as well. If you're worrying about how you're going to get everything done, you're going to be stressed and anxious. Instead, prioritize your tasks so you can tackle each task one at a time without all your other demands tugging at the edges of your brain.

For this to be successful, you have to focus on the present—no feeling guilty about the past or worrying about the future. Try to catch yourself when your mind seeps into the past or trickles into the future, and pull yourself back to the present.

Some people just can't part with their guilt and worries. If you're one of those people, choose a time during the day when it's okay to stress over anything and everything in your life. You need to determine the length of time you're going to allow yourself to worry and stick to that time limit. When your time is up, listen to some soothing music, go for a walk, read a book—the point is for you to change gears and a good way to do that is to come up with a strong break to signify that worry time is over.

Breathe Deeply

Get into the habit of taking deep breaths. Breathe in from your nose, out through your mouth, and make sure your breath reaches your belly. Pay attention to your breathing. What does it sound like? What is its rhythm? Breathing deeply like this will release tension and calm you down; paying attention to your breathing will keep you in the moment.

Take some yoga classes to learn about meditation, mindfulness, and how to regulate your breathing. Meditation is a discipline for your mind, whereas yoga is a discipline for your body. Both teach you to relax, and both can unleash your inner strength. Mindfulness is a discipline that requires you to actively pay attention to the present. You observe your thoughts and feelings without judgment while living in the moment.

Handy Tip

You may be thinking that it would be nearly impossible to stop the flow of your thoughts and slow down enough to pay attention to the rhythm of your breathing. Mindfulness would solve this by having you step back and observe your thoughts without getting involved with them. You wouldn't be trying to dam up your thoughts; instead you would be letting them flow without judgment or interference. At some point you'd probably notice your thoughts quieting down, becoming less stressful and intense.

Sleep

An important part of reducing stress is making sure you're well rested. That means you need to get enough sleep every night to feel awake and energized the next day. Your body won't accept getting just a few hours of sleep during the week and then making up for it over the weekend. It just doesn't work that way. Most people do best when they get seven to nine hours of sleep a night—every night.

Sometimes when you're under stress it's difficult to sleep. This can become a vicious cycle of being stressed because you're not getting enough sleep and being unable to sleep because you're stressed. One way to combat this conundrum is to keep a to-do journal. Whenever your busy mind is keeping you awake, write down your thoughts and tell yourself you'll deal with them in the morning. Putting aside a problem to be handled at a later time makes you feel that everything is under control. Now you can sleep.

When you wake up in the morning, look at your to-do list and carve out some time during the day to address your concerns of the night before. If you don't follow up on the promise you made to yourself, this exercise will not work.

There will be times when you'll be plagued by runaway thoughts during the night and you won't have anything to write with. That's when you force yourself to think about something nice. You push your worrisome thoughts out of your head with thoughts of having lunch with your best friend, walking your dog, dreams you have for the future, anything that takes you away from the negative. This takes a bit of work, and you're likely to find your thoughts running rampant again. Just gently guide yourself away from your stresses to the good things in your life. Soon this will become second nature to you.

Create a Schedule

A lot of stress comes from feeling like you have too much to do and not enough time to get everything done. The best antidote for this type of stress is to create a schedule. Your brain gets to stop working overtime when everything has its own time and place. Be sure you allow for emergencies and even for some down time. Set aside time for long bubble baths or lunch with a friend, whatever you enjoy doing. Spending some time on the activities you enjoy is essential to overcoming stress.

Handy Tip

Keeping a tidy house can be overwhelming. For most people, the mess builds over the week until they're faced with the gargantuan chore of bringing the house back to order. It doesn't have to be this way. Rather than letting things pile up, make a habit of putting them away as you move about your day. Try to train your children to do the same. Even if you're not a neatnik, you will feel better in a tidier, more organized home.

Exercise

A very important stress buster is exercise, which happens to be one of the easiest tasks to push aside. But the benefits of exercise cannot be overlooked and should be taken seriously.

A routine exercise regimen is necessary for optimum health. During stressful times, exercise is the best way to alleviate the physical symptoms brought on by psychological distress. Many people bypass exercising claiming lack of time. But that's a lot of hooey. We all have time for a twenty-minute walk during lunchtime or for some sit-ups and push-ups before taking a shower. Really, the only excuse for not exercising is laziness.

Exercise can take on many forms; you don't need an expensive gym membership to exercise. As already mentioned, walking and doing sit-ups and push-ups are exercises that you can fit into your everyday life. But if the thought of exercise turns your blood cold, you can play. Join a community sports team, take yoga or dance lessons, go hiking or biking, do any activity that gets you moving and you enjoy.

Handy Tip

Make anger work for you. The next time you get angry go for a walk or a jog. It's okay if you stomp your feet or mutter under your breath. Just let the anger flow through you, leaving a bit of it behind with each step you take.

The benefits of exercise outrank nearly any other form of stress reliever. Most of the benefits aids stress relief. Here are some examples of how we benefit from exercise:

➤ Releases endorphins, which make us feel peaceful—even euphoric—and they act like an analgesic

➤ Increases self-esteem

➤ Promotes sleep

➤ Gives us a sense of accomplishment

➤ Strengthens the heart

➤ Lowers blood pressure

➤ Makes us look better

➤ Increases energy levels

Eating right, exercising, basically taking care of your health will make you stronger and put you in a better position to handle the issues of post-divorce. You'll be setting a great example for your children as well. As a matter of fact, you should get them involved in exercising with you. It could be a great bonding opportunity!

Take Heed

Taking the time to care for your health means you may at times need to temporarily put your needs ahead of others'. Otherwise you may end up in the hospital, feeling depressed and mistreated, or feeling resentful. So don't skip breakfast because you need the time to get your children ready for school. Don't put off sleep to help a relative or clean the house. Don't put off exercising because you don't think you have the time.

Before beginning an exercise regimen, make sure you have a clean bill of health. Talk to your doctor about the type of exercise you're planning to do and find out if there's an exercise you should stay away from.

PART THREE

Enforcing and Modifying the Decree

CHAPTER 9

Modifying Your Decree: The Financials

In This Chapter

➤ Modifying child support terms

➤ How to handle debts

Life isn't static; no matter how carefully your divorce decree was written up, changes in life will require changes in the decree. This chapter will cover modifying the financial aspects of your decree starting with child support and moving on to how best to handle debts.

Child Support and Alimony

Hopefully your decree is written clearly enough that both you and your ex understand who is supposed to pay what amount and when it's due. If this is a problem, you must get a handle on the terms of your decree as soon as possible. You are bound to its terms whether you understand them or not. You can hire an attorney to interpret your documents for you; some law firms offer this service online for a nominal fee.

Take Heed

Do not guess or round down when it comes to what is owed according to your decree. Court orders require exact compliance.

The Payment Schedule

Once you are clear on the terms of your decree, you need to determine if you need to rearrange your life so you can comply. For instance, if you are paying child support, your order may require you to pay $350 biweekly. Biweekly means every two weeks, which adds up to a total of twenty-six payments in each calendar year.

What do you do if you get paid only once a month or on the first and the fifteenth of every month? You need to plan ahead and save enough money so you can send the appropriate amount on the proper date according to the terms of the order.

If your circumstances have changed and your paycheck's arrival doesn't sync with the terms of your decree, you still have to pay according to the decree's schedule; you can't just change the pay schedule to suit your circumstances. For one, a court order such as a decree can be changed only by a judge; you can't do it on your own. Plus, changing the pay schedule could result in the accidental underpayment of support. Now we'll do a little math to show how this can cause a problem.

Divorce Vocab

An arrearage is a payment that is overdue. If you are in arrears, you are behind in your obligations; in this case you would be behind in your support payments.

The decree is to pay $350 biweekly. Following this schedule there are twenty-six payments per year: $350 × 26 = $9,100. If payments are changed to the first and fifteenth of the month, there would be twenty-four payments per year: $350 × 24 = $8,400. Without intending to, the payer has created a $700 arrearage for the year. If undetected for, say, six years, the arrearage becomes $4,200 plus interest!

The payer in our example would have to ensure that the twenty-four payments would add up to the same amount as the twenty-six payments. To do that, each payment must be $379.17 (rounded to the penny). Most of the accidental child support arrears are created by this very error.

What do you do if you're reading this and have just realized that you have an arrearage? I recommend that you carefully do the math and gather documents (pay stubs, checks, bank records, child support payment logs from the child support agency, and so on) that support your math. Put everything together and confirm the total amount you think you owe. Then you have two choices:

1. Contact your ex in writing, set out your math, and offer to repay the money at whatever amount per month you can truly afford.

2. Open a separate bank account in which you deposit the money owed and approach your ex either when you have the total amount due or are sued for the arrearage.

You will want to take the safer route, which would be the first option—unless your ex is angry and vindictive. Being up front and honest will build good will and trust.

If you take the second option and wait until you're sued for the money owed, you may be able to negotiate a lower dollar figure since you will be paying in a lump sum. Your ex might be willing to take $3,200 on the $4,200 and declare the arrearage satisfied. If you are ever in this position, be sure to document the agreement very carefully; any slipups in documentation may make it easy for your ex to argue that you still owe $1,000!

If support payments are always late, you and your ex could work out other arrangements. This is tricky because you'd be altering the terms of a court order, which should be done by a judge. The courts do not usually get upset if both parties mutually agree to change their payment dates so long as it doesn't create an arrearage that someone complains about.

Take Heed

Don't make up your arrearage by giving gifts or otherwise giving a little extra here and there. Gifts do not count toward child support in many jurisdictions.

One way to protect yourselves in this scenario is to write up your agreement, get it notarized, and file it in your closed divorce case, which most clerks will agree to do (some won't). Remember, though, this is not a court order but it will give you at least a sliver of protection. A better way to protect yourselves is to get an attorney to draft a consent order for you and see if a judge will sign it, officially changing it without anyone having to file a new lawsuit, which can be expensive.

Avoiding Late Payments

Let your ex know if you're going to be late making your support payments. Sometimes the courtesy of the warning will buy you some extra time and understanding. But try to offset this possibility by planning ahead and setting aside money for a rainy day. If something happens to your source of income, you'll have a buffer that will allow you to make your support payments as well as pay for your own living expenses.

If you're the recipient of child support payments, being helpful to your ex will make your child support process smoother. There are many different ways for you to receive your support check. Talk to your ex and see what works best for him. If he hates you, the idea of physically writing a check to you every two weeks could drive him insane in just a few months. A better process would be for him to authorize his bank to withdraw money from his account and deposit it automatically into your account; he won't even notice it's happening. Another option would be for the payments to be automatically taken out of your ex's paycheck and deposited into your account.

There was a time when deducting child support from a man's paycheck, a practice initiated by what's called an income deduction order, negatively impacted a person's (often a man's) reputation at his place of work. These orders were used only on men who refused to pay their required child support, thus marring their reputation. This practice is now a normal way to make child support payments. There is no stigma to this practice and an employer cannot discriminate against an employee for having an income deduction order.

Having money transferred from your ex's bank account to yours is another great way to collect child support. Open a separate account just for this purpose if you want to keep your own bank information private. Nothing is to go into or out of that account except what's needed for child support. This will eliminate any potential accounting issues should any disputes arise.

Never use cash to pay for child support. Accounting issues are likely to arise if there is no official record of the transaction, and the payments could be disputed. When you pay by check, you have your ex's signature and the bank's stamp to prove how much was paid and when it was paid.

Take Heed

Offsetting is the practice of using money owed to offset money due. For instance, if you owe your ex $500 and he owes you $100, you offset his $100 by paying him $400. The problem is that offsetting can really mess up your accounting and it makes it difficult to account for the amount of child support paid if this ever has to be audited. Anyway, offsetting is not allowed by the courts for child support and will get you into trouble!

Enforcing Child Support Payments

You have your order but your ex isn't paying. The first thing you do is figure out how much you are owed, or, better yet, get a printout of what is owed according to your child support agency account. Then you need to send a letter to your ex demanding that he pays what he owes. Copy template 9.1 Demand Letter for Unpaid Child Support in the Appendix, fill in the blanks, and send it off.

You will note that the letter is very simple. Many people mess up their demand letters by making them too complicated or mixing unrelated items into the financial demand. You simply need to state that there is an order, what is due on a regular basis, and what is overdue by your calculations. Then you request that your ex pay what he owes within ten business days or submit a proposed payment plan for your review if he cannot pay the balance in full in ten business days. You state that if your ex refuses to pay or an acceptable payment plan cannot be reached, you will pursue the matter through the legal system and seek an award of legal fees and expenses for an attorney, which you estimate would be at least $1,500. Then you wait. There are only a handful of responses:

> ➤ Your ex pays! Congrats! Do not gloat. Send him a letter thanking him for the payment (see template 9.2 in the Appendix) and confirming for his records that his child support account is current as of this date.

> ➤ Your ex pays part of what he owes and asks for time to pay the rest. Document the payment and balance, and work out a reasonable payment plan for what is still outstanding.

> ➤ Your ex proposes a reasonable payment plan. Send back a letter accepting the plan (see template 9.3 in the Appendix) and monitor payments for compliance. If he falls off the plan, repeat the cycle starting with a new demand letter.

> ➤ Your ex sends a crazy payment plan. Send back a letter declining approval of his plan (see template 9.4). State your best counteroffer. If he accepts, send him a version of template 9.3 (see Appendix). If he refuses the counteroffer or doesn't answer, proceed to file suit.

> ➤ Your ex just plain ignores you. You do not have to ask or beg again. I recommend you obtain an attorney to put together your lawsuit for filing and service.

Modifying Your Child Support

Throughout life, circumstances change. The needs of a four-year-old are quite different from the needs of a sixteen-year-old, for example. If what you get for child support is consistently less than your child needs, don't hesitate to go to court to modify your terms.

If you are fairly certain that your ex's annual income has gone up by more than $5,000 since your original order and your child's needs have increased, your request for modification will likely be successful. The catch is how much your income has changed since the original order.

Take Heed

If you are violating other terms of the order when you request a modification of your child support terms, expect to get a counterclaim against you for whatever you are doing wrong.

Many states use an income shares model, which uses the proportion of each parent's salary to determine the amount of child support required. For instance, if you make $30,000 and your ex makes $60,000, your combined income is $90,000. You make one-third of this total income; your ex makes two-thirds. A spreadsheet is used to calculate the basic child support obligation, or cost, of each child. You pay one-third of this obligation; your ex pays two-thirds. If either parent's income changes, the calculated proportion of obligation changes, and a modification in child support is in order. It's probably not worth pursuing, though, if the increase would be under $100 per month.

The first step you take once you've determined that your ex's salary has changed significantly is to send him a letter requesting his voluntary increase of child support (see template 9.5 in the Appendix). I usually recommend offering the ex a deal. There are many ways to go with this, but as an example let's say your research calculates that child support should increase from $700 to $1,000. You might offer to allow your ex to make the increases incrementally—say he pays $800 for four months, $900 for the next four months, then the full amount of $1,000 from that point on. If he agrees, you can either hire an attorney to draft your consent of modification of child support and handle the modification lawsuit, or you can figure out to how to do this on your own.

If your ex ignores or refuses your request, your lawyer can use the consent of modification of child support letter to try to get an award for attorney's fees. This shows you were trying to cooperate. It is important to send this letter so your ex can't say that if you had asked nicely, he would have agreed to the adjusted payments to avoid paying your attorney's fees.

The Decree's Effect on Debt and Money

The decree covers three main debts, which are credit card debt, property settlements, and payments to third parties like school or daycare tuition. Let's take a look at these debts one at a time.

Take Heed

Keep in mind that if the debt settlement program involves letting the debt that is in your ex's name go bad so you can then attempt to negotiate a reduced lump sum payment, you will need your ex's permission because this tactic would reflect on your ex's credit.

Credit Card Debt

The divorce decree doesn't make credit card debt go away, but it can change each party's obligation to the debt. You are responsible for paying off credit cards that are in your name only, as is your ex for cards that are in his name only. If the card you are in charge of is in your ex's name, then you are likely to be "awarded" the debt and will be responsible for paying off the card. You may want to look into debt settlement programs if you can't keep up with the debt; you don't want to be responsible for damaging your ex's credit.

It is difficult for you to work with credit card debt if the card is not in your name. Hopefully, your decree expressly gave you access to the creditor with the rights to contact and communicate about the debt. If it didn't, you need to get your ex to put you on the account so that you can always access information about the debt. Many people transfer their ex's credit card so it's in their own name to eliminate these issues. Once the debt is in your name, absent intentional fraud, you can try to restructure the debt in the way that works best for you.

In general, for most financial planning the two immediate goals are to pay off credit card debt, which is almost always at high interest rate, and put aside money for emergency expenses. Some people focus on paying off the credit cards and accept the risk of not having an emergency fund. The benefits of having no credit card debt cannot be underestimated, though. Your credit score is higher when your credit card balances are under 50 percent— under 25 percent is even better. Reducing the amount of credit used in relation to the total amount of credit available will increase your score.

If you find yourself always on the edge or paying these credit card debts late, you should ask someone who is good with money to help you set up a budget that will get you out of the hole in three years or less. I have found that when someone has to work longer than three years to get financially stable, the motivation to pay off debts diminishes sometime before the goal is met.

Be careful of credit counseling agencies; they are not all the same! See "Chapter 1: Resources for Learning to Manage Money" in the Appendix for some sources that can assist you. If you have the money but still seem to pay your credit cards late, it would be a good idea to set up an automated clearing house (ACH) payment.

Divorce Vocab

An automated clearing house is an electronic network for financial transactions, the most familiar being direct deposit for paychecks. To make automatic debt payments, you would be involved in monthly direct debit transfers from your account to the bank that holds your debt.

Another way to take care of debt is to negotiate with your ex, if your relationship is on good enough standing. Your ex may actually be more comfortable paying off the debt himself, especially if you have something of value you could swap such as a tax dependency exemption for an additional child for a few years. Discuss options with your ex, and if you agree to some kind of swap or trade-off, put it in writing and get it notarized. File the agreement if the clerk's office will allow it.

Property Settlements

A property settlement simply is a division of assets ordered by the court during a divorce. If the court determines that your ex owes you money as part of a property settlement, a payment due date will be determined. If the settlement involves a lot of money, your ex will be given more time to pay partly because liquidating assets can take weeks. In such cases, I like to send reminders of the upcoming obligation perhaps six, three, and one month in advance.

It's a good idea for you to ask your ex to confirm that he is on track with obtaining the funds for your payment when these reminders come out. Too often when people wait until the last minute, all they get are excuses for why the money isn't yet available.

Whenever possible try to secure another asset while waiting for a big payoff. If your money is not secured and you see your ex liquidating the assets that you thought would likely be used for your future payment, definitely send a letter of inquiry. At least if you don't receive payment by the due date, you'll have the letter as proof of your diligence.

But what do you do if you owe the settlement and you don't have the assets? The best course of action is to inform your ex as soon as possible, and then pay what you can. At that time, be prepared to tell your ex how you plan to pay the balance. You can, of course, ask the court to modify and reduce your property settlement, but you would need to present a very good argument.

Take Heed

Pay attention to the tax consequences of your settlement payments. If you are not sure how to claim them, solicit the advice of a tax professional.

Overdue Payments to Third Parties

The parent who is obligated to pay third parties like schools and daycare centers must pay consistently and in a timely fashion. If the obligated parent in your case happens to be your ex and he pays the school directly, be sure to get a receipt or have access to proof of the account being maintained properly. This is important because a missed or late payment can result in lost class schedules, lost enrollment, refusal to transfer necessary school records, and embarrassment for you and your child.

In cases where your ex is not paying the school bills as required, make sure you have invoices from the school or daycare. If you have to step in and pay all or part of the bill, make your payment distinguishable from your ex's.

It's worth having a conversation with your ex if you have continual problems with these payments. Ask him if there is something he can do with his budget to make sure this obligation gets paid first. You may need to take your children out of private schools and high-end daycare centers. Although this isn't an ideal solution, removing the burden of high-cost schooling can be a relief for all involved.

CHAPTER 10

Modifying Your Decree: Change in Status

In This Chapter

➤ How to change your decree when you or your ex remarries

➤ Changing your decree when you or your ex moves

➤ Safety provisions in your decree

In this chapter we will look at how to change your decree if you or your ex has a change of status such as getting remarried or moving away from the area.

Modifying Your Decree to Accommodate Remarriage

A common get requests from noncustodial parents who have remarried and want to file for primary custody. They want to show the court that their new marriage and home are now much more stable than the custodial parent's present situation.

If you're faced with this request as the custodial parent, it is important for you to consult with an experienced custody attorney in your state to clarify your state's laws. Keep in mind that courts are not interested in fostering multiple child-custody modifications.

Generally, the strongest case against your ex's attempt at modifying your decree on the heels of his remarriage would be if there is something wrong with his home or parenting, or if there is something especially beneficial about your home and parenting. Often the law requires that you demonstrate the first before it even considers the latter. Again, it is worth consulting an attorney to determine how your state and particular courthouse address this type of modification.

Handy Tip

While no one likes to talk about it, there are communities and specific judges who have well-known views on custody. Is this right or fair? No, but it is what it is. You'd much rather know beforehand if the state laws or the judge will likely make your case more or less difficult.

On the flip side, a lot of custodial parents want to modify their decree because they do not like who their ex married. This is not a legal reason to modify a custody arrangement. As mentioned earlier, the new partner needs to have caused observed and provable harm. Yes, it is harmful if the new stepdad plays favorites toward his own kids. Yes, it's harmful if the new stepmom doesn't pay attention to your daughter's sensitive nature and makes her cry daily. And no, the situation is not likely to rise to the level of provable harm that a court will respond to.

When you have transition issues with a new family dynamic, that is more a matter for counseling or coaching. If you have "they are just plain mean" issues, your ex and his new spouse may not agree to go to counseling, but you should still send the children to give them a safe outlet to vent their frustrations. Feeling helpless is an awful thing for a child in this situation.

The counselor can make recommendations regarding your child's visits with your ex. If the counselor makes recommendations that your ex refuses to follow, then you have something you can file suit about. You then have a neutral professional who states that doing things differently is in your child's best interests, and you have documented resistance.

In strong arguments for a modification stemming from a problematic remarriage may include the following:

➤ The remarried ex resisted a third-party counselor's recommendations.

➤ The remarried ex refused to cooperate with the children's counselor.

➤ The ex married someone with a criminal record who is specifically dangerous to children.

➤ The ex married a current and provable drug user (has current and/or multiple DUIs).

➤ The ex's new spouse physically abused the children, and there's documentation to prove it.

➤ The ex committed provable domestic violence on the new spouse or the new spouse committed provable domestic violence on the ex (proof can be tricky without arrests, restraining orders, or multiple 911 calls).

The fact that your ex's new partner hates you is not sufficient reason to seek a modification. Even if she was the person who broke up your marriage, in fact, especially if she broke up your marriage, you must have real grounds to show this person will harm or cause harm to befall your children.

Modifying Your Decree to Accommodate Moving Away

When the primary parent moves, lots of things happen all at once:

> ➤ The children move
>
> ➤ The schools and daycares may change
>
> ➤ The parent's work schedule may shift
>
> ➤ The commute for visitation is changed
>
> ➤ Finances may be impacted so there may suddenly be child support issues

If the noncustodial parent moves, at least the children stay put, but all the other changes can occur.

Giving Notice

Most states have rules specifying how far in advance a parent should notify her ex of her intention to move. Although it may be a short time period like thirty days, it is better, with only a few exceptions, to give more rather than less notice. If your ex is not crazy, giving more notice is more respectful, gives a longer period of time for him to adjust, and more time for you to come up with a joint plan, if possible.

If your ex is crazy, dangerous, or just looking for a reason to take you to court, it's not a great idea to give him more notice. In those cases, just comply with the law and hope the shorter time period will make it harder for him to cook something up or hire an attorney to challenge the move or sue for primary custody.

Keep in mind that if your ex is truly crazy, he'll sue no matter how much advance notice you give him, so be prepared for a challenge. If you know you have this kind of ex, you need to prepare well in advance of your move and make sure you are collecting all evidence of his crazy behavior, fully complying with the court order, and generally cleaning house.

What if you are reading this book and you're planning a move and you've just realized your notice is going to be really late? Postpone your move if you can so you can at least give close to a one-month notice. But if you can't postpone your move take all of these steps:

> ➤ Write your notice and include your new address, contact information, and all the new information you have on the children's schools or activities, babysitter, and so on. Mail it today, keeping a copy for yourself, of course.
>
> ➤ Send your ex an e-mail of this notice with a read and delivery receipt.
>
> ➤ Call your ex to inform him of your plans; record the call, if possible

Be apologetic in your notice; you really are in the wrong. In this situation, it is a great idea to offer better than pot sweeteners. Extra summer time or letting that parent have the kids the last week before the move are all good ideas. Ask your ex point-blank if there is something you can do (short of leaving the kids) that would help him with this transition.

None of this may save you from a court filing alleging you were hiding your move. If the court agrees with your ex, you can be in for a difficult fight. I have seen courts decide to give temporary custody to the slighted parent while the case was going on. Custody cases can easily go on for over a year, so do not underestimate the importance of a temporary placement decision.

Divorce Vocab

A standing order is a rule that is enforced by the court until it is officially changed or withdrawn. It can apply to any type of case pending in court.

Moving with Your Children

After giving notice of your move to your ex, he's likely to serve you with papers to modify custody; he may even try to get full custody. Do not panic. Just because he's taking action doesn't mean he will win.

Your first step is to figure out whether you may still move with the children or if the court requires the children to stay in the jurisdiction. You will need an attorney for this kind of battle. It would be dangerous for you to move away with the children if the court's paperwork (often termed a *standing order* or *domestic order*) requires a court order before the children can be removed from the court's jurisdiction.

If you are so restricted, the first thing to do is to try to negotiate so that you can move with your children and return for all court proceedings at your own expense. Your attorney should attempt to get permission from your ex to do this. If he doesn't agree to this, your attorney may have to ask for an emergency hearing to get the court's permission for you to move with your children.

Keep in mind that you can always move alone; it's unconstitutional for anyone to restrict your right to move. Decisions about children, however, can't be made until a hearing can be held to decide the issue. You could, for instance, move during summer and leave the kids with your ex for their summer vacation and travel back and forth for court. Most primary parents do not like this idea, and I am not fond of it myself, but it can work well in some cases.

I have had custodial parents end up turning down promotions, quitting relocated jobs, and canceling moves to get out of a move-based custody fight.

Often the person who is moving offers "extras" to the parent staying behind, thinking a spoonful of sugar will help the move get done. Only you can know if this will work. Generally, it is a good idea to approach an ex in a sympathetic way and offer what you can without hardship or too much inconvenience.

I have seen parents who are moving a ten-hour drive away suddenly offer to do all the transportation and guarantee a visit every month. The finances must make sense too. If the trip is far enough, it's going to require a flight. If your children are below a certain age, you may have to fly with them or pay extra fees to have them escorted. Even if the flight for one child was minimal, $300, for instance, that would add up to $3,600 in one year of monthly visits. Factor in how stressful it's likely be for a child to travel once a month every month for the next seven years, and you're making a very expensive proposition.

I do think it is appropriate to sweeten the pot with an eye to getting an agreement without a fight; after all, you are the one moving the kids. Easy offerings include the following:

➤ Cell phones for the kids, if appropriate

➤ E-mail accounts

➤ Skype accounts

➤ Web chatting

The Visitation Schedule

Usually the visitation schedule changes after a move. It is more common for long-distance visitation to occur during the lengthy holidays and vacations (spring, winter, and summer breaks). Often the noncustodial parent gets an option on all the three-day holidays from school also.

Be mindful if your ex wants to come to your location because he is going to need a hotel and rental car. These expenses are valid (you don't want him staying in your house!) and can be used to adjust your child support. So figure out the expenses likely to be accrued by your ex during a visit, multiply that number by the number of visits planned during a year, and subtract that from what you get for child support. Be prepared for your support to take a hit. The court does not have to give dollar-for-dollar credit, but it often does.

What if you're the noncustodial parent and you're the one who plans to move? The notice provisions and suggestions outlined above also apply to you. You would want to start by looking at your anticipated schedule and finances. You need to look at the support amount you are currently paying and figure out how much it will cost you to travel back to visit with the kids. It's better to underestimate here.

Figure out the costs, the kind of things you'll need to visit (airline ticket, rental car, hotel, and so on), and a calendar to look at prospective visits over the next year. Once you have this information, you need to send it to the custodial parent and invite a discussion. Hopefully, you can come to some kind of agreement.

If both parents work out the details without a fight—congratulations. But you are not done yet. Remember, you have a court order that doesn't match your new agreement. This type of event is significant and should be protected by the issuance of a new court order.

One party will have to file a modification suit. For legal advantage, I recommend that the parent who's moving file it. Some jurisdictions have rules regarding how many modifications a person can file within a certain time period. Since the moving parent is instigating the change, I prefer she "use" one of her allotted modifications. She can have the agreement already written, signed, and notarized even before she files. I recommend that at minimum a family lawyer be engaged to review an agreed list of terms and write a draft of the agreement, or review whatever you have drafted and agreed to.

Take Heed

Some things people agree to are not legal. They cannot be put in an agreement because they are either unconstitutional, such as the mother will never move again and if she does the father gets the kids, or unenforceable, such as the father promises to love the children's dog. An attorney specializing in family law can guide you through these nuances.

Be thorough. Your agreement should be drafted with an eye toward closing loopholes and with as much specificity as you can manage to eliminate interpretation fights later on.

When courts rule on who should pay for visitation costs, they take each person's income into account. I have seen several angry fathers who had to carry more of the travel costs because they out-earned the mothers.

Following Safety Provisions in Your Decree

Safety provisions are not included in all decrees. So before going any further, find out whether your decree includes any safety provisions. A common clause, which I require in all my decrees, is called the separate existence clause. It may read like this:

The parties hereby mutually agree to live separate and apart, and each shall be free from the interference, molestation, authority, and control, direct or indirect, by the other as if single and unmarried. Each party may reside at such place as he or she, in his or her sole absolute discretion, may select, subject to the terms of this Agreement. Both parties agree that they shall not molest, harass, or interfere with the other whatsoever, nor shall either of them attempt to cohabit or dwell with the other.

A beefed-up clause involves restrictions on third parties and may include prohibitions on contact. If you have this clause, it is a *de facto* restraining order. I find that the police always respond better to an emergency when the victim identifies that there is a court order restraining the ex from harassing her. Use your order if you're being harassed by your ex.

Take Heed

Keep in mind that a piece of paper does not protect you from anything; you protect you. You have to be aware, track events, and know the protections that you are entitled to and insist upon them. Too many police departments are unwilling to take constant, petty harassment seriously—you have to insist you need help from the police and seek escalation of the issue if you feel you are not being heard or protected.

What to Do if Your Decree Doesn't Have a Safety Clause

You have to start from scratch if you don't have safety provisions in your decree. You have to document the efforts you make to get your ex to leave you alone, and you may need to send him a cease and desist letter (see template 10.1 in the Appendix). It is important that you do a great job documenting anything and everything that happens to you. Here are some examples of what should be documented:

➤ The back door is open when you were sure you locked it

➤ The computer is turned on when you know you turned it off

➤ The dog was let out of the yard

If there is any question that your residence has been compromised, it is critical for you to get in the habit of backing up your evidence to a separate location so that your hard work, tape recordings, videos, and handwritten irreplaceable logs do not just "disappear" one afternoon. I have seen this too often. Be vigilant.

Sending that cease and desist letter can trigger retaliation by some people. It's a catch-22. If you don't make your position clear, the court may not take your claim seriously or may be more inclined to give your ex a mere slap-on-the-wrist warning. I know many people who didn't want to poke what they view as a sleeping dragon. I point out that the dragon can't really be sleeping if he is stalking you. Still, it may make you feel better to engage a lawyer for the task of sending a knock-it-off-or-there-will-be-consequences letter.

I do not view it as necessary to send more than one stop-terrifying me letter. So if you're still having problems after you've sent the letter, pursue other options. One such option is to get a temporary protective order (TPO) or a temporary restraining order (TRO). If your ex is just mean, a TPO will likely be enough of a threat to stop him. If he is crazy, however, the TPO may accelerate the situation, and if that's the case, nothing was going to deter him anyway. Rather than being a deterrent, then, the TPO sends the message that there will be consequences, often a no-bond felony, if he is caught violating it.

The scary fact is that if someone is willing to swap his freedom to get to you, he will get to you eventually. If you have a Terminator-like ex, you must take drastic measures. Consult with people at a domestic violence shelter, especially find someone there who has experience with this kind of person and knows how they operate. The shelter may have some resources you can tap into. Also seriously consider hiring a private investigator to document your ex's activities.

If your ex has proved difficult and you are going back to court, you should see if you can get any of the following stipulations added to your new court order:

➤ A separate existence clause, discussed above.

➤ Meet at a neutral location for child exchanges. People used to use police and fire stations for this, but that may be a bit stressful for the mild offender. A fast-food restaurant closest to your home is usually a good choice.

➤ Forbid in-person or hand delivery of anything. Instead, deliveries are to be made via mail, courier, or sealed envelopes in the child's bag.

➤ Adults shall communicate in a respectful manner and shall not by manner, tone, or language degrade or disrespect the other parent.

➤ All nonemergency communications shall be by e-mail.

➤ All communications between the parties are restricted except for those pertaining to the children.

➤ Neither party may enter the other's home.

➤ Both parties are to remain in their vehicles during the transfer of children.

➤ In the event that the parent receiving the children for a visit is more than thirty minutes late, the visitation is cancelled or the time is taken off the next visitation period.

➤ Your ex must take an anger management course or have an anger control assessment or full mental health assessment (these are always easier to get if you agree to undergo one also). Always request input into the choice of examiner. You must do what you can to make sure your ex cannot select his examiner and that the examiner is someone who can detect a clever liar or sociopath.

➤ Restrict your ex from coming to your home, job, and children's school.

If you are staying in the former marital home, it's always a good idea to do the following:

> ➤ Change all the locks, garage door openers, and consider bracing and blocking devices on weak doors or sliding glass doors.

> ➤ Tell your immediate neighbors that you are divorced and if applicable, tell them your ex should not be there and if seen to call the police (or at least call you—people hate to get too involved).

Handy Tip

If your ex agrees to undergo a mental health assessment only if you do too, consider agreeing to it only if he pays for the assessment when you test healthy.

➤ Install inexpensive interior and/or exterior security cameras.

➤ Buy a locking gas cap for your car.

➤ Photo document the entire home and its contents, and store photos outside of the home to be used in case of vandalism or theft.

➤ Adopt a medium to large dog, if you can offer it a good home. Dogs are a great deterrent and can act as an alarm if there is an intrusion, plus they are great company. Check out PetFinder.org for help adopting.

➤ Buy some self-defense items. Don't buy a gun if you aren't going to be comfortable using one, but pepper spray, wasp spray (which sprays 25 feet and will drop or slow most any attacker), an aluminum baseball bat, a Taser, a stun gun, a water pistol with bleach, or a panic button alarm system are great choices.

What to Do About an Annoying Ex

Your ex is not dangerous, but he is annoying—what do you do? Again, document all the annoying instances to build your case. Although tedious, this is necessary. Having witnesses is also helpful. If your ex gets predictable, having your priest, rabbi, or reverend over to see his handiwork is dynamite in court.

Sometimes, these kinds of exes will ease up if you let them know that everything is being monitored and retained for evidence. For instance, let's say you are in a state where you can legally record your ex without his knowledge. More often than not if you start a conversation by telling him that he is being recorded, he will behave. Keep in mind that once you tell him you're recording him, you must assume for the rest of your life that he will be recording you (and the kids) too.

CHAPTER 11

Modifying Your Decree: Property and Children

In This Chapter

➤ Enforcing your house and property decree

➤ Enforcing and modifying child custody

This chapter continues the discussion of modifying and enforcing your divorce decree. In particular, it covers enforcement of house and property, as well as child custody issues as it applies to the order.

Compliance Problems with the House and Property Order

Unfortunately, it is common for a divorce to finalize with one party still living in the former marital home or retaining property such as a time share. Some people find themselves in the position of still having their name on the mortgage or debt for the property, but it's their ex who is responsible for keeping the payments current. The problem with that scenario is that if the ex fails to pay the note on time, it can hurt the other party's credit. If you're in this situation, you hopefully had a clause drafted into your decree that addresses some safety measures such as the following:

➤ You should be allowed access to the mortgage holder so you can check the status of the payments.

➤ There should be a provision that requires your ex to notify you if he's late making the mortgage payment or if he fails to pay it at all.

➤ You should have the right to make the payment yourself if necessary, and your ex must have to pay you back.

Take Heed

Don't sit on those letters! Send them out right away. Note on each letter if it's a second or third notice for this delinquent payment. You're building your evidence. The letters show the court that you want to protect your interests in this matter and that you have done all you can do. Now you need the court's intervention.

Don't panic if you don't have those clauses in your decree; I'll show you how you can work around this problem.

Dealing with Late Payments

Any time you find out that your ex was late making a mortgage payment or that he skipped out on it entirely, you need to send him a letter demanding that he pays the mortgage on time (see template 11.1 in the Appendix) or a letter demanding that he makes the mortgage current (see template 11.2 in the Appendix). You will need to include the name and address of the payee, the payment due dates, and the total amount owed, including late fees. Send the letter by first class mail or by e-mail.

Enforcing the Order

If your ex doesn't respond to your letters does nothing to rectify his delinquent or missed payments, you may have to file suit to protect your remaining interests in the home and your credit. You can add the following paragraph to the last demand letter you send just before you file suit:

Be advised: You have failed to come into compliance with our court order. Repeated attempts to obtain your compliance have been unsuccessful. It is necessary to obtain the intervention of the court to enforce the divorce decree. Once filed, I intend to seek recovery of my attorney's fees, which may be in excess of $1,500. Further, I will seek the full extent of sanctions available to this court for contempt. No further efforts will be made to obtain your compliance before filing suit. Govern yourself accordingly.

Whether you plan to hire an attorney or represent yourself, you need to have the following at the ready:

➤ A copy of your complete divorce decree (with the judge's signature and clerk's filing stamp)

➤ Copies of all of your written demand letters

➤ Copies of any other communication you have had on the issue (if it was verbal, you may just jot some notes to summarize the gist and date of each conversation)

➤ Mortgage statements and notices that reflect the current amount of the debt and what is necessary for the debt's reinstatement to current status

➤ Proof of your out-of-pocket costs relating to the failure of payment

The demand letters should be attached as exhibits to your complaint. Your jurisdiction may have slightly different requirements, but you're off to a great start with the items from this list.

Enforcing the Maintenance of the House and Terms of Sale

In many cases, the home shared during marriage is going to be sold after the divorce. Some decrees have clauses that require the responsible party to keep up the maintenance of the house. In most cases the responsible party is the ex-husband. Even if it's your ex's responsibility to maintain the house, you need to keep a close eye on its condition. An angry ex may try to retaliate against you by allowing the house to fall into disrepair.

Just as you do with any other violation of the decree, you need to send your ex a letter to put him on notice of your intentions to require compliance. Take pictures, or otherwise safely and legally document the state of the property for your evidence. If your ex refuses to comply with the decree, you may ask him why he isn't keeping up the property. The excuse will be that he doesn't have the money or the time. Incorporate the excuse into your second notice, using words such as:

After I sent you the first notice and inquired on the phone when the condition would be corrected, you advised me that you did not have the money to fix it. While I understand it may be a challenge, we need to have an understanding regarding when the condition will be addressed. Please provide me a date or plan to get the repairs done on or before (choose a date that is seven business days from the date of the letter).

In this scenario, you're the bad guy; how dare you require your ex to comply with a court order? Do not be bothered by your ex's resistance. Remember, he doesn't like you. Even if you let him slide for six months, he will be upset the first time you meekly ask about the house. It's better to address the issue right away.

Take Heed

Most decrees do not include the right to periodically inspect the house to ensure it is being maintained properly, so you will not know about any interior damage that there may be.

Child Custody Issues

When children are involved, emotions run high. Following the child custody order of your divorce decree can end up being a nightmare for both of the parents, one of the parents, or the kids.

The good news is that in general, parents can do anything they each agree on that veers from the decree. So, if you and your ex decide to handle custody arrangements differently, you're free to do it. The problem arises when one parent insists on following the document to the letter, and the other wants it changed.

In this case, the custodial parent needs to clearly communicate his or her preferences and intentions. As the custodial parent, you should let your ex know that there are only three ways to handle child custody arrangements after divorce:

➤ Follow the decree to the letter

➤ Make agreed-upon changes, but either parent can insist on following the decree.

➤ Disregard the decree and wing it

You can go on to explain that there are advantages and disadvantages to each option, and then tell him which option you prefer.

Handy Tip

It's best to strictly follow the decree if your ex is crazy, dangerous, or untrustworthy. There may be ramifications later, when you need him to compromise on an issue. But if your ex isn't the compromising sort in the first place, that may not matter!

Keep the following in mind:

➤ Even if you compromise, agree, and constantly do things differently from your order, you still have the right to insist that your ex follows the order. It is best to give some kind of notice that you are about to require strict compliance, if you never have before.

➤ Your children's wishes do not control or trump the order. Your ten-year-old refusing to visit and hyperventilating on the floor does not give you permission to alter the order and skip your ex's visit.

➤ As you do in other situations, it is best to document when your ex does something wrong or refuses to follow the decree. You may need it in the future for evidence.

We often hear fathers lament that they are kept out of the loop by mothers. The best course of action you can take if you don't have primary custody of your children is to proactively seek out information:

> ➤ Contact your children's schools and daycare centers to make sure you are on their pickup list, emergency contact list, and have privileges to see the children at school and talk to their teachers and counselors. Ensure that your phone number, e-mail address, and mailing address are in the schools' systems so that you receive all school correspondences. Check in with your children's teachers once a quarter to make sure everyone is on track and that the teachers know you're involved.

> ➤ Contact your children's medical providers to ensure they have your phone number, e-mail address, and mailing address.

> ➤ Purchase an all-in-one fax machine for the custodial parent to copy pertinent documents for you. Be sure to discuss this purchase and your intent to be helpful before buying the machine.

> ➤ You may want to consider subscribing to one of the websites designed to help divorced parents communicate and share their child's information with each other by providing a secure and centrally located calendar for both parties to use. See MyFamilyWizard.com or ParentingTime.net.

The Schedule

Help your children get used to their visitation schedule by getting them their own calendar. At the beginning of every month, mark the days they'll be spending with your ex, so they can see what to expect for the month. When lives have been turned upside down like theirs have, a lot of comfort can be had by knowing what to expect.

Try to at least occasionally honor your older children's schedule preferences. They can mark their preferred schedule on their calendar, and bring the calendar with them during their next visit with your ex. They can work out some alternative schedules that could have them home with you for the weekend of the big school party.

Any schedule changes should be communicated to your ex right away, and vice versa. Some decrees only require giving reasonable notice for any schedule changes. This is, of course, rather vague, and leaves it up to you to use your own judgment when determining what "reasonable" is. Giving same-day notice to another parent has been found reasonable if the notice was given as soon as the person knew of the change. A good rule of thumb is to treat your ex the way you would want to be treated. If you'd want three to four days' notice of any schedule changes, then give your ex that much notice.

> ### Take Heed
>
> When working around schedule conflicts and visitations, you want to take the moral high ground. Being uncooperative hurts your children more than anyone else and damages your character in the long run. Plus you don't want to give your ex more ammunition for labeling you the bad guy.

Visitation

Visitation is one of the biggest issues faced by divorced couples with children. It's important to understand that the noncustodial parent is the only one who can enforce his visitation rights. That is to say the custodial parent cannot sue her ex for not following the visitation order. The custodial parent, however, can seek to modify the decree.

Let's look at examples of some visitation issues based on cases I have litigated:

> ➤ The mother has custody and won't let the kids see their dad after he's remarried his former mistress.

If the divorce decree does not include a specific prohibition regarding the mistress (we call her the Barbie in our office), the children cannot legally be kept from their father. Although the father has a right to enforce visitation, he should pay attention to how his children are responding to their stepmother and perhaps voluntarily seek family counseling for everyone. If he won't do that, the mother can seek to file a modification to try to compel some counseling and perhaps a temporary modification of the visitation schedule until the children's emotional needs are stabilized.

> ➤ The mother makes the children available to the father although she doesn't like him, but the father doesn't make the effort to see his children.

The father sought to have the mother held in contempt, which was denied because the mother could prove that she made the children available. Apparently, the father liked telling people he was being denied access to his children as a way to explain why his kids weren't with him more often. For reasons unknown, he would not ask for his full time and keep them the full time.

> ➤ The father has the child in his care. Mom reappears after years of absence and demands the return of the child, which causes the child to have a nervous breakdown and be hospitalized.

In this case, the father had been raising the child and paying child support to the mother. Once he stopped paying child support, the mother returned and demanded the child back.

The mother still had legal custody, so the child had to be returned to her, which caused the child to have a nervous breakdown. The father had his hands tied because he hadn't wanted to rock the boat by changing the custody order. To avoid all this turmoil, he should have modified the custody order years before.

> ➤ The father has custody and mom visits every once in a while but now wants more regular access to the children. The father won't agree to it.

Take Heed

If a parent out of anger denies visitation based on bogus claims of the children's emotional distress, the parent can be found in contempt of court for denial of visitation. It's best for you and your children not to act on your anger-fueled compulsions.

As the custodial parent, the father feels that his ex shouldn't just pop in and out of their children's life. So when the mother pops back in, he stonewalls her requests to see the children on a more regular basis. The father can be held in contempt for his interference; the mother could seek to enforce the order granting her visitation. The court will generally protect a parent's right to reestablish a bond with a child, so it would've been better for the father to work something out with the mother. The father can file and seek a modification to try to accomplish this if necessary.

When it comes to enforcing custody, denials of visitation, and similar issues, you should hire an attorney. If you cannot afford one, at least arrange to pay for a consult with an experienced family lawyer to help you prepare for handling your case on your own. This kind of service is often called unbundled or à la carte legal services. See if it is available in your state.

Divorce Vocab

Unbundling is the process of breaking something into smaller parts. An attorney is often hired to take a case from beginning to end. But she can also unbundle her services so clients can pick and choose exactly which service they need. It's like eating à la carte in a restaurant. Instead of ordering a dinner that includes salad, soup, entrée, and dessert, you order only those items in the menu that you actually want. This is a good way to save money.

Modifying the Child Custody Decree

All jurisdictions have requirements that must be met in order to file a modification. The clear requirement is that there has to have been a substantial change of circumstances since the order was initially issued. So if you've asked for a modification that was turned down, a certain period of time needs to pass before you can request the same modification.

But keep in mind that the only time you need to go to court to request modification to your child custody decree is if your ex refuses the change. If he goes along with what you want, then you can stay out of court. If you find that you do need to take your ex to court, you need to be prepared.

Before you file your modification take out your original order and examine it carefully. The moment you sue your ex, he can counterclaim to try to hold you in contempt for the slightest infraction of that order. If you find that you are doing something that violates the decree, you need to stop and fix it, or figure out a way to minimize its impact.

For instance, a mother might sue a father for a modification of custody to reduce his visitation based on the fact that he doesn't visit. The father would most likely counter by trying to hold the mother in contempt for denial of visitation. He may also throw in that she was supposed to refinance the house within twelve months, but it's been thirteen months and she hasn't refinanced yet. The mother should take care of the refinance issue before filing for modification if at all possible.

Handy Tip

Once you're divorced, the odds that you will at some point need to go back to a family lawyer are very high, especially if your divorce was rife with conflict. So if you think there's any possibility your case will ever require modification, start saving your money right away so you'll have the funds to hire an attorney when you need one.

When preparing your case to modify the child custody decree, make sure you have all your evidence gathered together. You may want to try your case to a friend or two to make sure there are no holes in your argument or what you've gathered as proof. You are, after all, very close to this issue, so you may not be able to see things clearly.

The most common mistake people make is referring to instances before the divorce to back up their modification request. Even predivorce instances that have never been mentioned before can't be used. The court will only consider circumstances that occurred since the divorce decree had been issued when ruling on a modification.

Take Heed

Any modification request is a new and separate court action, so your ex needs to be located and served and the court that presided over your divorce might not be the court and judge who hears your modification.

Communication Rules When Modifying Your Decree

Most divorced people ended up divorced in part because they could not communicate. So who thinks being divorced makes you a better communicator? Adopting some communication rules as soon as possible will be of assistance here:

➤ Never yell at each other: One or the other of you may be recording the conversation.

➤ Never curse at each other: Again, one or the other of you may be recording the conversation.

➤ Never hang up on the other parent: Even if your ex is yelling and cursing don't hang up. Politely excuse yourself and say that you'll call back later.

➤ E-mail: E-mails serve as a record of your communications, plus both you and your ex are less likely to say the crazy things people say to their exes.

➤ Stay in the present: Don't bring up old issues, even if you know you're right. Your ex either won't care or won't listen anyway.

➤ Don't lecture: You don't like to lecture and it never did any good anyway.

➤ Don't cry: Often crying leads to more attacks.

➤ Listen: A lot of what your ex is saying will be aggravating, but he could provide nuggets of useful information or have legitimate requests.

➤ Accept that your ex's communication will never improve: You couldn't fix him when you were married.

➤ Apologize: As soon as you realize you've made a mistake, apologize.

➤ Put a limit on your time: At the start of your conversation, let your ex know you have only x number of minutes to talk.

➤ Sound nice, and then sound about three times nicer: This just might set a pleasant tone for your conversation.

➤ Never fight with your ex's new spouse: You shouldn't be talking to the new wife about your children anyway. If the new wife causes a problem, take it up with your ex.

➤ Set up a regular communication schedule: You can check and respond to any e-mails from him on Monday nights, for instance.

➤ Keep your schedule: If something unexpected comes up and you can't keep your obligations to your children or your ex, tell your ex as soon as possible.

➤ Don't quote the decree on the phone: You want any information that requires quotes from your decree to be written.

➤ Let your ex talk to the kids when they are with you: Tell your ex in advance when you'll be calling to avoid misunderstandings.

➤ Limit conversations: Covering one topic per conversation will keep things simple and less problematic.

➤ Agree to disagree: Take the high road and stop arguing when you can without it causing a problem.

➤ Trade with your ex: Make a bargain that you'll work on one thing that really bugs him, if he'll work on one thing that really bugs you.

➤ Stay away from delicate topics: If possible, stay clear of topics you know will elicit a fight.

➤ Avoid talking when either of you are in a bad mood: Let your ex know if you're in a bad mood so he knows something besides him is aggravating you.

➤ Send your ex the information before discussing it with him: This will lead to a more productive conversation and will keep your ex from being on the defensive because he doesn't have all the facts.

➤ Agree to always show respect to each other in front of the kids: If you're always dissing each other in front of your children, they will feel confused and caught in the middle.

➤ Agree that emergencies require a phone call: If one of you can't be reached via the phone, texts, e-mails, and notes in the mailbox are to be tried next.

➤ Agree to coordinate schedules: Don't talk to your children about upcoming activities before you've cleared the schedule with your ex. You don't want to build their excitement only to disappoint them in the end.

➤ Keep your divorce conversations private: Children don't need to be privy to unpleasant adult conversations; discuss your divorce issue when your children are not around.

➤ Agree to always stay in touch: It's important for both parents to know how to reach each other for the children's sake.

➤ Agree never to cut off your children's access to the other parent: Even if your child is being punished, he should always be able to get in touch with the other parent.

➤ Compliment your ex: Say something nice from time to time about your ex; it's good for your karma and helps to keep the peace.

➤ Use your words: Many people communicate negative emotions with tone and attitude, snippiness and temper. Learn to use your words to express yourself rather than show your irritation; you're more likely to get results.

➤ E-mail an agenda: Before you talk, send your ex an agenda of the points you want to cover; it will help keep you on track.

Enforcing Communications

The best way to police your conversations with your ex is to clandestinely record them—if you are in a state that allows it. Second best is to preserve voice mails or get a witness to your conversations. If you can arrange it, a neutral witness is better than your sister or best friend. People like ministers, attorneys, teachers, and investigators can give a convincing affidavit of what you are enduring.

If verbal abuse is a problem, keep a log of every instance. The log can be as simple as a dated list or it can be detailed on an Excel sheet. This should be a detailed log that records every instance you were called a name, you were threatened, and so on. Back up your log with phone bills and printed e-mails, and you'll have the evidence you need to give you some relief.

PART FOUR

Handling Your Ex

CHAPTER 12

How to Handle an Angry Ex

In This Chapter

➤ Handling an angry ex's communications

➤ Handling an angry ex in public

➤ What to avoid when dealing with your ex and why

Dealing with an angry ex can be frightening—terrifying, even. The sheer power of anger coupled with the size advantage most men have over women can be downright paralyzing. In this chapter we'll go over ways you can cope with and minimize the effects an angry ex can have on you.

Tracking Communications with Your Angry Ex

Angry exes seem to find nothing else to do than talk at (not to) you, threaten you, torment you, and otherwise aggravate you. How do you deal with that? That depends on which form he uses to communicate with you—by phone, texts, or e-mails. There are different ways for dealing with each of these.

Handy Tip

Your ex seems to enjoy sending you nasty letters and e-mails, and making anger-filled phone calls to you because he wants to aggravate you enough to lose control and make a stupid mistake. Yelling and screaming back at him makes him feel smug, and as far as he's concerned, he's won that round. Try to stay cool, and you'll take the wind right out of his sail.

Keeping a Log

Your best bet is to turn the process of communicating with your ex into a scientific process. To start, Use template 12.1 in the Appendix to start keeping a log of the communications that you had from your ex over the last few months. Notice in the template that there are places to identify the severity of the communication and its type (e-mail, phone call, voice mail, letter, hand delivery, etc.).

There is also a place in the log to note the alleged purpose of the communication. For instance, if your ex calls and curses you out and it has something to do with your child's upcoming student-teacher conference, you could note that in the alleged reason box. Also, jot down what you think might have motivated the call or at least influenced the mood or emotions of your ex. For example, if child support was just increased, you might note the child support increase as a possible factor.

One reason it's important to log in these calls is to remove the emotions from the communication. A tried-and-true way to lose weight is to keep a food journal and write down every single thing that you eat. Then you start to pay close attention to the process and not the emotions. Your ability to adjust your food cravings increases. The same is true of a money journal or money log whereby you write down every single penny you spend; your ability to control your urge to spend increases. When you keep a log of your communications with your ex, you'll receive the following benefits:

> ➤ An increase in your ability to control your urge to react to what your ex is saying

> ➤ Evidence of your ex's behavior if (more likely when) you should have to return to court

> ➤ You'll feel empowered by having control in an abusive situation

Recording Your Conversations

In some states it's legal to record conversations without the other person's knowledge or permission. This, of course, is a priceless tool to bring to court. Before you do any recording, though, you need to find out whether secretly recording your conversations with your ex is legal where you live.

Even if you live in a state that allows this clandestine recording, that doesn't mean it's legal to set a wiretap. A wiretap is a recording device that picks up the conversations of third parties. An example is leaving a recording device in a room where your ex and his father will be talking so you can record their conversation. This would be in violation of wiretapping laws and would carry criminal consequences.

If your state does allow people to record conversations without the other person's permission, you've just acquired a very powerful way to protect yourself against the abusive communications of your ex. The benefits you get from recording conversations are similar to the benefits of keeping a log. But now you have evidence you can present in court that demonstrates both what was said and how it was said. A lot of abusive people may not use abusive words, but the tone and manner in which they speak, the decibel level of their voice, can constitute abuse.

Put it in Writing

Let's say your ex calls to tell you he will be late dropping off your child. When you question why he's late, he begins to yell and scream at you. He may be yelling at you just to let off steam and you just happen to be, conveniently, at the other end of the phone line, or you may have said something that set him off.

Did you point out that this is the fifth time he's been late, that this affects your child's homework, sleep patterns, or sports practice? The reason you bring these facts to light is that you think it may change the way your ex behaves. It won't. Your ex would have to be a reasonable, sane, and good-natured person. He's not.

Instead of voicing your concerns, put them in writing. Your ex will likely feel less affronted and not so much as though he's being put on the spot. A letter also preserves a record of your communications for future use.

Take Heed

Unless you're recording (legally) your conversations with your ex, he will deny most of what you claim was said between the two of you. After all, you have no proof. That's why it's important to get into the habit of corresponding with your ex in writing.

Writing Letters

You can use e-mails for your more casual interactions with your ex, but sending a letter has more of an impact and may be taken more seriously. You've probably been told that any letters you send to your ex should be sent via certified mail. That's because with certified mail requires the recipient's signature—proof that he's received the letter. But you should also send the letter through the normal USPS channels.

People hate having to make the effort to drive to the post office to pick up and sign for certified mail and some routinely refuse to do so. So I recommend you send letters to your ex by certified mail as well as regular US mail. If your ex refuses the certified letter, you can still say that he received the letter that was sent via regular US mail.

When writing a letter to a volatile ex, it's best to stay as matter-of-fact and formal as possible. Start your letter with something like, "I wanted to call to your attention to our conversation on (insert date)." Then you unemotionally describe what took place during the conversation between you and your ex. For instance, if your ex insisted on screaming and yelling even though you asked him to stop, you could write, "During the conversation, you raised your voice and would not stop yelling despite my many requests that you do so."

Be careful. You are not trying to sound like a lawyer. But you don't want to sound totally like yourself either. The letter should have a slight tone of formality to it and should be short and to the point. People, including exes and judges, have a tendency not to read longer letters. You want your ex to respond to the letter by changing his behavior, but it's more likely to be used to document your ex's temper. If you make the letter too long, too dense, too abusive, too argumentative, and involve all sorts of different points, you will make it very hard for your ex and a judge to follow.

Keep your letter on point. Don't write a letter demanding that your child be returned on time, and then go into a discussion of the cheating he did seven years before. The minute a judge sees such a mixed letter, he will begin to disregard it and you. It marks you as an angry person who is holding a grudge and may even be using the letter as a vehicle to get some revenge. So keep your letters short and sweet and clear. It is better to write three letters on three different topics than it is to write one five-page-long letter.

Handy Tip

Any letter you write to your ex should stand alone. References to things outside of the letter that require your personal knowledge may confuse the reader. Always remember that a judge is your final intended audience.

Text Messaging

Are you getting nasty text messages from your ex or his family? If so, you need to know how to preserve and print the messages as soon as they start arriving. You want to get text messages onto a piece of paper in a way that doesn't look like you typed them or had the opportunity to manipulate the words. In other words, don't prop up your phone and type the messages on your PC, and then print them out. In many cases you can send text messages to an e-mail address, and then print them.

Most cell phone providers do have a way for you to get text messages off your phone. You need to be quick, though. Some cell phone providers retain text messages for only a certain period of time. Find out how long your text messages will stay on your phone or in the system before they are deleted. There is nothing worse than finally getting a court date three months from now and discovering the offensive text messages have vanished two days before trial.

You need to analyze your behavior with your ex to make sure you're not setting off any triggers. If you did something to set off your ex, and it's documented in an e-mail or text trail, you need to reconsider your evidence. Always remember that your ex can have the same information that you do. In fact, your ex may have a copy of this book! You do not want to bring in an abusive text string only to have your ex prove that you were giving as good as you got.

Once you print out the offensive text messages, you should forward a copy to your ex, telling him that his behavior is unwelcome and constitutes harassment. (Note you should not contact him if there is a restraining order, only if one is not in place.)

There's nothing wrong with returning a text saying please don't text me or please do not text me and curse at me. However, most people do that instinctively and it usually doesn't work. Send your formal cease-and-desist letter. You can send a text notification that says, "I am sending you a formal cease-and-desist letter requesting you stop texting me," and then follow up by actually sending a letter. See template 10.1 in the Appendix, cease-and-desist letter, which requests the sender stop all contact with you, including text and e-mails. Since you do not have a restraining order and still have children, you cannot tell your ex not to talk to you at all. So you want to use the modified or limited cease-and-desist letter. See template 10.1 in the appendix whereby you request parameters for certain types of communications, which you set out clearly in the letter so there can be no confusion.

In general, make sure that you document and preserve the offensive communications in case you need to prove at a later date that they were abusive. You must create and constantly update your log, which in itself can be submitted as evidence of the abusive behavior. Remove anything that could be construed by your ex as a trigger for his behavior. You do not want to give him easy excuses for why he was misbehaving. And finally, you want to tell your ex very clearly that you wish him to cease the abusive communications.

Handling Angry Exes in Public

There is no one-size-fits-all solution to dealing with a person who is willing to display his temper in public. It's up to you to determine just how much public anger you can and will tolerate. Much of this decision depends on where you are and who else is being impacted.

Some hot-button locations include the following:

> ➤ Your child's school: Parent-teacher meeting, open house, after-school activity
>
> ➤ A point of transition for your child: Your home, your ex's home home, school, or a neutral drop-off point
>
> ➤ Your job
>
> ➤ Grocery stores
>
> ➤ Places of worship

Any public show of anger and aggression is both frightening and humiliating. Let's take a look at what you can do depending on where you are.

When Your Ex Behaves Badly at Your Child's School

There are particular issues surrounding any sort of violence on a school campus. The sheer number of children who could be harmed by an out-of-control angry person is enough to get everyone's attention.

The first step to minimizing danger is to determine if the facility has regulations regarding behavior. A great many schools have protocol for misbehavior by parents. You also want to know if the school will have security present during the day and during after-school activities. It is important that you know in advance what type of assistance you may receive should a true emergency arise. If the school doesn't supply any such assistance, you may need to request special assistance prior to events.

Your child's function should be free of cursing, glares, nasty comments, inappropriate sharing, yelling, and all other abusive communications between you and your ex. Of course, it should be free of abusive communications between your ex and your child.

At least if your spouse misbehaves under these circumstances, there are other people present. Do not be afraid to ask anyone who is around when your ex acts inappropriately to serve as a witness or write you a short note about what he saw. This will add to your evidence for future litigation if it becomes necessary to reign in your out-of-control ex. Let's face it; if you married a crazy person, pride has no place in your heart or in your vocabulary.

Responding to an Angry Ex

When your ex is on a rampage, what do you do? How should you act? Crying and acting hysterical is like throwing gas into a fire. If you want to encourage your ex to keep acting abusively, then just give him what he's looking for—signs that he's upsetting you. Your emotional reaction to your ex's angry behavior shows him that he can still control you.

Fight Back by Doing Nothing

Instead of allowing your ex to push your buttons, convince yourself that it's not necessary for you to respond to his anger. The urge to tell him off may be nearly overpowering, but don't do it. Stay physically and mentally still during a verbal attack, and then it will be easier to prove that you didn't do anything to provoke it.

Although in general a bystander's first inclination is to stay out of the fray, it's human nature to want to assist a helpless person who is being attacked. So when your ex chooses to pitch a fit in the lobby at your child's piano recital, don't join in. Other people in the lobby will be more likely to step in and help you out. Ideally, though, it's best you walk away when you're being accosted, if the situation allows it.

Fighting back will get you nowhere; you're dealing with someone who is being highly irrational. Your ex is not going to suddenly stop his ranting because he understands that what you're saying happens to be true. So resist the urge to fight back, and your ex will look like a complete out-of-control lunatic.

Film the Encounter

If your ex insists on acting a fool in public, you can do what every teenager in the country does when a scene is unfolding—film it! Invest in a decent camcorder or use your smartphone. Keep it at arm's reach at all times. When the crazy hits, you hit record. I have discovered that one way to cool down an angry ex is to tell him that you are recording him. He's likely to reduce the bad behavior to avoid giving you ammunition to use in court.

Take Heed

In most cases, an ex who loses his cool is not doing something illegal. But if you see that your ex is stepping over the line, don't hesitate for one moment to call the police. Don't wait for the intensity to escalate and don't debate it with him.

Protecting Yourself at Work

If you know your ex is volatile and may appear at your place of employment, plan ahead. Explain your situation to your boss or someone in your human resources department.

You don't have to lay everything out—just outline your situation so they are aware of the potential danger. It may be uncomfortable for you to do this. The upside is that the courts will take it seriously if your ex acts out at your place of work.

Another preemptive step you can take is to write a cease and desist letter (see template 10.1 in appendix) to warn your ex away from your place of work. You may want to provide a copy to your employer as an extra precaution.

Handy Tip

When you're out in public and your fuming ex comes looking for you, don't run and hide. Stand next to a crowd or even a group of people. Your ex is less likely to do you harm when there are people about to witness his behavior.

What to Do When You're Out and About

You have to go to the grocery store, to church, to the park with your kids. What do you do if your ex repeatedly shows up at any of these places and creates trouble? The easiest way to avoid your ex in this case is to change your schedule and venue, if you can. If you have always shopped on Sunday after lunch at the same grocery store, shop on a different day of the week at a different grocery store. Better yet, vary when and where you shop weekly or biweekly.

What to Avoid When Dealing with an Angry Ex

Some things you just should not say or do when your ex confronts you. Here are the top five:

1. Pushing his buttons: Doing or saying what you know will rile up your ex will keep you in the fighting loop.

2. Bringing up old problems from your marriage: The court will view you as holding a grudge if you regurgitate old problems—that's not good.

3. Involving the children: Keep the fight between you and your ex as much as possible; your children should never be involved.

4. Expecting your ex to have improved since the divorce: You are sure to be disappointed.

5. Comparing the present to the past: Thinking about the past leaves you mired in your marriage and in negativity.

Pushing His Buttons

You have all witnessed grade school children picking on another child. They find something that one child is sensitive about, like their weight, and they tease the child about it constantly. More than likely, the bantering leads to a fight.

Divorce Vocab

To push someone's buttons means to know how to elicit an emotional reaction from that person. It can have negative or positive connotations. The connotation is definitely negative when you push your ex's buttons; you know exactly what to do or say that will annoy or anger him.

You know what bothers your ex, and you use this information as a shield when you're being attacked. Sometimes you attack first. If you have an ex with anger control problems, chances are you'll be locked in a fighting loop. Your ex is not likely to choose to stop fighting with you. The only way to reduce conflict is for you to make changes.

You may think that it's not fair that you have to back down first, but here is an instance where you can take some control to benefit your sanity. You can control to some degree how your ex acts by not pushing his buttons.

Pushing his buttons can make your ex feel as though he now has license to pick on you. He may even use this in court as the reason he is not controlling himself—you're pushing him to anger.

Bringing Up Old Problems from Your Marriage

Even sane people don't like to be reminded of bad times and poor decisions. So your ex will definitely not respond well if you bring up his past digressions.

Let's start by examining why you bring up instances such as the car he paid too much for that broke down a month later, plunging the family into debt. Why would you bring that up three years after the divorce, and six years after it happened? There can be valid reasons for you:

➤ You may still be paying on that debt and are struggling because it!

➤ You are watching your ex make a similar bad decision right now and want to stop him.

➤ You want to use the past screwup as a reason you are saying no to something right now.

If you were left with the debt after the divorce and have to pay it on your own, your ex most likely does not feel your outrage or sense of unfairness. So your complaining about it won't accomplish anything. Your ex is not going to volunteer to pay it off for you and he is not going to apologize six years after the fact if he hasn't already. So, although your feelings of frustration are valid, there is no good reason to bring up the issue again and again.

You'll be just as ineffective if you're trying to stop your ex from making another bad decision. Let's take a quick, practical look at the situation:

➤ Your ex doesn't like you.

➤ Your ex doesn't trust your judgment.

➤ Your ex thinks you are out to get him or you're out for revenge.

➤ Your ex doesn't want to be told what to do by anybody—especially not by you.

So, even if you have good intentions, without a court order you need to be hands off where your ex is concerned, even if you know he's about to make a big mistake, and even though his mistakes have a direct impact on you. If your ex buys another car that turns out to be a lemon, he may have to use money that should be paid for support to fix the car. Can you prevent this? Probably not.

Your best bet is to offer to be a sounding board for his upcoming decision and try to be unemotional. If your ex takes you up on it, do not attack him; just try to get the information to him for consideration. Stay matter-of-fact in your approach, and tell him what you think. There doesn't need to be an argument. For example, you can tell your ex that you don't want to put money into his new business because the last business didn't work out. That's it.

Involving the Children

You know that you should keep your kids out of fights between you and your ex. But ask yourself if you've said any of the following to your ex during a fight:

➤ "That's why the kids don't want to see you."

➤ "She gets this from you."

➤ "Why don't you tell him that he can't play soccer because you didn't pay for it this month."

➤ "I know you said it; the kids told me you said it!"

➤ "Why do you think he can't concentrate in school?"

➤ "You never do what you say. You don't have to see them cry. I do."

These statements do not convey information as much as involve your kids in your fight. Most angry exes would take this information and question your children, maybe even vent anger at them.

You do need to tell your ex when something impacts the children, but it shouldn't be when he's angry or during a fight. Your ex is more focused on his anger and what he wants to hear, not on what you are saying. You may think that you had communicated the issue to your ex, but he won't remember or acknowledge any of it.

Stop giving your ex important information during fights and he may learn that you will communicate only when the two of you are not fighting. For some of you this means you will stop talking almost entirely! That's okay. That's what e-mail and letters are for (creates a better evidence trail).

The above statements have dual meanings that come across more effectively when spoken with a clear head during calm times:

➤ When you say, "That's why the kids don't want to see you," you're in fact trying to say that your ex's behavior hurts the kids and is destroying their relationship.

➤ When you say, "She gets this from you," you're trying to tell your ex to cut her some slack because she isn't doing it on purpose.

➤ When you say, "Why don't you tell him that he can't play soccer because you didn't pay for it this month," you're trying to explain that you feel like the financial bad guy, and your child won't understand that you rely on his dad to pay for soccer.

➤ When you say, "I know you said it; the kids told me you said it," you're reminding your ex that there are consequences when he says bad things around the kids.

➤ When you say, "Why do you think he can't concentrate in school," you're pointing out that your ex's behavior disrupts your schedule and affects his schoolwork.

➤ When you say, "You never do what you say. You don't have to see them cry. I do," you're trying to explain to your ex that too much uncertainty takes away your children's structure and makes them feel like they can't depend on or trust us.

Learning to get your message across in the least adversarial way increases the chances of it being met with less resistance and getting through to your ex.

The Pitfalls of Expecting Your Ex to Improve

The only reason people change is because they perceive the value of the change and want to make the change. Don't expect your ex to change for any other reason than that he wants to. Here's a list of off-base reasons some people have for expecting their ex to change:

➤ You've changed

➤ The kids need him to be a better parent

➤ His family now understands that he's the problem

➤ He got in trouble for some of the things he did

➤ He can

➤ He should

➤ It would make life easier

Expecting your ex to change only leads to disappointment, which you then blame on your ex. I constantly tell my clients that they bring on their own stress by expecting people to behave outside their normal character. Do not expect a snake to walk; it does not have feet, and it won't do it.

Your ability to manage your personal expectations is at the core of how you change your life. Just as you do not expect a two-year-old to do well on an all-day shopping trip, do not expect your ex to suddenly become the stand-up guy he has never chosen to be.

Take Heed

A farmer was out working in his fields and found a very sick snake. He was a kindly farmer and a good person, so he took the snake into his home. He fed it and cared for it each day. And each day the snake seemed to get a little bit better. After a month, the farmer picked up the snake and was happy to see it had healed entirely. "You are healed Mr. Snake, you can go free," said the farmer. "Thank you," said the snake, and then bit him.

The snake was acting within its character. It was doing what it knew to do. Intentions and wishes rarely counteract core values and beliefs. If your ex is a snake, don't be surprised when he bites.

Comparing the Present to the Past

No good comes from making comparisons between the past and the present. Most people don't make this sort of comparison unless they feel that life is worse now than it was in the past. This kind of negative focus does not motivate anyone to improve on the present conditions.

For instance, you used to own a beautiful home in a great school district and now live in a rental in a district where the goal is just to graduate its students. Focusing on what you no longer have only serves to make you depressed. It makes you feel like a failure. It makes you angry. These negative emotions will make you more likely to push your ex's buttons, bring up old problems, involve the kids, and complain about your ex's failure to change. In short, comparing the present to the past can make it easier for you to do exactly what you need to avoid doing!

What does this comparison do for your ex? It will not make him calmer. It will not make him communicate more. It will not protect your children. It will not make him change. Start breaking the comparison habit today.

The best way to get rid of a negative habit is to replace it with a positive one. I recommend that you place a loose rubber band around your wrist. Every time you catch yourself comparing your present to your past, snap your rubber band and imagine that you are "snapping yourself out of it." You don't have to do this hard; pain is not the goal. The goal is to notice the habit, put a stop to it, and remind yourself to redirect your thoughts to something positive about your present circumstances.

 # Sharing Custody of Your Children

The area that generates the most stress after a divorce is working with your ex on all the issues that impact your children. If your ex is angry, crazy, or just plain unreasonable, it sets the process up for failure. There are some things you can do to improve your situation. They won't work perfectly for everyone, but they should grant you some small measure of relief.

Co-Parenting

When both parents in a divorce cooperate in raising their children, it's called co-parenting. The benefits of co-parenting are that both parents can be a strong influence in their children's lives, sharing time, information, and making decisions jointly and with the best interests of the children in mind. It usually requires some control of emotions.

Co-parenting is a marvelous thing when it's done right. Parents who are best at co-parenting often have resolved or let go of the lingering issues that distract other couples. Co-parenting is likely to fail in cases where there has been physical abuse, domestic violence, or extreme emotional abuse.

How to Make Co-Parenting Work

You and your ex need to lay a foundation for a co-parenting relationship to be successful. Here are some ways to establish that foundation:

➤ Both parents have to believe that the other has something valuable to offer the children and that the other parent's time with the children is important and desirable.

➤ Both parents have to work out a fair time schedule for their children.

➤ Both parents have to follow the stipulations of their agreement.

➤ Both parents have to give a heads up in a timely manner to the other when plans change or emergencies arise.

➤ Both parents need to reinforce to the children the positive benefits of the other parent.

➤ Both parents have to avoid letting the children observe or hear parental discussions, friendly or not.

➤ Both parents have to resist fighting the children's battles with the other parent—the children should be encouraged to resolve their issue with that parent directly.

➤ Both parents must be flexible to the other's changing needs.

➤ Both parents must make all decisions based on what is in the children's best interests, even when it is to his or her disadvantage.

➤ Both parents need to separate their emotional baggage from parenting decisions.

➤ Both parents must be respectful to each other.

➤ Both parents should make all important decisions or changes together.

➤ Both parents need to make it as easy as possible to share the children's possessions and to fix mistakes.

➤ Both parents must share information about the children as they receive it.

➤ Both parents must pay on time whatever they agreed to or are obligated to pay.

➤ Both parents should select and enforce the teaching of important values to the children.

In *Psychology Today*'s "Divorce for Grownups" blog, Sam Margulies wrote the article *Co-Parenting after Divorce*, which gives these six successful tips on making co-parenting work (read the article at www.psychologytoday.com/blog/divorce-grownups/200903/co-parenting-after-divorce.com):

1. Residential proximity: Co-parenting by divorced parents who live near each other is most successful partly because the lives of all involved are minimally inconvenienced.

2. Economic parity: Fair financial responsibilities for each parent are important to successful co-parenting. Child support guidelines may not be adequate. Divorced parents should review their budgets to ensure that each household is sufficiently funded.

3. Intelligent scheduling: Schedules should allow both parents time with their children and time for themselves. The children need time with each parent and stability. Everyone needs to be flexible to allow for conflicts and unexpected schedule changes.

4. Acceptance of different styles: Co-parenting requires tolerance and acceptance of different parenting styles. For instance, you may think that an 8:30 bedtime is important for your children, and your ex may feel it's perfectly fine for the kids to be up until 10:00. Both of you need to accept the other's decisions—unless, of course, they may cause harm to the children.

5. Acceptance of each other's new spouses: The children should be encouraged by each parent to like and accept their new stepparent. It will be difficult, or even impossible, to co-parent if the children are uncomfortable in either home. And each parent needs to keep any jealousy they're feeling in check.

6. Effective conflict resolution: Divorce leads to many changes for both parents and children. Coordinating new schedules and new logistics can be difficult. Co-parenting requires the ability of both parents to resolve their differences in a friendly and respectful manner. Sometimes a mediator may be needed to help resolve more emotional or complex conflicts.

Take Heed

Children who are constantly exposed to parental fighting are most likely to have difficulties in life. They don't feel safe in such a toxic atmosphere. If you have to fight your ex, do it when the children are out of the house.

Here are some particularly toxic comments that you must avoid saying to your children (from "Co-Parenting through Separation and Divorce: Children First." North Dakota State University. http://www.ag.ndsu.edu/pubs/yf/famsci/fs565w.htm):

➤ "If you don't behave, I'll send you to live with your father/mother."

➤ "You're lazy/stubborn/bad tempered, just like your mother/father."

➤ "I could get along better here by myself."

➤ "If you weren't here, I could …"

➤ "Sometimes I wish I'd been the one to skip out."

➤ "Your mother/father put you up to saying that."

➤ "Your dad/mom doesn't love any of us or he/she wouldn't have left us."

➤ "You can't trust her/him."

➤ "He/she was just no good."

➤ "If she/he loved you, she/he would send your support checks on time."

➤ "If your mother/father is five minutes late again, you're just not going with her/him."

➤ "If you don't like what I buy you, ask your father/mother to do better."

➤ "Who would you really rather be with, Mommy or Daddy?"

➤ "Now that you're the little man/little woman of the house …"

➤ "Someday you'll leave me too, just like your father/mother. Promise me that you'll never leave."

➤ "You're all I have. You're the only person I can rely on."

➤ "Over my dead body!"

Parallel Parenting

In my years of practice I have seen countless judges yell, threaten, punish, and even take children away from parents who could not cooperate with each other. They ignored the obvious fact that it takes two to cooperate. If my client was willing to cooperate and the other parent was not, we would be doomed to fail in our court ordered mission to parent cooperatively. Recently, a saner approach called parallel parenting has evolved.

Some of you cannot make any decision jointly with your ex, large or small, obvious or not. Any attempt to come to an agreement on a parenting decision spirals into an argument. There are those who become emotional any time they just think about dealing with their ex. Unfortunately, this exposes the children to ongoing conflict at a level that is guaranteed to cause them present and future mental health problems.

Take Heed

Children who are exposed to an inordinate amount of anger and fighting between their parents may develop some serious stress-related physical issues, such as bed wetting, regression, aggression, hair loss, depression, anxiety, sleeplessness, or even nervous breakdowns and suicide attempts. Make every effort to keep the arguments between you and your ex completely out of earshot of your children.

Parallel parenting is a form of joint child custody that allows each parent to raise the children independently with as little input or consultation from the other parent. Each parent has the authority to make decisions regarding their children while they are in that parent's custody. It gives each parent the opportunity to raise their children and be involved in their children's lives when the parents cannot work together. Communication between the parents is not encouraged, and when it can't be avoided, it is usually done via e-mail or other form of writing.

The parallel parenting agreement spells out very clearly who has authority to make certain decisions and usually requires the other parent to be informed of those decisions. A third party may be enlisted at the beginning to make sure that the agreement covers as much as possible so neither parent has to instruct, request, advise, or demand the other make a decision a certain way. The plan must be as detailed as possible so that any loopholes, vagueness, or ambiguities are ironed out from the start.

With parallel parenting, the children have two separate parenting realms. While this may sound unusual, adapting to two different homes, two different sets of rules, bedtimes, homework routines, and so on is actually better for a child than the continual conflict that arises when their parents can't get along or agree on anything.

Each parent leaves the child to the rules and dominion of the other parent when in their care and never questions the child about what goes on in the other home. In this way, each parent can parent as he or she feels is best.

Setting up a parallel parenting agreement is best done at the time of the divorce, but you can revise your agreement to include parallel parenting if things are truly that bad between you—as long as your ex agrees. This is another instance where getting a third party involved to act as an intermediary may be a good idea.

A word of warning: you may have a hard time finding an attorney familiar with parallel parenting. Do some Internet research and be prepared to explain parallel parenting to the judge if you are not in a state like California, which was an early adopter. It may be beneficial to have a counselor on board to provide you with a written recommendation to ease the judge's introduction to parallel parenting if he or she has never heard of this kind of arrangement. See the resources on parallel parenting in the Appendix.

Counseling

Learning how to deal with your new life, the changes you see in your children, and your ex is a lot to handle. Counseling can help you and your children through this transition.

Counseling does not carry the stigma it once did. These days it would be difficult to find someone who has not been exposed to counseling either personally or through someone he or she knows. The advantages of counseling include the following:

> ➤ There are many different kinds of counseling, and at least one will likely fit your needs.

> ➤ There is flexibility in the costs of counseling—it's possible to find group counseling or clinics with a sliding fee scale that will be affordable for you.

> ➤ There are a variety of personalities and counseling approaches; you are likely to find a combination that will work for you.

> ➤ There are counselors who work evenings, weekends, and even by phone—check the Internet or ask for a referral from a friend or physician.

Counseling for Your Children

Getting counseling for your children can help them develop their coping skills and attain emotional stability. The latter is no small trick when their world appears to be so unstable to them. You will have to investigate your options to see what kind of counseling is best for your children and be aware that one child may need one type of counseling and another child may need a different type.

Generally, you have a choice between group therapy and individual therapy. Groups are composed of kids who have similar divorce issues. They're a good choice especially for teenagers who feel more comfortable receiving help from their peers. It also helps reinforce that they are not the only kid in the world with dysfunctional families.

Individual therapy is the traditional type of therapy where the child meets individually with a counselor. It is critical that the child bond to the counselor. Many factors can affect this bonding process, including the counselor's age, gender, race, sports interests, and whether siblings see the same counselor.

When introducing your children to counseling, tell them that you are going to try different counselors until you find one they are happy with. This will give them the assurance that they have some say in the process, which can go a long way toward getting their cooperation.

Counseling for Your Ex

Unless you have a court order mandating your ex gets counseling, you can't force him into it. If you do have an order that requires family or co-parenting counseling, just remember not to try to do the following:

➤ Make your ex sorry for what he did

➤ Punish your ex for all that has happened

➤ Turn your ex into you

The goal is to improve concrete aspects of the way your ex communicates and interacts with you and your children. This can be achieved in many cases if you are careful not to push for your agenda and just let everything take its course.

If you don't already have a court order for counseling, then you didn't push for it because you wanted to get through the divorce more quickly, your judge wasn't a fan of counseling, or you presented your evidence and were denied. If you were denied, you will need your ex to do several crazy things to establish a pattern so that you can prove that counseling is in order. You will need to document his behavior carefully, hopefully with the help of impartial witnesses like teachers, doctors, other parents, neighbors, and so on. Getting an order for an ex to be evaluated or receive counseling post-divorce is tricky and should be handled by your local family law specialist.

Using Technology to Communicate

It was hard enough for you and your ex to communicate when you were married, but now there are multiple, separate schedules and fewer incentives than before. Consider taking advantage of some of the advances in technology to make things smoother.

Web-Based Communication Services

Several companies offer a web-based calendar and communication service that can act as a bridge between you and your ex and give you a neutral

Handy Tip

Several different companies offer web-based calendars and other ways for divorced parents to communicate. Two of them are www.ourfamilywizard.com and parentingtime.net. You can find others by doing an Internet search.

place to post information. You can post questions, updates, and even contact information for school and medical events. Communicating this way is impersonal, free of stresses and arguments.

Video Conferencing

In addition to companies that offer centralized scheduling and information websites for divorced families, there are video conferencing services. One such company is Skype.

Skype is a VoIP (Voice over Internet Protocol) application that allows users to make voice calls, transfer files, send instant messages, and hold video conferences over the Internet. Calls to other users within the Skype service are free, while calls to both traditional landline telephones and mobile phones can be made for a fee using a debit-based user account system.

Skype can be a good way to supplement communication between a parent and children who live far from each other or are traveling. Many report that the phone calls with their children are generally longer and more satisfying when the video option is included. This can be especially important when children are young and their attention span is limited.

Even though Skype has grown in popularity, concerns have arisen about its safety for children. A quick Internet search will bring up many websites that go over safety tips for protecting children using Skype.

Cell Phones

Cell phones are great for keeping parent and child connected, but they don't come without potential pitfalls for the child. A child needs to be mature enough not to get sucked into text messaging all day long, talking on the phone incessantly, and even playing games when they should be doing schoolwork or sleeping.

You will need to set some rules and boundaries for your children to follow before giving them their own cell phones. There are companies that can help you do this. One such company is kajeet.com. It offers a variety of parental controls, GPS tracking, and even what it calls a wallet for both you and your children to help them learn financial responsibilities.

It's essential to set some rules for your children, establishing guidelines and consequences that go along with cell phone use. Spell out what you will and will never do (like pay any overage charges or put the bill in your name), what you may consider doing, and what your children must do in exchange. Discuss cell phone rules with your children and how the following scenarios may impact their cell phone privileges:

➤ The child's grades slip below the acceptable level.

➤ The child gets into serious trouble.

➤ The child is involved in any kind of trouble stemming from use of the phone like a car accident or sexting (sending of sexual texts).

➤ Your ex says he is going to stop paying for the phone and you do not want to or cannot pay for it.

➤ The phone is lost or damaged.

➤ The child breaks rules covering maximum time spent on the phone, maximum number of texts, and late night phone usage.

➤ How and under what circumstances the phone shall be removed for punishment.

➤ Who pays the overage charges if the child runs the phone beyond its air time or text limits.

The biggest reason cell phones become a headache is because no advance planning is done to address these very common situations.

CHAPTER 14

Alternatives to Going Back to Court

> ## In This Chapter
>
> ➤ Choosing not to fight
> ➤ Mediation as an option to conflict
> ➤ The arbitration alternative
> ➤ Preparing for future litigation

You cannot entirely prevent ending up in court again after your divorce has been finalized, but you can take steps to lower the odds as much as possible. If you and your ex find yourself at an impasse, however, there are alternatives to going back to court. A basic change you can make is to decide to fight only about those issues that matter the most to you; let the others go.

Picking Your Battles

People fight over a lot of things that in the long run don't much matter. Sometimes our ego keeps us from backing down. You have been conditioned by your marriage to fight, and the divorce decree didn't sprinkle you in magic old-habit-breaking dust. You are used to fighting with your ex. You are not used to letting things go.

The very simple cost of peace is to learn which battles are worth fighting for and which ones are not worth the cost, even if you win them. To get the hang of this, I recommend you call a one-sided truce. It is one-sided because you are not going to discuss it with your ex. Refuse to fight for ten days. Refuse any challenge or aggression that does not flat out physically endanger your children. Revel in the power (yes, choosing not to fight feels powerful) of your choice.

Keep a chart or list and jot down how many things come up that you don't react to. This ten-day "diet" of peace will convince you that you can determine what you want to do regardless of the situation. Your ex may try to bait you. Laugh it off. Write it on your list. Feel strong. This is what is meant by rising above your circumstances.

If avoiding a fight is new to you, here are some examples to help you get started.

> ➤ Ex: I need to bring the kids back early; something came up, are you at home?

You: Yes. Can you get them here in the next half hour?

You did not point out that you have things to do, that he never spends time with the kids, that having the kids back early ruins your plans to get a few things done without them in your hair, and you did not say no to force your ex to use his time with the kids. You did not argue.

Do not worry that letting this go will set a precedent for your ex to walk all over you. All you did was go along with the change in plans and decline to fight.

> ➤ Ex: Things have been a little tight. I won't have your check for another week or two.

You: I understand. OK, I'll call you next Saturday, and you can narrow down the date for me. I will need to know when it is coming to adjust my bills.

You did not point out that it is always something or that you don't believe things are that tight for him. You did not yell, curse, hang up, or otherwise display negative emotion. You did not argue about when you would have the check, and you did not accuse him of doing a poor job with the child support.

What you did was acknowledge his statement and make a definite and reasonable request, and then the issue is closed.

> ➤ Ex: I have been telling you for years that you need to get that car taken in, and you never listen. I'm not going to help you when it breaks down. You just don't spend your money wisely, and I always have to bail you out. This is how it was when we were married.

You: Hmm. I hear you. I see why you believe that. I do have to get back to (work/the kids/dinner/a project I have going) now. So, I'm going to run.

You did not question the validity of his statements, argue, use a sarcastic tone, or disagree with him. You did not bring up any of the multiple hurtful things he's said or push back.

What you did was acknowledge his thoughts (crazy or not) and excuse yourself—you rolled with it.

Let's say your ex wouldn't let it drop and goes on.

> ➤ Ex: Don't try to avoid this! I am tired of you avoiding everything. You need to deal with what's going on. You do this same thing with the kids, and they've told me they've had it with your *@?!

You: I hear you. I am not somewhere where I can talk right now. I will not avoid any issue we have that impacts the children. I will call you on (pick a date) so we can talk calmly. I will send you an e-mail before then with the issues I think we have to discuss; you can send me back anything you think I missed.

You did not react to the nasty language or the escalation, start arguing, meet him at his emotional level and fight, ignore the one part of his ranting that was valid (to discuss a child's issue).

What you did was redirect the fight to another date and time of your choosing. You also asked him for his input—everyone, especially narcissists, loves being asked for their input. You did this in a way so that when you send your agenda, it will be welcomed because he will want to review and revise it. It will get you on track to use an agenda to work things out. This helps keep the talking on topic and to a minimum.

At the end of your ten days, check your list and see what was thrown at you. Do you notice any patterns? Did you see that by not responding, some of the situations just went away? Was there anything serious that you still needed to deal with? Notice that even if something happened that you have to address, you will be addressing it calmly. If you didn't have to resist more than three invitations to fight, extend your ten-day trial period by another ten days. You need to practice.

Inevitably, some things will be too serious to ignore. Some examples include not giving the children medicines at all or on schedule, leaving the children unattended, not paying support or always paying late, and always altering the visitation schedule. If you have tried gentle diplomacy to no avail, you may want to consider the use of alternative dispute resolution methods such as mediation or arbitration.

Mediation

You and your ex are at an impasse. You are unable to see eye to eye on an issue or on many issues. The thought of going back to court turns your stomach. What do you do?

One non-adversarial way to solve disputes outside of the courtroom is through mediation. This way of settling a legal argument enlists the help of a neutral third party—a mediator.

The mediator is an impartial facilitator who meets with both sides and works to find a mutually agreeable solution to the conflict. Mediation has a structure, timetable, and dynamics that informal negotiation lacks. The mediator does not have the legal power to impose or enforce a decision, though, that's up to the parties involved. If the issues can't be resolved by a mediator, the next step is to file a lawsuit.

Divorce Vocab

Arbitration, although usually used in business, is another way besides mediation to resolve conflicts in divorce without going to court. The arbitrator is more like a judge than a mediator in that arbitrators have the power to decide cases. Unlike with mediation, where the opposing parties make the final decision, the arbitrator has the final say.

Mediators use various techniques to open discussions and help opposing parties reach an agreement. Attorneys develop relationships with good mediators and will be able to help you select one who will be a good fit for your case. I tend to prefer strong-arm mediators who really make an effort to help both sides see where they are not being reasonable.

Mediation does work. I have settled cases with mediation that had seemed hopeless. Here are some tips to help you prepare for mediation so you have a better chance of a successful outcome:

➤ Make child care arrangements for the whole day. You do not want to interrupt a process that is working because you have to pick up the kids, or be preoccupied with the logistics of how to get your kids home.

➤ If you go through mediation without an attorney, have a law firm on call in case you need a quick bit of advice. You will need to set up this agreement and make financial arrangements for it in advance of your mediation.

➤ Make a list of the big issues you want to discuss and the little issues involved with each big topic so you don't miss anything.

➤ Charge your cell phone and laptop.

➤ Dress nicely even though you're not going to court and there is no one to impress. Women often feel better if they're dressed nicely when they face their ex. Keep in mind that you're not dressing up for your ex; you're dressing up to feel professional and confident.

➤ Eat before leaving the house and bring lunch and snacks with you. Mediation can take hours and hours. If you are starving, you will be more irritable and distracted.

➤ Bring your legal file with you and any documents you may even remotely need. You don't want a smooth-running mediation to be postponed just because you don't have the exact cost of the summer camp, health insurance, or braces quote with you.

➤ Park in an all-day lot or somewhere else that won't require you to move your car or feed a meter after a certain number of hours.

Handy Tip

Obvious or not, there are some reactions you should avoid during mediation:

➤ Do not make a big deal of something that is important to you; that's like waving the "take it from me" flag.

➤ Do not let your emotions get out of control.

➤ Do not gloat or celebrate when you get something you want.

During mediation, you're allowed to meet with the mediator on your own, without your ex being present. These meetings are usually called a caucus. Ask for a caucus with the mediator whenever you need a break from your ex. In fact, you can ask that an entire mediation be conducted so that you and your ex are in separate rooms. If you have a history of not getting along or domestic violence, ask for this kind of mediation in advance. Be sure to confirm that it has been set up this way and the mediator assigned to the case is aware of it.

Here are some tips to help you during mediation:

➤ Do not bring other people with you into the mediation room—it will just cause problems. You can have someone waiting outside the room for moral support, and you can call whomever you'd like from your cell phone during breaks.

➤ Do not let other people make your mediation decisions for you.

➤ Do not let what your ex says during mediation bother you. A lot of that inflammatory talk is just pure habit or is said intentionally to put you on tilt so you'll do a poor job negotiating. This is a great time to practice the truce project described earlier in this chapter. Focus on extracting the facts and discard the rest.

➤ Do expect to feel like you were hit by a truck when you wake up the following day. Often buyer's remorse sets in. Your deal, if you reached an agreement, cannot be changed. Be aware when striking your bargain that it is final.

Keep in mind that the mediator is not a judge. He or she cannot make you or your ex do anything; the entire process is voluntary. Even if you are ordered to mediation by the court, you can't be ordered to settle.

Your ex may not have this advice, so he may try to use the mediator as a judge or cheerleader with the goal of getting someone else on his side to agree on how awful you are. Breathe deep. The mediator won't go along with your ex and you'll live through it.

Take Heed

The legal system encourages mediation. To get people to talk openly and settle their case, everything discussed in mediation is considered to be confidential. If your ex says he makes more money than he had claimed before, you cannot make the mediator come to court and testify to that.

Future Litigation

In a perfect world, you will return to court only if and when you are ready to go. If you follow the concepts set out in this book, you will eliminate the main reason for fearing court—being unprepared.

It is best to prepare for future litigation now. If it never happens, then you got lucky. If it does happen, however, you can feel smug in that you had been planning for it in advance and are prepared.

Here are some of the preparations you should make:

> ➤ Start a legal piggy bank fund for an attorney. Your goal should be to have $2,000 set aside within two years, which means putting aside about $83 a month. Think if it like an insurance payment. If you are bad at saving, take $1,000 from your next two tax refunds or windfalls.

> ➤ Get into the habit of documenting everything in every legal way you can, including tape recording, video recording, saving and printing out e-mails, and print screens of social networking pages. If an incident occurs, get affidavits from willing witnesses right away.

> ➤ Change your attitude from being nervous about going to court to feeling confident because you'll be prepared. The best way to win a war is to be so well fortified that no one wants to fight you.

➤ Address your weaknesses to make you a stronger person and to make any complaints your ex may have against you illegitimate. If you do get called out, you can prove that you fixed, resolved, addressed, improved, or eliminated whatever your ex complained about. Taking care of your issues can prevent the need to go to court.

➤ Form a relationship with the attorney you want to represent you. This doesn't mean try to date him; it means get to know him and his staff, his practices, and how his retainers and fees are determined. This is a lifesaver if you need a quick question answered.

➤ Tell your ex that you want to work on resolving your problems without going back to court. Do this in writing (and keep a copy) so you can prove that you weren't trying to fight. And don't put that statement in an e-mail filled with nagging, hate, complaints, and other negative trappings.

➤ Always conduct yourself so that your behavior and choices can be explained to a judge without fear. This goes double for your writings. Assume your ex keeps everything you write, so don't sound crazy or mean, and don't curse, threaten, or willfully fail to follow through on your promises.

➤ Take responsibility for your actions. If you make a mistake or do something wrong, admit it and fix it right away as best you can. Most people think this would make you more vulnerable, but it actually makes you sympathetic and likeable, traits that are rare in courthouses these days.

CHAPTER 15

Protecting Yourself During Litigation

In This Chapter

➤ Gathering evidence

➤ Mistakes to avoid

➤ What to do if you've been arrested

Going to court to face an ex can leave some people feeling helpless and vulnerable, especially when there are no funds to hire an attorney. What do you say? What should you bring with you? What will you need?

This chapter is designed to give guidelines for preparing evidence to those who will be representing themselves in court.

Gather Your Strongest Evidence

You probably have bags full of papers you want to use as evidence against your ex. But what do you think you're going to do with that bounty of proof, dump it on the judge's desk? Judges don't have the time or the interest to wade through an unorganized mess of potential evidence. It's better to sort your papers and other evidence into a sensible accounting of your ex's transgressions.

E-Mails

Find a pattern among your pieces of evidence. Let's say you have thirty-two e-mails. Perhaps seven of them are angry and nasty in tone. Pick the worst one as an example. Maybe fifteen of the e-mails are regarding changing visitation at the last second. Pick one clear-cut example that doesn't require a lot of reading. Maybe the rest are all aimed at making you feel bad about the divorce four years ago. Again, pick one that is representative.

Out of those thirty-two e-mails, you should have three to show the judge as evidence of your ex's behavior. You can refer to the total number of e-mails you received in each group within a specific time period. Don't throw those other e-mails away, though. Be prepared and have the additional e-mails sorted into three stacks, ready for the judge just in case he or she asks for them.

Take Heed

Pay attention to the condition of the documents you plan to use in court as evidence. If you have a document that is barely readable, consider whether it is critical to your case. If you present it in court and the judge can't read it, it may be disregarded and your account of what it says may even be questioned.

Choose evidence that proves your point with the least amount of speaking, thinking, reading, or explanation. Do not make or expect the judge to work hard on your case. Who knows what mood the judge is in or whether there is something occupying his or her mind. Do not require or expect to get 100 percent attention from the judge.

Do not write on your evidence and original documents. This drives courts, judges, and attorneys crazy. If you've already written on your credit card statement from last year, so be it; but do not highlight it, draw arrows on it, circle parts, and so on. If you feel the need to notate a piece of evidence, do so on an identical copy only! Evidence that has been written on has technically been tampered with.

Several days before your court date, lay out your evidence on a table. On 1 × 1-inch sticky notes, write either Plaintiff's #_____ or Defendant's #_____. Place the sticky note on the bottom center of the original document. You can handwrite the label on the copies if you like. Place each copy under its tagged original.

Photographs, Logs, and Journals

If you have a bruise, photograph it. If somebody tears your clothes, keep the clothing. You have to keep this evidence. You can't throw it away. You can't say, "Oh, my baby sister's neighbor's cousin saw it." The best evidence is the actual object. So if somebody punches your nose and you bleed on your shirt, keep your shirt and take photos.

Keep logs and journals that describe your arguments, what you were arguing about, money flow, money discussions, child support and alimony payments because they can be used as evidence in court.

Police Reports

When you call the police, request a formal police report—especially if it's regarding a domestic violence incident. Some police officers are reluctant to do the paperwork required to file a police report. In that case, get the officer's name and badge number and make sure you document it because if you have to call the officer's supervisor, you're going to need to prove that you actually called the police for help in the first place.

Creating a Trial Book of Evidence

Creating a trial book is a good way to keep everything organized. In a three-ring binder or presentation sleeve, add your evidence, placing colored paper or some other sort of divider between each type of evidence. If you have a lot of evidence, it's a good idea to create an at-a-glance chart to place at the front of the book (see template 15.1 in the Appendix).

Once your evidence is organized in the book, mark whether each was accepted or not. You should also use this book to jot down notes about the evidence your ex has offered and whether it was admitted or not.

All this preparation may sound like busy work, but in court on your big day you will be distracted and nervous. You'll feel more confident knowing that all your documents are at your fingertips. Also, you can take pleasure in knowing that you have an organization system similar to what your ex is paying his attorneys thousands of dollars for.

Handy Tip

Sometimes the trial evidence is kept by the court, and sometimes it's returned. Both scenarios are normal, so don't be surprised if after all your hard work preparing your trial book, the court decides not to keep it on file and returns it to you.

Witnesses

Witnesses brought by litigants without lawyers tend to be woefully underprepared and often talk too much. Judges hate cases with a lot of witnesses. Generally one witness is enough. If you have three or more witnesses, it appears as though they are just cheerleading, telling everyone how great you are, which is not helpful to a judge unless your character is in question. Having many witnesses saying basically the same thing is not helpful and can be annoying to a judge.

Sort your witnesses just as you sorted your document evidence. To determine your most powerful witness, ask yourself who you would choose to testify if you were allowed only five minutes. If you are in a case so complex that it legitimately requires three or more witnesses, you should hire a lawyer.

If you do decide to go forward without an attorney, check out our website at www.upickupaylegal.com for affordable videos that will help you and your witness prepare for court. See Chapter 19 for more information on going to court on your own.

A Few Common Rules

You should be aware of the potential pitfalls and rules you may face by going to court without an attorney. Here are a few:

➤ Make at least two copies of each piece of evidence because you must share your evidence with the opposing side before you present it to a judge.

➤ Since you're not an attorney, your evidence may not be accepted. Your ex or his attorney, if he has one, may object to your evidence. If he objects, he has to give a reason, and then you have to respond to his legal objection. "I really want to use it" is not a proper legal response. You have to argue (legally) or explain why your evidence or document is proper for the court to see.

➤ The hearsay rule trips up a lot of people representing themselves. If you are directly quoting someone else, he or she must be present in court to say it. The court doesn't want to rely on what you say that person said. Think about it; what crazy things could your ex make up that someone supposedly said about you?

Divorce Vocab

Litigation is simply the judicial process by which rights are enforced.

One way around this is to present the information without attributing it to a specific person. For example, it's hearsay if your report that the real estate agent said the house is worth $175,000. But you might be able to get away with just stating that the house is worth $175,000.

Constant Call to Court

Your ex has plenty of money and a seemingly big desire to take you to court again and again. What do you do? Document, document, document.

The best way to address an ex who is repeatedly filing suits against you is to construct a detailed chart of all the litigations, how they ended in your favor (hopefully), and show that your ex is just harassing you with all these lawsuits. You must be able to show a judge quickly and easily that when litigation is filed by your ex, he never (or rarely) prevails and is often warned about his behavior by the judge.

Make a habit of having all your hearings transcribed by the court reporter to create a reviewable record. This is an extra expense that can run $30–$70 an hour, so be sure to ask how much it is; the cost is due at the end of the hearing. Having a hearing transcribed also encourages the judge to be on slightly better behavior.

The transcription is not typed up automatically; you have to request that it be typed, and this can cost hundreds of dollars, so be certain you need the whole record if you request it. You can ask to have just a section of a hearing typed up, like the opening statements and the judge's ruling. And you don't have to have it typed out at all; you can just have it taken down and saved for future need.

The reason you want to get in the habit of having your hearings transcribed is that your ex is bound to slip up and lie, and the transcript is your proof of what he said under oath. If you can prove to a judge that your ex has lied, the judge will likely be more motivated to act.

Hire an Attorney

Get the best attorney you can afford, but be sure to get someone who you can stick with over the years. It is valuable to have one attorney long-term when dealing with an angry ex for the following reasons:

➤ There is less of a learning curve

➤ It will save you money in the future

➤ It's a subtle positive sign to the judge when a person is able to keep the same lawyer over time; it shows the lawyer believes in you and you are meeting your financial obligations to the lawyer

What if you can't afford a lawyer? If your ex is determined to keep throwing money at the courthouse and any attorney who promises to harass you, you need a strong lawyer to devise a strategy and create a line of defense between you and your ex. This will cost you a good bit of money, but it can be looked at as an investment in preventing future litigations.

One option you have is to ask for your ex to pay your attorney's fees because of the disparity in your incomes. While you may be allowed to seek an award of fees at the start of a case to enable you to protect yourself, I see a number of judges who like to wait until the end of the case to consider the awards. This is not good news for you. Your lawyer may have to make a very strong argument for an early (interim) award of fees to keep you represented.

Try to get as much information on your ex's finances as possible not just because it will bother him, but because you need to be able to show the disparity of your incomes.

Common Mistakes that Will Make Your Ex Sue You

Here are some things to avoid because they are like waving a red flag in front of a bull and scream, "take me back to court!"

Money Issues

Money is a huge point of contention for many couples, whether married or divorced. Divorce, though, can bring out the worst in people where money is concerned. If you have the bigger income, don't do the following:

➤ Take a vacation, especially a nice vacation

➤ Purchase a car, especially a nice car

➤ Purchase visible accessories such as jewelry, car rims, fancy cell phones

➤ Buy big-ticket luxury items such as a flat screen TV, a new gaming system, new furniture

➤ Lend money to other people

➤ Buy fancy gifts for anyone

➤ Move into an expensive home or apartment

➤ Show favoritism on support payments if you have children from different marriages

➤ Quit your job

Visitation Issues

Children are another huge source of contention between exes. You both love your children, but they sometimes get caught in the middle of power moves made by either or both parties. Don't let that happen. So when your children are at stake, do not do the following:

➤ Move farther away (if possible)

➤ Move your new significant other into your home

➤ Threaten to take your ex to court—just do it if you have to

➤ Involve the police unless absolutely necessary

➤ Hide the children with other family members to avoid visits

➤ Play games with court-required communication between a parent and child by claiming the child is always busy, asleep, in the shower, and so on, as a means to keep your ex away from your child

➤ Tell your ex that your new spouse or significant other is a better parent than your ex is (even if it's true)

➤ Tell your children if they don't like your rules they can go live with your ex

➤ Exclude your children from your ex's wedding (without a court order)

➤ Block visitation on critical holidays

General Issues

Many of the general behaviors that may instigate your ex to sue you are really based on common sense. Here are a few things you should not do if you want to avoid being sued by your ex:

➤ Start a scene in public

➤ Fight with school officials (dealing with school officials when they are wrong takes finesse, not intimidation)

➤ Let your child skip school or be constantly tardy

➤ Hide medical records, procedures, visits, or other critical health information

➤ Let your child call your new spouse (or anyone else) Mom or Dad in place of your ex

➤ Ground your child from the phone and include your ex

➤ Take away your child's cell phone without telling your ex or ensuring he still has a way to communicate with your child

➤ Send your child out of town or state (like to Grandma's or camp) during your ex's visitation time without agreement

Arrests

On the off chance that something goes terribly awry or you make some very bad decisions and you get arrested, what do you do? It all depends on where you are in the divorce court process.

Recently Arrested for a Divorce-Related Issue

Get a lawyer, quick! In fact, you are likely to need two attorneys—a family lawyer and a criminal lawyer. Yes, this will cost you a lot of money. But if you haven't been in trouble before, the odds are good that a competent criminal lawyer can get you off lightly.

Be careful of using one lawyer for both your divorce issues and your criminal issues. There are some attorneys who can handle both and it would save money, but you're increasing the risk of criminal liability or loss of custody.

By acting quickly, your lawyers can figure out how best to arrange damage control for you before the case goes on a civil calendar (with your ex) or a criminal calendar with the prosecutor. There are times when what you are doing in one court impacts how the other court is inclined to proceed, so intelligent coordination here is a must.

Take Heed

If you are obligated by the court to disclose your arrest and your ex found out that you failed to do so, he could add this oversight to the criminal act. Discuss this with your family lawyer.

Recently Arrested for an Issue Unrelated to Your Divorce

If your ex hates you, he will use it in some fashion to make his arguments to the court. If your arrest truly is unrelated to the divorce, you can handle it quietly, and you are under no court obligation to disclose it, you may have gotten lucky.

At this point, you may want to take a hard look at yourself and seriously consider rehabilitating yourself. Go to counseling, get a job, resume attendance at your place of worship. This is a great time to turn a corner, not just metaphysically but to show the courts that you now know that you did wrong and are interested in doing better.

This is a good time to work on other improvements. Enroll in online parenting, anger management, and co-parenting courses. Hopefully, the efforts you are making will be genuine and motivated by a sense of humility.

Be careful about how you proceed if you were arrested and it wasn't your fault. Everyone says that! Even if it's true, you will sound like you are avoiding responsibility. Ask your attorney how best to deal with this issue, as it will depend on what you are charged with and what the evidence (not your opinion about the evidence) shows.

Arrested in the Past for a Divorce-Related Issue

In general, courts don't want to hear about what happened in the past before the divorce decree was entered, but arrests are often the exception. A common divorce-related arrest is for domestic violence.

I have represented a lot of fathers who were unjustly accused of domestic violence. No matter if you actually did the deed or not, if you were arrested or found to violate an order, you are guilty of the act in the eyes of the court. So you have to be careful about loudly protesting your innocence to the court; it will come off worse than if you had "accepted" what you had done and rehabilitated yourself. This is similar to people who were wrongly convicted and never got paroled because they didn't show remorse—because they didn't do it!

Sometimes you have to improve your situation at the expense of being right. Get counsel from a lawyer to work out this dilemma so you are comfortable with your decision. Just know that saying to a judge that you didn't commit that crime you were arrested for seven years ago and your wife had lied and gotten away with it won't go well for you. It can be interpreted by the judge that you think the court is stupid.

If your ex likes to keep beating this drum, keep emphasizing your rehabilitation progress. Stay in counseling or in your faith community, where people will vouch for you. Document how well you've been accepted and trusted by these people since your rehabilitation. Keep this document for a rainy day.

You can always directly ask your ex (preferably while running a voice recorder if legally permissible) what you need to do for her to accept and move past your mistake. You may be surprised by what she says. She may be nice, which is good for your files; she may be nasty, which is also worthy of documentation. She may actually tell you what you need to do. If she does, do it—as long as it is reasonable. This would give you an excellent defense against future pestering.

Arrested in the Past for an Issue Unrelated to Your Divorce

You were arrested in the past and have fulfilled your obligations related to that arrest. Hopefully, by now you have been able to overcome your arrest socially and professionally. The best way to defend yourself if the arrest is brought up in litigation is to calmly and unemotionally state that it happened a long time ago, you did everything you were supposed to do, and you have not been in trouble since.

CHAPTER 16

Choosing an Attorney when Going Back to Court

In This Chapter

➤ Whether to hire the same attorney when back in court

➤ Court costs the second time around

➤ Types of fee arrangements

Your divorce is final, but it hasn't necessarily put an end to the strife between you and your ex. There is so much more coordination and so many more rules that need to be followed as you manage visitations and financial duties. It's almost inevitable that problems arise as you and your ex adjust to the new court-ordered guidelines for your lives. Sometimes the only way to solve these problems is to go back to court.

The big question that most people face in this situation is whether to hire the same attorney they used for their divorce. In this chapter, we'll go over what you need to consider to determine who would best represent you in court the second time around.

To Hire or Not to Hire the Same Attorney

When you know you'll be going back to court for a divorce-related issue, your first task is to determine if you want to hire the attorney who took you through your divorce. Of course, whether you rehire your previous attorney depends on how your original divorce proceedings went. Obviously, if you felt like you were hit by a truck, you are not going to sign up for that attorney's protection again.

Ask yourself some questions if you're on the fence about hiring the same attorney who saw you through your divorce. Did you feel comfortable with your lawyer? Did you feel your lawyer had enough skill to represent you, or do you think another more skilled lawyer would have improved your outcome?

Handy Tip

Although an attorney's skill level is, of course, extremely important, the trust you have in your attorney can be just as important to the outcome of your trial.

Financial Considerations

Financial aspects come into play when deciding whether to rehire the lawyer you had for your divorce. For one, many reputable lawyers refuse to work for someone who has an older debt that is still unpaid. So you may find yourself stuck if you still owe money to your former counsel. But if you paid your last lawyer, you may be able to get some helpful credit terms. Lawyers often extend more flexible payment plans to returning clients who have made timely payments during prior cases.

Another financial benefit to returning to your divorce lawyer is that the lawyer is familiar with your case so it will take less time to come up to speed on your current case and will cast you less money.

A new lawyer would need to review prior court documents and maybe even the entire court file. The more complicated the matter is that you're facing; the more detailed the attorney's review of the previous files needs to be. You also need to be 100 percent certain that you have the entire file. The only way to be sure is to go the courthouse and print the whole thing or check it against your records—the one page you are missing could mean everything!

Geographical Considerations

Geography is also a valid factor. If you have moved since your last case, you may no longer be located near your old lawyer, making pairing up again inconvenient. Even more of a concern is where you have moved. The lawyer may have to litigate in a county or local community that he or she does not commonly work in. Some judges in the more rural courthouses have a natural suspicion of people bringing in the "slick, big-city lawyers." Worse yet, some small counties have rules that only a local practitioner is likely to know about. Also to be considered is that the farther your lawyer has to travel for court, the higher your fees are likely to be.

Bulldog Lawyer vs Settler

This is a trick question—you need both. Many people set out to acquire the bulldog attorney. Yet another group sets out to find an attorney who will be reasonable, aim to get the trial over with and thus keep the fees in check. Anytime a lawyer is limited to taking just one of these approaches, you should be concerned. Your attorney should be able to put on both personas with equal success. You never know when a case will turn from easy settlement to a tooth and nail fight, or vice versa. Most attorneys, though, have a clear strength and will not be shy about telling you what it is.

If you had a bulldog-type lawyer for your divorce, consider whether that approach is needed this time around. If it isn't needed, have a frank talk with your attorney to determine how skilled he or she is at using a quieter method. If your divorce attorney doesn't seem to be the right fit for your current situation, move on.

The Cost of Going Back to Court

An attorney has to read the client's file to give an accurate retainer estimate. But I can help you by setting out some price ranges. Please keep in mind that these are ranges as of the writing of this book and cannot possibly cover every case and every state. Also, a myriad of factors can affect and increase the cost of a retainer. Here are some rough numbers:

> ➤ Motion for contempt: $750–$3,000; varies with complexity and metro area
> ➤ Modifications of child support: $1,000–$4,000; varies if payee is self-employed and with metro areas
> ➤ Modification of final decree: $1,500–$4,000; tricky motions to get granted and can be complex
> ➤ Protective Orders: $750–$3,000

So for most situations, between $2,000 and $3,000 is an estimate of the cost of going back to court with a competent family lawyer. This fee range doesn't apply if you have aggravating factors. Aggravating factors can be one or more of the following:

> ➤ Crazy people
> ➤ Crazy lawyers
> ➤ Criminal goings-on
> ➤ Domestic violence
> ➤ Thievery
> ➤ Self-employment
> ➤ Custody factors

Each of those aggravating factors can increase the cost of your case.

Take Heed

A modification of final decree is often requested by someone who hired a lawyer who didn't get the job done to that person's satisfaction. Such changes are usually not possible.

Divorce Vocab

A retainer is a fee that is paid to retain, or have access to, a professional's services and advice on an as needed basis.

The most expensive service a family lawyer offers is usually fighting to change the custody decree. Custody case retainers can start, as of the writing of this book, at somewhere between $3,500 and $7,500. You rarely find a flat fee rate in custody cases because there are too many variables.

The fees are affected by the attorney's hourly rate. Newer attorneys in a large metro area may be billed around $150 per hour. The generation of bulldog lawyers who trained me have rates over $400. In general, the more you pay, the more experience you are buying, which is a good thing.

If money is tight, it's better to have a younger and more affordable lawyer than no lawyer at all under most circumstances. However, you want to steer clear of attorneys who have not been practicing the majority of their time for the past two years in family law. Many other attorneys will dip their toes in family law to make a little extra money thinking it is not that hard. These lawyers are dangerous to you and to your case! Do not hire your cousin the real estate lawyer. Find a real family lawyer.

Types of Fee Arrangements

Since we are talking about cost, we need to explain retainers and the different kinds of post-divorce fee arrangements that you can have.

The various fee arrangements include the following:

➤ Standard retainer: The client pays an up-front predetermined amount that reserves the firm's legal time for the client's matter and is an estimate of the funds required to complete the matter. The final fee may differ greatly, depending on unforeseen or undisclosed circumstances in the case. The client takes the risk that fees may exceed the retainer and additional monies will be owed to the firm. This risk is balanced by the possibility of a refund of unused funds that exceed the minimum fee or outstanding balance, whichever is greater. The balance bears interest.

➤ Flat fee: The client pays a set up-front predetermined amount that acts to reserve the firm's legal time for the client's matter and represents the only funds required to complete the matter. The final fee may not differ. The upfront fee is usually high to include the likelihood of the matter becoming more difficult and expensive. This is balanced by the possibility of the legal work exceeding the amount paid. The client pays no interest with a flat fee.

➤ Modified flat fee: The client pays an up-front predetermined amount that acts to reserve the firm's legal time for the client's matter and represents the only funds required to complete the matter within a preset fee range. The final fee increases to the next preset fee if the actual fees exceed the original fee range. The client and firm equally divide the risk that the upfront fee may be slightly lower or slightly higher than the actual fees incurred. The client pays no interest where fee paid as agreed.

Ranges of legal costs incurred might look like this chart:

$1,500–$2,500   Fee: $2,000

$2,501–$3,500   Fee: $3,000

$3,501–$4,500   Fee: $4,000

$4,501–$6,000   Fee: $5,250

$6,001–$8,000   Fee: $7,000

$8,001—   Fee: By agreement only

➤ Modified contingency fee: This arrangement is not available for divorce clients by law. Where this arrangement is possible, the client pays an up-front reduced amount that acts to reserve the firm's legal time for the client's matter, and the firm is thereafter entitled to a percentage of the amounts recovered, 33⅓ percent when there is no litigation and 40 percent when litigation is necessary. The client and firm share the risk that no recovery may be made and the reduced up-front fee is all that is paid. The client pays no interest when the original fee paid is agreed upon.

➤ Pure contingency fee: This is possible in a post-divorce case, such as the collection of a child support arrearage. In that case, there is no up-front fee of any kind, and the attorney bears the expenses on an ongoing basis. If there is no recovery, the attorney does not get paid or recover time or monies expended. If there is a recovery, the firm receives the agreed upon percentage (often 33–40 percent, but subject to local customs) and gets reimbursed for any out of pocket expenses it paid in advance. The client receives the balance after the firm is paid and reimbursed.

PART FIVE

Lawyers

CHAPTER 17

How to Pick a Great Divorce Lawyer

In This Chapter

➤ What kind of attorneys are there?

➤ Who to get and why

➤ Who to avoid and why

We've determined the kind of client you are, now we'll take a look at a few general personality types of lawyers. This will give you a chance to recognize what type of lawyer you've worked with before and make sure that you have a good fit for your personal challenges in the future.

Kinds of Attorney

People can spend a lot of time with their attorneys when they're immersed in a case. Some people need their attorney to have certain traits, and some attorneys work better with a certain type of client. Being aware of these personality traits and what they may mean to your case can be important. Here are a variety of personality types you're likely to find among attorneys:

➤ Fog horn: Attorneys with this personality trait are pompous, brag about connections, usually older, fixed in how they like things done, and have predetermined ideas about some issues (like women and custody). They are not always interested in pesky things like details because they pretty much know how your matter should shake out. They will pressure you and everyone else.

➤ Susie Sensitive: These attorneys make you feel so comforted because their empathy flows like water. They are sensitive, and you can easily hurt their feelings. If you get an overbearing opposing counsel, touchy judge, or evil ex, these lawyers are going to struggle and be distracted by the emotions and the wrongdoings. These attorneys should never be matched with clients of similar temperament because nothing will ever get done.

➤ Table Pounder: These lawyers have a strong personality and want to go to court on the first day. They are comfortable in court but not usually good at negotiations and mediation. They are likely to cause things to escalate so they can go to court, where they are in their element. These attorneys will bulldoze through a case, which can feel good until you get the bill! If they decide they are right (which is most of the time), they will not listen to their client. People who get offended will not work well with this kind of attorney.

➤ Overbooker: These tend to be solid lawyers, if only they had about ten fewer cases. They are popular, getting many referrals, but they take in more clients than they should so your matter is always on the back burner. An overbooker responds better to crises than to normal issues due to their backlog. Do not select this attorney if your matter is time sensitive.

➤ The Decorator: These attorneys have beautiful offices, and their clothes and cars are impeccable. Your documents look nice, but the depth of knowledge and content is not there. These attorneys are for simple matters only. They are usually found among younger lawyers.

➤ The Columbo: Rumpled with messy desk, these attorneys know everything about your case so don't be worried, but they won't put forth any effort. They are good lawyers unless your case requires finesse. They are uncomfortable with excessive emotion—do your crying outside the office.

➤ Part-Time Family Lawyer: These attorneys are waiting for their two-year personal injury case to settle. Since they need to pay rent and eat during that time, they take on "easy little" divorce cases. If anything starts to get out of hand or speed up, they will be flustered or aggravated that their "easy" case now requires work. Everyone should avoid this lawyer; there is no telling where they acquired the small store of information they have. They certainly have no patience with the emotions that go with divorce work and resent interpersonal requirements.

➤ Star Student: These lawyers are great in their offices, where they can research and ask other attorneys questions, but they freeze up in court and in any other live situations. They are not good trial lawyers. They are not mature enough to work a complex case, as well as deal with a client's emotions, the opposing counsel's pressure, and the court.

➤ Burned Out: Lawyers who have experience and are comfortable in the courtroom but have grown to hate what they do are burned out. They are not good with clients who are continuously emotional, as this is part of what's burned them out. If you are rational and unemotional, a burnout can be a good lawyer.

➤ The Called: These attorneys usually have a spiritual component or a fundamental sense of right and wrong that is offended by crazy people. They fight against the rising tide. They have skill and passion. These are great attorneys to have on your side, but they are getting rarer. They will tolerate more emotional baggage than almost any other type of attorney (but you should still hold back on the drama).

Bedside Manner

Along with personality traits, your attorney's bedside manner will be critical to your stress level. Some people need their attorney to be matter-of-fact and serious; others need someone whose shoulder they can cry on. Most people thrive with an attorney who has a mix of bedside manners to address various situations. The point is to be comfortable with how your attorney speaks to you, responds to your questions, requests (or demands) information from you, and handles misbehavior from you. If an attorney's manner rubs you the wrong way in the beginning, it will only get worse. This would not be the right attorney for you.

Who to Hire and Why

Without a doubt, you should hire the most experienced family lawyer you can afford. Money really shouldn't be your primary consideration. You want someone who specializes and is experienced in family law and has a good track record. Here are questions you must ask every attorney before you hire one:

Take Heed

Many lawyers will profess experience in a variety of law specialties. But practicing law is one area in which being a Renaissance man is not such a good trait. For an attorney to be able to maneuver through the maze of divorce proceedings, he or she needs have been immersed in the study of family law. Be sure when you go to court, you have the expertise of a highly qualified family lawyer.

➤ How long have you practiced family or domestic law?

You want a lawyer who has practiced family law for at least two years. You'll find a good balance of knowledge and affordability with an attorney who has five to ten years of experience. If you're dealing with a more difficult case, you'll want a more seasoned attorney with ten to twenty years of experience. Attorneys who have been in the business for over twenty years are what I call silk stockings attorneys. They may belong to well-known firms and are expensive—maybe even overpriced—but they are very, very skilled.

➤ Who trained you to do this?

Ask lawyers who have been practicing for less than five years who trained them to see if they just came out of school, couldn't get a job, so opened a law firm. Although this scenario doesn't mean a lawyer is unqualified to take your case, but the foundation built by strong formal training by a more experienced lawyer is always preferable.

➤ What percentage of your practice is family law work?

The attorney you want representing you should spend at least 65 percent on family law; the higher the better.

➤ What other kinds of law do you practice?

If the attorney practices other types of law, make sure they're at least somewhat compatible to family law. Be careful of criminal lawyers practicing family law part-time; the paperwork requirements for the two areas are very different, and you may not get the sensitivity you want for your personal issues from someone who defends violent criminals. I have found litigating against criminal lawyers slows the case down and costs more money.

➤ How do you find your clients?

An attorney who gets clients primarily by word of mouth is likely to be excellent. Be wary of someone who does not list references from past clients or other attorneys. One advantage of the divorce rate being over 50 percent is that many people have worked with a divorce lawyer, and most will tell you happily whether they thought theirs was competent or not.

Handy Tip

If you can't get a recommendation for a good family lawyer from anyone, call the bar association in your state. Every state bar has a group of specialty lawyers. Find contact information for the president of the family law group, and call to ask for recommendations.

➤ How many days do you spend in court each month on average?

An active family lawyer is a trial lawyer and goes to court often—about two to six days a month or more on average. If months are going by without the attorney going in front of a judge, there is something wrong and this attorney is not for you.

➤ Do you like to go to court?

Believe it or not there a plenty of attorneys who are scared of going to court or hate the hassle of trials. You may get an honest answer. If your case is courtroom bound, weigh this heavily. A good negotiator or hand holder does not a great litigator make.

➤ Do you handle high-conflict cases such as those that deal with domestic violence, threats, and visitation interference?

An attorney who practices at this level will make you feel safer if your matter starts to sour.

➤ What were the fees for your worst case ever? How long did the case take?

With this question, you are trying to determine if the attorney has handled a heavy-hitting case that dragged everyone through the mud. Fees on extreme cases, depending on your location, will be at least $30,000 for a trial that lasts longer than about two years.

➤ What experience do you have in my county?

Some local courthouses are just chock full of rules an outside attorney can never learn in a timely fashion. You want to find out if your attorney feels comfortable practicing in your county and whether he or she has some credibility with the county's judges.

➤ What do you dislike the most about your divorce work?

With this question, you are trying to find out what the attorney hates and determine if you are likely to do that very thing. You want to make sure you are a good fit.

➤ What do you like the best about your divorce work?

You want to know the attorney's motivations for doing divorce work. The best divorce lawyers view their work as a calling—the money is just not worth the stress.

A Word about Location

Hiring a lawyer who's close to you is ideal, but as a practical matter you shouldn't need to be at your lawyer's office that much.

Law offices are definitely not set up for walk-ins. You can't pop in just to see what's going on or to ask a question. Lawyers generally have plans for every minute of every day so if you stop by without an appointment, you will be interrupting work and your visit will not be appreciated. So location doesn't belong high on your to-hire list when shopping for a lawyer.

Location can be a factor if you and your attorney live in different counties. Attorneys don't necessarily know the ins and outs of the laws in counties outside of those they generally do business in. And people in some smaller counties resent big city lawyers. Of course, if your rural area doesn't have any competent attorneys, then go with the best city lawyer you can find.

Lawyer Availability

After you've found an affordable lawyer with expertise and good recommendations, you need to find out about availability. Before you retain an attorney's services, ask about caseload and how your case would fit in.

An attorney's availability is particularly important if you have an emergency or something that needs to be addressed in the next couple of weeks. If you have a hearing that is already scheduled, restraining orders, TPOs, or if you have anything that's time sensitive, you need to be sure your attorney of choice has a clear slate to take on your case.

Following Rules

For attorneys to meet deadlines, research cases, and get to court on time, they need to be disciplined. To be disciplined, an attorney's office must have rules and procedures that the staff adheres to. Clients, too, have specific roles to play, with their own structure and set of rules.

Take Heed

True deadlines are scarce these days. Even the seemingly drop-dead tax deadlines have a work-around. But the legal system offers us one of the rare cases where true deadlines exist. When your attorney says your court date is in two weeks and he needs your documents in five days, he's not kidding; he needs your documents in five days. You can't mess with the schedule.

Rules make you more confident, and they make attorneys more successful. An attorney who has rules, especially someone who has established protocols for what clients are supposed to do and not do, will be able to control your case and reduce your stress.

So, when you're evaluating attorneys note whether the office and its staff is structured and disciplined.

Methods and Operations

You'll be able to work better with your lawyer if you understand the typical office protocol. Attorneys' offices tend to be busy places. With the set deadlines of court dates, the onus of getting prepared and armed to face opponents in court is fully in the hands of lawyers. But clients need to cooperate to keep this world of tight schedules, emotions, and deadlines on track.

Phone Calls

Phone calls can be a touchy subject. Your attorney's office should return your calls within one day, two days max. Notice I said the office, not the attorney. Each attorney balances multiple clients and won't necessarily be able to return your call personally. The staff is trained to handle most matters and it saves you money. You really don't want your attorney calling you for everything when he or she is billing at $330 an hour!

Phone calls need to be controlled. Legal work is interrupted every time a client calls with a question, and if a client calls multiple times a day with questions, well, that sure can take the wind out of an attorney's sails, slowing down progress on your case and others.

Ask your attorney about using e-mail to communicate your questions. You can gather your questions throughout the day and send one e-mail in the afternoon. Your questions can be handled all at once, which will save you money and reduce stress in your attorney's office. Good attorneys have a high obligation to control their clients' access to them, in order to secure their quiet time, their planning time, their uninterrupted work time.

When something is really important, you should be able to get your attorney on the phone, but your attorney, not you, gets to determine what's really important. Your job is to hand over information to the office, and then to let your attorney address the problem. If you trust your attorney, then you trust him to determine when he needs to get you on the phone. Good attorneys are careful with their time and your bill.

Meetings

A law firm is not equipped for surprise visits. An unplanned meeting is usually unproductive. Questions usually need to be looked up, thought about, or researched, which usually isn't done on the spot. So always set up meetings in advance. Call your office and ask for a meeting. Explain why you want to meet so your attorney can be prepared.

Handy Tip

Attorneys who are protective of their time, are mindful of your money.

Client Requirements

The attorney-client relationship goes both ways. For your case to go smoothly, you have work to do too. Be sure you ask your attorney the following questions:

> ➤ What do you expect me to be responsible for?

> ➤ How would you like me to contact you?

> ➤ How often should I contact you?

> ➤ What types of issues should I be contacting you about?

> ➤ What can I do on my own?

Court Preparation

Once you've hired your attorney, ask about the court preparation protocol. I love the saying that life, obstacles, and challenges are 90 percent preparation, 10 percent perspiration. The attorney who trained me, Donald Weissman, Esq., had been a lawyer for thirty years at the time, and he said, "If you prepare a case to settle, it'll try. If you prepare a case to try, it'll settle." So we always prepare cases as if they are going to court, because that way we're never surprised, and that way we're never unprepared.

Standard preparations for court include the following:

> ➤ Always aim to arrive a minimum of thirty minutes before your court time.

> ➤ Be at court before your attorney arrives.

> ➤ Do not be late. Traffic is not an excuse, weather is not an excuse, a sick baby is not an excuse. A court date is a court date, is a court date.

> ➤ Make sure you have turned in all the documents your attorney needs to be reviewed and copied well before your court date.

> ➤ Ask your attorney to prep you for court before the case is called.

Emergencies

Emergencies happen in family law, so you want an attorney who is calm and has a protocol for dealing with emergencies. Here are a few common emergencies you should go over with your attorney:

> ➤ Failure to return a child on time

> ➤ Threats and harassment

> ➤ Utilities being cut off for nonpayment

Find out what method your attorney uses for responding to emergencies. You're looking for clear instructions and a somewhat standard response.

Read and Understand Your Contracts

A contract is a binding agreement between you and your lawyer, so you need to fully understand its terms. It includes terms of agreement regarding the amount of the retainer and the financial or other consequences if the contract is prematurely canceled (is your money refundable or not). Clarity and understanding is key to lowering your stress level and promotes honest feelings. Terms of your contract may include the following points:

> ➤ The attorney's rate: This includes the billing rates, frequency of payments

> ➤ What the attorney is charging for: An itemized list of what will be charged to you, such as postage, travel expenses, detectives, and so on

> ➤ Details of how the attorney plans to handle your case

> ➤ What is expected of you

The more detailed the contract (up to a point) the fewer surprises there will be as your case moves forward. This is good for your stress level and for your relationship with your lawyer.

Who Not to Hire and Why

Having the right attorney is about 70 percent of the battle in a divorce case. Having the wrong attorney can really set you up for failure before you even get out of the gate. How do you know which attorney's to stay away from?

Recommendations

Word of mouth is a good guideline. If you hear people complaining about their divorce attorney, take heed. But keep in mind that highly skilled attorneys can have personalities that rub people the wrong way. Get to the bottom of the complaint. If the problem is with the attorney's performance, cross him off the list; otherwise note the complaint, but keep that attorney on your list.

If you have trepidations about an attorney but he or she has an impeccable record, express your concerns during your first interview, and weigh the answer when it's time for you to make your choice. An attorney who won't discuss your concerns openly, should be crossed off your list.

Check Bar Records

A great resource right at your fingertips is the state bar. You can look up lawyers' records online at your state's bar website. You can find out how long they've been in practice, their status (whether they are active practitioners), where they earned their degree, and whether they have any disciplinary actions in their history. Cross all lawyers off your list who have ever had any disciplinary actions taken against them.

Take Heed

We all like to think consequences follow wrongdoing. But there are some crazy, evil attorneys practicing law who have no dings on their record. Any competent family lawyer could tell you who these attorneys are, and many will if asked in a general way.

Using Price as a Guide

Avoid cheap so-called attorneys. You can find people on sites like craigslist.com who advertise to do legal paperwork and divorce paperwork for you at ridiculously low prices. The prices are so low because the advertisers aren't lawyers. They may not even be paralegals. On top of that, this activity is considered to be the unauthorized practice of law—it's illegal. If the bar knew about it, it would punish and sanction those people. So stay away from the little $125 preparation deals; they are usually sketchy.

Divorce Vocab

A paralegal is someone who has the education and training to perform certain legal tasks under the direction of an attorney. A paralegal is not an attorney, and any fees charged to the work of a paralegal should be less than those charged by the attorney.

You also want to avoid attorneys whose fees look suspiciously out of line with everybody else's. If you know that a divorce like yours should cost somewhere between $2,000 and $4,000 and someone quotes you $800, it should be a red flag. I've had people call and tell me that they had a horrible first lawyer. He didn't show up for court, he forgot to file papers, he was nervous and angered the judge, and so on. When I ask how much he charged, I usually hear a fee that's around $500. Good attorneys don't get out of bed for $500! What you save in money, you're increasing in risk.

Avoid Generalists

When you work with a generalist, you're not getting someone with expertise in family law that can make a difference in your case. There is nothing wrong with an attorney being a generalist; it's just not the right choice for people going through the complicated maze of divorce. In a smaller town, you may see more attorneys who practice many types of law because there are fewer attorneys to fill the niches. However, 95 percent of the time you're going to be safer with a specialist than you would be with a generalist.

Avoid Lawyers with Bad Attitudes

All attorneys are busy, or at least the really good ones are, so don't be put off if you're put through some screening processes. But pay attention to the attitude of the people you're talking to—the attorney and the staff. Ask yourself the following questions:

> ➤ Do they sound like they're being helpful?

> ➤ Are they trying to direct you the right away?

> ➤ Do they really listen to you, or are they just doing their job?

> ➤ Do they have passion or drive?

You may even ask the attorney why he or she became a family lawyer. You want to figure out what the attorney's attitude is going to be. It's important for your attorney to have a positive attitude, because you probably won't!

Most clients have a negative attitude. What happens if both you your attorney have a negative attitude? Chances are your case is doomed. There will be no energy driving the case—no ambition to see it through to a positive end. You should be looking for an attorney who seems happy practicing law. Attorneys who can't be happy in their skin, in their office, with their staff, and with their choice of profession can't help you get to a better place.

Avoid the Scorched Earth Lawyers

The scorched earth policy comes from the military and originated thousands of years ago. The expression refers to a war tactic that burned to the ground anything that could be useful to the enemy. There are attorneys who will destroy everything so they can win their cases. This strategy is usually unnecessary and can hurt even those who are not in the crossfire. It's best to stay away from this type of lawyer.

CHAPTER 18

Getting the Most Out of Your Divorce Lawyer

> ## In This Chapter
>
> ➤ Translating attorneys' actions
> ➤ The right lawyer for you
> ➤ Saving money

As much as you'd like to, you can't just sit back and let your lawyer do all the work. You must play an integral role in your case. There are ways you can get the most out of your lawyer, and ways you can sabotage your case. The best way to keep from tripping up your case is to keep unfounded fears at bay.

Understanding Your Attorney

After the financial aspects of the attorney-client relationship have been addressed, many clients wrestle with gaining trust in their attorney. The world of courtrooms and judges and litigation as a whole is quite foreign to most of us, and divorce may be the first experience many have with the legal system.

It's easy for neophytes to misinterpret their attorneys' words and actions, so we'll take a look at what could be going on with the attorney and how to address it, if necessary.

Your Lawyer is Being Nice to the Opposing Lawyer

Clients often believe that attorneys cannot fight as zealously as possible if they are friendly with each other. They may view it suspiciously if their attorney chats with the opposing attorney in a friendly way, does something nice for the other side, or refuses to believe evil of the other lawyer.

Rival sports teams gives us the best analogy. When quarterbacks are pitted against each other for the highest prize their sport holds, does that mean they should push or trip each other when they meet in public? No, of course not. Should they slander each other to the press? No. Must they hold actual hate for the other? No. Lawyers are like quarterbacks. Some lawyers are friends with each other, some are acquaintances, and some are mortal enemies.

Do not ever assume that because your lawyer is nice to an adversary that he or she is selling you short. Often, better deals are cut between lawyers who are friends than can be won fighting tooth and nail in the courtroom. If you are concerned, ask your lawyer directly if he is comfortable litigating your case with the opposing attorney. Ask him if there is any advantage or disadvantage to this attorney representing your ex.

Your Lawyer Doesn't Get on the Phone with You

Your case is your entire life, but it is only a part of your lawyer's work life and case load. So your attorney will almost always feel less passion, less focus, and less dedication than you would like. You have a right to an attorney who cares about you and your case and gives it enough time and attention to help shape a favorable outcome.

To ensure an attorney's dedication to your case, ask how much time and attention your case will receive before you hire him. He should be able to tell you generally what to expect. You then have a basis for comparison as you're going through your case. If you're getting less than promised, then you are right to feel slighted and should take it up with your attorney.

There are two things to take into account from your attorney's perspective:

1. Your attorney may not get on the phone with you to avoid running up your bill

2. Your attorney may prefer an alternate means of communication. My office is very e-mail driven; you have to e-mail me to get me as I am rarely physically working in the office.

Handy Tip

If you want an attorney's attention, put your concern in writing. Attorneys are neither able to nor encouraged to ignore a complaint in writing.

You have a right to ask questions, receive answers, and convey new information. If you have a means to do this and your case is progressing, your inability to talk to the attorney frequently may not be detrimental. However, if your personality will lead to your losing your trust in your attorney because of the absence of consistent communication, you must address it.

Your Lawyer Wants to Settle

You're looking forward to your day in court and presenting all your evidence, but your lawyer sees a way to settle the case without much to-do. A bit anticlimactic, isn't it? You're all set for a fight and it just fizzles. Your lawyer obviously is not doing his job, right? Wrong.

Approximately 90 to 95 percent of all civil cases settle. A lawyer would be remiss not to look for a way to settle your case and avoid the staggering costs of going to trial. In most cases, a client's desire to go to court is more about airing out the grievances they've suffered at the hands of their ex than getting justice.

Good lawyers know that it is just not that simple. Things are very often not fair and don't work out the way they should. Thus, they focus on dealing with the devil that they know, versus the one that they don't.

Ask your lawyer up front whether he thinks you will get a chance to put forth all of your accumulated evidence. You will find that much of what you want to present is either not presentable or does not have enough bang for the buck to take up precious court minutes. However, as I've already said, it's best to be well prepared. I was taught that if you prepare a case to settle, it will try; if you prepare a case to try, it will settle. Find a lawyer who is willing to prepare your case for trial. Then when it settles, you will know that you received the best possible outcome.

You Wanted Your Lawyer to Lead a Fight

You may have imagined a cutthroat lawyer showing no mercy as he goes after your ex in court. How disappointing it is when you see your lawyer acting downright polite in the courtroom. Really, though, you want an attorney who will not be intimidated and will provide a strong defense, putting in work where work is needed and paying attention to detail while pushing to get the very best outcome possible.

Generally, attorneys who are vicious and stubborn with their opponents will be vicious and stubborn with their clients too. You want an attorney who is versatile, who can finesse a settlement, sweet talk court staff, and shred people under cross examination.

Your Lawyer Agrees with Your Ex and Is on His Side

No one tells clients this, but you are not always right. When you are wrong, it is the obligation of a good lawyer to tell you that and to disagree with you. If your lawyer does whatever you want even when you're wrong, you have a misguided lawyer. When your lawyer disagrees with you, he is truly earning his fee. It is not easy to tell people what they do not want to hear.

Your Lawyer Doesn't Understand What You've Been Through

Your lawyer is human, and it's hard for him to listen to your story of hurt and betrayal over and over again. Lawyers tell clients to keep their focus in the present because their work is in the present. There is a practical reason to focus on the matters at hand: judges do not want to hear the history.

Your attorney should be familiar with the nightmares you lived through because it gives him insight into where you are emotionally and what kind of adversary he has. Outside of that, the past tends to cause problems when dragged around in the present like a dirty security blanket.

Take Heed

You are already divorced. By most laws, what occurred before your divorce decree has been addressed and is not to be brought up again. So if you're back in court for an increase in child support and you bring up that your husband cheated on you five years ago, you'll aggravate the judge. He may believe you're holding a grudge and begin to doubt the sincerity of your motives for being in court, even the truth of your testimony.

You Want Your Ex Punished; Your Lawyer Must Make It Happen

The only way anything will happen in your case is by agreement or by judge's order. Notice that neither of those options permits a single lawyer to "make it happen." If your ex is stealing money from a college fund, your lawyer cannot make it stop. He can ask your ex to stop. He can threaten consequences if your ex doesn't stop. He can ask the court to take a look at the matter.

Too often clients believe they are buying results and not efforts and time. Lawyers don't sell results; they sell their time, knowledge, and effort to influence outcomes. Before you complain about your lawyer, make sure you're not expecting him to do something that no lawyer can do.

You Don't Want to Pay Your Lawyer to Talk to Your Lying Ex

Your lawyer has to talk to the other side. Doing so is part of fighting for you. No, it doesn't make you feel good when you see the bill. If you suspect your ex is trying to run up your bill, let your lawyer know your concern so he can take steps to keep the billing down. Also know that you can get in trouble should your lawyer stonewall, or refuse to communicate with, the other side. If the court finds out, it could charge you with all or a part of your ex's legal fees and deny your request for your ex to pay your fees. In short, it is not worth the money to play the avoidance game.

Your Lawyer Isn't Discussing Strategy with You

I hate to let this particular cat out of the bag, but in most cases in family law there isn't a whiteboard full of strategic notes. This is not a class action suit. It is not a corporate takeover (although it might feel that way to you).

The "strategy" has more to do with interpersonal communications and negotiation approaches. Some clients feel let down that their lawyer's "plan" is just to make a reasonable offer based on the facts and see how the other side responds.

Also keep in mind that you are the client, not co-counsel. If you want to be as close to the driver's seat as you can get, you need to find an attorney who prefers this for their client model. There are attorneys for every different kind of client and it's important that you find a match at the beginning or there will be problems.

"The lawyer keeps pushing me to give up more and more and it's not fair. They aren't giving up as much as I am."

Divorce Vocab

Stonewalling is the term used to describe an attorney who refuses to cooperate with the opposing side or otherwise evades or obstructs the legal process.

Handy Tip

Several workers were hired at 9 am and promised a full day's wage. They were happy. At lunch, the foreman hired three more workers and promised to pay them a full day's wage. The morning workers began to grumble. At 3 pm, with just a few work hours left, the foreman hired three additional people and promised them a full day's pay. At the end of the day, all received a full day's pay. The morning and lunch workers were angry. They felt it was not fair that the workers hired at the end of the day worked less than they did and received the same pay.

The fact that others got paid the same to do less work does not make your portion less fair; it just makes them more fortunate. Learn to be indifferent to the good fortune of your ex, it means you are not emotionally attached to him anymore.

"The other side does whatever they want and if I mess up anything I get in trouble…"

Anytime you say "it's not fair," just remind yourself of how you roll your eyes when you hear your children say that. The facts of each case vary so much that you have to rely on the expert you hired to look at the whole and decide how to handle it. Often the reason you are upset about compromising is because you are compromising for a jerk. No one likes that, it just *feels* wrong. Also, your resistance is based on what has happened in your past, and your lawyer is more focused on your present.

Your Ex's Lawyer and the Judge Seem to Be Friends

Let's assume you are right and the judge is friendly with your ex's lawyer. Most of what you would want your lawyer to do would make you and your lawyer look silly and desperate. Even worse, the judge could get the idea that you believe him to be biased based on his behavior. Judges hate to be accused of bias, especially when they have none. If your attorney handles this wrong, it could backfire and make you both look paranoid.

The real concern is whether the friendship will affect your case. Judges may give their buddies little courtesies, but they do not bend the law for their friends. Yes, there are cases where illegal dealings are going on, but they are not very common.

You've Paid for a Lot, But Not Much Has Been Resolved

Clients pay for time and effort, not for results. Have letters been drafted, sent, and read? Have court dates been scheduled, and complaints filed and reviewed? A lot of money can be spent before serious momentum can pick up in a case.

Ask for a written bill to be sent out at regular intervals. Review the bill carefully. If you don't understand it, write the office and ask for clarification of the current bill and more specificity on future bills.

Most often, this concern is related to mismatched expectations. At the start of your case, tell your attorney what you want to see and expect to happen. It's even better to put all of that in writing and get the attorney's feedback. He should be able to tell you if you're grasping at straws or being too optimistic about your likely outcome. Remember, you want to hear what he tells you especially when he disagrees with your expectations. If your attorney isn't delivering what he promised, you have better grounds for being upset.

Prehiring Checklists

Four out of five times attorneys do a good job and the client is just freaking out. But a lawyer can screw up a case. If you are experiencing an issue, bring it to your lawyer's attention and ask for a discussion. Prevention, though, is the best way to deal with these issues.

During your search for an attorney, prepare a notebook with questions you can ask attorneys during an interview and a place to record their answers using the questions and organization in the following templates as a guide.

Client Confidential Notes

Here are some questions you can ask yourself as you are researching attorneys to interview:

➤ What is the most money I can spend on an attorney?

➤ Who recommended this attorney?

➤ Does the attorney have a good record with the State Bar Association?

➤ Does the attorney appear to be disciplined in his or her work? (This is supported if the attorney asks you to be disciplined.)

My Attorney Information Sheet

Photocopy the following questionnaire and give it to prospective attorneys before you complete the hiring process. They may think this is a bit odd, but when they understand that it will set expectations and prevent future problems, they'll probably ask for a blank copy to add to their office paperwork!

The answers to these questions will give you valuable information about the attorney and will be a major tool for you to use when deciding who you should hire to represent you.

My Attorney Information Sheet

1. What is your direct expertise in the areas I need?

2. What is your availability to take on a case like mine?

3. What is your bedside manner?

4. If I am crying on the phone you will:

A. _____ Prefer I calm down before we talk.
B. _____ Talk to me briefly, and then continue when I am under control.
C. _____ Hop in and pull me together.

5. My spiritual beliefs are:

A. _____ Not an issue.
B. _____ I rely heavily on my faith to get me through the day.
C. _____ I believe in God but don't need any spiritual support from the firm.

6. Are your spiritual beliefs similar to or in support of mine?

Y N

7. What is office procedure for taking my phone calls?

A. _____ Call when you have a problem.
B. _____ E-mails are preferred over phone calls.

8. Phone calls/messages are usually returned within: _____

9. What is office procedure for responding to my e-mails?

10. What is office procedure if I want a meeting with the attorney?

A. _____ Phone request.
B. _____ E-mail request.
C. _____ In person request.

11. How will your office keep me up to date on my case?

A. _____ Periodic phone updates.
B. _____ E-mail updates.
C. _____ Copies of all documents.

12. What do you require me to do or complete before we go to court? _____
_____
_____
_____

13. What other requirements do you have of me?

_____
_____
_____

14. What do you want me to do in an emergency?

_____
_____
_____

15. What is your retainer (cost estimate)?

_____
_____
_____

16. Is it a flat fee? _____

17. What does the fee cover?

_____

_____

_____

18. What doesn't the fee cover?

_____

_____

_____

19. Do you accept payment plans? _____

20. How likely are we to exceed the retainer? _____

21. If we do exceed the retainer, can I get on a payment plan? _____

Money Savers

The following advice can save you money and your sanity. It will also keep you on track with your case and in sync with your lawyer. Some of the advice may be hard to follow, but it will be worthwhile in the end.

Collect Files from Previous Court Hearings

If you have files from previous court hearings, get copies from the court clerk. It is pretty dangerous for a lawyer to rely on a file that's produced by a client because some documents may be missing. You don't want to be in a situation where your ex's lawyer refers to a document that is missing in your file. Neither does your lawyer.

A good money-saving shortcut to make for your lawyer is to add summaries to your large files to reduce the time an attorney would need to go through all your paperwork.

Handy Tip

If you have a big file or a lot of history and litigation behind you, summarize the important points. Here's an example:

"On such and such a date, I filed X, and X happened. The judge ruled X. He found him in contempt, and then he filed X against me, and then the court dismissed it."

Summaries will reduce administrative time and save you money.

Save Your Questions for One Phone Call

Making multiple calls a day to your attorney is financially wasteful. Jot down your questions as they come up, and when you have a few ready, then call your attorney. Even better, ask your attorney if e-mailing is an acceptable way to communicate. You can refer to e-mails if you need to and your attorney can respond at a time that's good for him.

Get Your Family Under Control

Your family can be your worst enemy in a divorce case because each member seems to have an opinion. When that opinion differs from the attorney's, family members start dialing the law firm to complain. Every phone call adds to your bill.

It is absolutely inappropriate for anybody other than you to contact your attorney's office. Attorneys are bound by attorney-client privilege. An attorney can't reveal information that was expressed by his client. If an attorney discusses your case with a family member, or anyone else, the attorney-client privilege is voided. That person, then, can be subpoenaed to testify against you on the matter discussed.

Keep Your Emotions to Yourself

Your emotions can color how you see and interpret things. If you can, quiet yourself down before addressing what you think is going on. You may find that a rational, unemotional outlook changes your whole landscape. Emotions can also become expensive. When you spend time with your lawyer venting your feelings, you're spending money in the form of the lawyer's hourly fee. You're also not doing anyone any good, especially not yourself. If you need to vent, find a good counselor.

Give Your Attorney Authority

You need to give your attorney the authority to settle your case, if you want to settle. The best way to do that is to state an acceptable range of whatever it is that is being negotiated. So instead of saying that you'll accept $800 a month in child support, give your attorney a range of, say, $700 to $800 to work with. Then when your ex offers $750, your attorney knows that's acceptable to you and accepts it. Without that range, your attorney would need to take the time (translate: money) to consult with you before moving ahead.

Follow Instructions

Follow your attorney's instructions to the letter, whether they are complicated or easy. If you don't understand why you need to do something, ask. Many times lawyers give instructions to clients that need to be done for their court appearance. The court won't take excuses, so your lawyer won't accept excuses from you. It costs you money every time your lawyer to stop what he's doing to get after you to do what you were instructed to do.

Not following instructions can have disastrous results. I'll give you an example. I remember four occasions when I got temporary protective orders for my clients—two women and two men. They did not follow instructions.

When you have a restraining order, you may not talk to the other side. That means no texting, no typing, no semaphore, no pigeons, no notes under the door, no social media interactions, as well as no talking. You may not respond to the other person.

It may seem harmless to just respond to someone, but the consequences can be severe. The court may believe you tricked it in getting your restraining order, that you're just trying to set someone up to go to jail, and it can penalize you. All four of these clients didn't follow directions and communicated with the person who caused them to get a restraining order. Of the four, both men went to jail and one of the women was yelled at and charged all fees.

Turn in All Assignments on Time

Attorneys often operate on a tight schedule. For instance, if I say I need your assignment back by Monday at 9 am, I may be scheduled to look at your file at 10:30, take your assignment, draft an entire letter from it, and get it out. If your assignment isn't in on time, I can't write my letter. Let's say you send it in the next day. I'm in court and don't have time to get to your case. Now it's two days later, you're screaming because nothing is happening. Then on Thursday, the opposing counsel calls and does something crazy because he never got his letter. I've been unable to get the letter to him because you didn't turn in your assignment on time.

When your attorney gives you deadlines, it is to make certain that your case gets worked on during the schedule he has set up for it. If you miss your deadline, it may be days before he can reschedule it. You may end up being charged a rush fee or at overtime rates when you finally do turn in your assignment.

Check E-Mail and Voice Mail Regularly

Do not make your attorney's office chase you, which means check your e-mail, voice mail, and paper mail often throughout the day. If your computer breaks down or your phone dies, let your attorney know about this. Whenever your attorney needs to hunt for you, it costs you money. It wastes time and can causes delays.

Arrive at Court on Time

There are no excuses; despite weather, traffic, or any other extenuating circumstances, you must be at court on time. You need to be at court well before your scheduled time in case your attorney wants to prepare you or give you any last-minute instructions.

I have had more than one case where the client was late so the judge made our case sit all day. We sat in the back of the courtroom until every single other case had gone. Your attorney probably charges you hundreds of dollars an hour, so being late can cost you a pretty penny.

Bring All Documents to Court

Always, always bring all your documents to court. Never show up for court with just a smile and your purse. Be ready for anything. You never know when your case may go off on a tangent. And don't rely on your attorney to have all your documents. You may have forgotten to send something or your attorney may have spilled coffee on your file. Usually the court needs to see the original documents, anyway, and you have the originals. Any missing document could mean that you need to reschedule your trial, and that costs money.

Answer All Allegations Without Venting

If your ex says he wants your Cadillac and you don't have a Cadillac, don't spend time on the phone or space in a document complaining that you don't have one; simply state that you don't have a Cadillac. If you've sold it, simply say so. Just answer the question.

If you're getting letters full of lies from the opposing counsel, just point out the statements that are lies, why they are lies, and if or how you can prove that they're lies. Keep it simple and to the point. Stay matter-of-fact and don't let your emotions run the show. It saves money and saves your lawyer the aggravation of your drama.

Read All the Documents Sent to You

You need to keep up with your case, and there's no better way to do that than to read all your documents. Ask your attorney to send you copies or scans of all the documents related to your case. If you are getting all your documents, you should never have to call your lawyer to find out what's going on, which can be another expensive expenditure for you. Keep up with your case and make sure you file all your documents so they'll be organized and ready when you need to go to court.

Don't Listen to Your Friends' Legal Opinions

Friends mean well, but their advice and opinions may be way off the mark; they don't know the ins and outs of your case, and they don't know the law. Their advice may cost you a lot of money in additional attorney fees for all the time you spend on the phone with your attorney, resolving your unfounded concerns.

If a friend raises what you think is a valid concern, though, by all means talk it over with your attorney.

Give Your Attorney Spreadsheets on Complex Evidence

I require spreadsheets from my clients indicating child support payments, histories, and medical expenses. You can also make charts or graphs. None of this has to be extensive or complicated. All you need is something that shows at a glance what's needed.

For instance, if you're arguing that your ex owes you money for child support, you should know how much money. Go back through your records, bank accounts, receipt book, whatever you've got and make a chart with the month and year, amount due, amount received, and the arrearage for each month in question. You just saved yourself a lot of money; an attorney can charge a bundle for doing all of this because it takes time.

Transcribe Your Recordings and Summarize E-Mails

A lot of times I get evidence willy-nilly. People bring me Facebook printouts and hundreds of e-mails. When people have been recording conversations like they're supposed to, they could have over ten hours recorded.

Take Heed

Don't let well-meaning friends who don't have a law degree incite you to ignore or go against the advice of your attorney. You'll get yourself in trouble, and trouble costs money and stress.

Handy Tip

When recording conversations, make sure you're using a high-quality digital voice recorder with recordings that can be transferred via USB cable to your computer and e-mailed right to your attorney's office. It doesn't cost that much, and there's no point in using a cheap, low-quality recorder that's going to garble the critical piece of evidence you need.

To keep your attorney fees down, summarize and sort your e-mails. So if you have a stack of sixty pages of e-mails on one issue, write a summary on top that describes the issue, such as, "Threatened to quit job to avoid child support." Each stack of e-mails should have a summary at the top. Then all the e-mails should be indexed. This also saves money at trial.

Do not make your attorney sit and listen through three hours of recordings to find the twelve seconds when your ex threatened you. Transcribe it. You can informally type the transcription yourself, and highlight the pertinent sections. Although most courts won't accept this, you're doing the transcription for your lawyer. Later, your lawyer can make decisions about how to use the recording and transcription.

CHAPTER 19

Going to Court on Your Own

> ## In This Chapter
>
> ➤ How to do your own simple contempt
> ➤ Dealing with the clerk's office
> ➤ What to do and not do in the courtroom

Whether because of finances, simplicity of the case, or some other factor, you may end up representing yourself in court.

Let's say you have a domestic law court order that you seek to enforce, most commonly because the offender, your ex, has not paid child support, alimony, insurance monies, or other amounts awarded to you by decree. Just because you cannot afford $1,000-$1,500 in attorney's fees to start your case does not mean you cannot proceed. This section is designed to walk you through the process of filing your contempt and appearing in court on your own.

Every jurisdiction has laws that vary at least from other jurisdictions. The discussion here should at least give you an idea of the process. I cannot cover everything here, so if you decide to move forward on your own, you're accepting risks. However, in the case of most garden variety contempt proceedings, you will be much better off following this outline than listening to well-meaning friends, or, worse, attempting it on your own.

Divorce Vocab

In law lingo, *contempt* describes showing disrespect to the court often by not obeying the judge and the decree that was handed down.

Representing Yourself

Some cut-and-dried cases can be handled without hiring a lawyer, and there are plenty of instances in these cases when a layperson will likely do a fine job representing herself.

If you decide to represent yourself, you will hear yourself referred to as the Pro Se litigant, or pro se (pronounced *pro say*) *plaintiff*, which means "for self." The word plaintiff is related to the word *complaint*; it is your complaint that is coming before the court.

The defendant obviously is the person who sets out to defend him- or herself from your complaint. It is important to understand the following:

➤ What the court will expect to see

➤ What you must show or prove

➤ What you can do to help your case

➤ What you should avoid

There are any number of matters that you should not consider handling on your own—ones best handled by professional attorneys:

➤ Any time custody is at risk or in question, you should hire an attorney

➤ If you do not already have an order

➤ If your case is not clear-cut

In short, self-representation should be reserved for clear, uncomplicated cases; practiced in other instances may result in losses that could have been avoided by hiring an attorney.

You are free to consult with a local attorney in lieu of or along with using the following suggestions, which may not totally apply to your case or your area.

Do You Have a Valid Court Order?

Before you can take your ex to court for contempt, you must have the signed and filed order that he violated. Depending on your state, the order may be from a superior court judge; a magistrate judge, in the case of many protective orders; or the Supreme Court judges in New York. If your order is from another state, you will need to contact a law firm and pay for additional assistance because extra steps are required when the order you seek to enforce is not a local court order.

The order must have been signed by a judge and filed with the clerk's office of that county. You should not assume that if you have a draft of an order with no signature and/or no file stamp that this document has in fact been signed and filed. It may have been changed before it was filed. If you need a copy of the order or need to verify that your copy is valid, see the section on dealing with the clerk's office later in this chapter.

Do You Know Where the Offender Lives in Your State?

The general rule of law with a contempt action is that it should be filed in the same county court where the violated order was issued. The same judge who issued the order will be assigned to hear the contempt, if possible. You cannot proceed if you cannot find the offender, your ex, because offenders usually need to be personally served, or actually handed, the papers as notice.

Take Heed

In most jurisdictions, you need to personally serve papers to an offender when bringing him to court for contempt; you cannot just publish the fact in the local newspaper.

Do You Know Where the Offender Lives Outside of Your State?

If you have an order issued in your state and your ex has since moved, you still may be able to enforce it in your state under certain situations. This concerns jurisdiction (does the court have the right to order a person to follow its orders) and it is complicated.

You should consult an attorney for cases involving jurisdictional problems unless your ex lived in your state at the time of the prior order and/or still owns property in your state. If you have the facts right, your ex can be served with your papers by the sheriff department of the state in which he now lives. You would have to contact that sheriff department, find out where to send your papers and what payment is required for the service. Once it has served your ex, make sure you get the sheriff's department to return a notarized Affidavit of Service form to you.

Do You Have Money for a Filing Fee and Service?

Filing fees vary nationwide, so check with your county clerk in the civil division to find out what the fee is to file your contempt and have a sheriff serve the papers.

Service must be paid for, though. The documents must be delivered either by a registered process server, who needs a court order as permission to deliver the papers in some counties, or the local police, usually a sheriff. The amount charged for this can vary, but it is usually $25 to $75 for the police. Private servers can cost a lot more, usually over $75 per attempt. It is safest for you to use the police, who will usually also file the affidavit of service for you. However, a private server may be necessary if your ex is being difficult, hiding from the papers, or has to be served at a specific time.

In rare cases, the person being served cooperates with your lawsuit and may accept service. You can then either mail or personally give him the court filings, and he will take the Acknowledgment of Service form, have it notarized, and return it to you for filing. This usually happens when the ex is concerned about a sheriff coming to his home or job.

The whole process is delayed when this friendlier way of serving papers doesn't get the required results, which is why this method isn't often used. If you wish to try this method, though, be sure to send the accompanying Letter Requesting You Acknowledge Service form, which gives a deadline for the return of the acknowledgment to you. If your ex doesn't return it by the date you set, proceed with a sheriff or private process server.

If you receive your acknowledgment back and it has been properly signed and notarized, you must make two copies of it. Send the original with one copy and a self-addressed stamped envelope to the clerk's office for filing in your case. Keep a copy in case it gets lost in the mail.

Do You Have Proof that Your Ex Failed to Follow the Order?

You need to show the court proof that your ex failed to follow the order in question. If your order was for money you haven't received, you may use one or more of the following as proof:

➤ Bank statements

➤ Overdue bills

➤ Child support agency account statements

➤ Affidavit (notarized promise of truth)

➤ Your ex's bounced check

➤ Your letters asking for payment

An important part of your proof is your demand. Most people make their demands in person or on the phone, which gives them no evidence for court. Use template 9.1 in the Appendix, if you have not already made a written demand or if your written demand does not look similar. Keep a copy, as this demand will be attached to your motion for contempt as a primary exhibit.

Take Heed

I do not recommend witnesses as proof in court, other than yourself if you do not have a lawyer. Witnesses add complexity and more opportunity to aggravate the judge. In addition, subpoenas may be required, and that can become time-consuming and costly.

I don't recommend that you use witnesses in cases such as this, but if you must have a witness, have only one and be sure he is absolutely critical to proving what your ex did or did not do. For instance, if your ex was supposed to give you certain pieces of furniture and claimed they were stolen but he actually sold them to someone else, that person would be a valid witness. Your testimony alone would not prove your ex lied about the items being stolen.

Did Your Ex Fail to Comply on Purpose?

The court will consider an element called willfulness. Did your ex ignore the order on purpose to harm you, or did he have no choice? Your ex can be found in contempt for not paying if he didn't have the money, but the court is likely to be more understanding and much easier on him than if he had the money and was being spiteful by not paying.

Filing Your Contempt Motion

Now you are ready to begin work on drafting and filing your motion for contempt. You may have seen or found contempt forms on the Internet with check boxes. It is not wrong to use them, but it sends a message to the judge that you have had no legal help with your case. See template 19.1 in the Appendix for a motion for contempt form you can use that will look as though it was professionally drafted.

How to Get a Copy of a Prior Court Order

Before drafting your contempt form, you'll need a copy of the prior court order on which this contempt is based. Look up the clerk of court in the phone book for the county the order came from. Call and ask for the civil division. If you have your case number, read it to the clerk on the phone and ask for the filing or entry date of your order by its name. If you do not have the case number, give the full name or names used on the order and make a note of the case number when it is given to you. If you don't know the exact name on your order, describe the document you are trying to find. If your order is more than seven years old, your file may be in storage on microfiche, and otherwise not readily accessible. You may have to wait to get a copy.

The clerks are not allowed to give out legal advice (be very wary of any who do), and usually they won't fax or mail you a document from a phone request. If you can go to the clerk's office, do so and request a copy of the order in person. You will have to pay for photocopying.

If your order is old, check to see if you will have to request a copy of it prior to coming to the clerk's office and ask when it will arrive so you don't waste your trip. The order does not need to be certified. It should, however, have a file stamp date, be signed by a judge, and have the name of the court on it.

Divorce Vocab

Certifying a document requires a special stamping process, usually with a raised seal, to confirm authenticity. It is most commonly done on final decrees of divorce and is used mostly for name changes.

If you cannot go the clerk's office, it may be possible for you to request the copy by mail. Call the clerk as above and confirm your case number and order entry date. Ask the clerk if he would send a copy of your prior order if you sent the office a Letter Requesting a Copy of Prior Order form, enclosed payment for the photocopying, and a SASE. Be sure to get the name of the clerk to send it to, if possible, and confirm the payment amount, possibly by estimating pages to be copied. This may be the only way to go for people who live far away from the clerk's office or can't get time off from work.

Filing Documents With the Clerk

Before filing your documents, you need to call the county clerk and ask him whether contempt actions use the original case number or are assigned a brand-new one. Different counties handle this differently. When in doubt, the general rule is to use the old case number and case caption (the heading with the names and case number) as it looks on your prior order. If you do this wrong, it is not fatal to your case, but it may cause administrative hassles.

When your contempt motion is ready to mail to the clerk for filing, it should have the following:

> ➤ A summons with your case caption and your mailing address filled in: This formally notifies your ex that a legal action is being commenced against him

> ➤ The original petition for contempt plus two copies signed by you, with your exhibits attached: This tells the judge what is wrong and what you want done to fix it, and your exhibits are the first proof of your claim

> ➤ Notarized verification by you: You must swear under oath that what you are claiming is true

> ➤ A blank Notice of Hearing form: You want the court to set your hearing date with as little effort as possible, so you provide a form it can simply fill in, file, and return

> ➤ SASE for the clerk to mail back your file copies: As you are asking the court to send you documents, it is proper and quicker to give it the address and postage to do so. Most will not spend their own money to mail items to you.

> ➤ A letter to the clerk requesting filing: A letter should go with documents sent to the court asking what you want done with your documents, in this case, you want them filed for a Contempt action.

> ➤ A Request for Sheriff Service form and a money order to pay for the sheriff: You must show the court that you will get personal service for your ex. If you are forced to use a private process server, you do not have to send a sheriff request. If you are using a sheriff, you usually need to fill out the sheriff's Service form, which makes two carbon copies, returns the whole thing, and provides payment for the service at that time, usually the $50 (check to be sure how much it is).

> ➤ Payment for the cost of filing the motion for contempt, if there is one.

If you have to send a document for filing with the clerk later, like the Acknowledgment of Service form or private process server's Affidavit of Service form, it should have the following with it:

> ➤ The original document with original signatures and proper case caption, or it'll get lost

> ➤ At least one copy so it can be returned to you after it's been stamped and filed

> ➤ A SASE to get that copy back to you

Make sure to find out if there is a fee to file documents. Some counties have started charging $1 to file and will return your document if the fee isn't enclosed.

Take Heed

A clerk's office will never file a photocopy. All documents must be original and have the ink signature on them. But photocopies of other papers like your overdue bill proof or copy of your demand letter may be attached to an original (signed) complaint.

Specialized Family Divisions

Some counties have specialized family divisions, which have several differences from but are generally easier to navigate than the county clerk. These specialized divisions may have their own packets of forms for you to complete and send to your ex. They also often set their court dates differently.

For those counties with a family division, you need to send the original petition with three copies, one marked "courtesy copy for family division." This copy will get forwarded to the special family division to be assigned a judge, and then set on that judge's calendar.

The family division may send a thick packet of materials to both parties at the start of a case. If you are sent both packets, be sure to mail your ex his packet immediately with a letter saying "here is your county packet." Make a copy of that letter and keep it as proof of mailing it. This packet contains a lot of material that you must read through and complete as best you can by the dates set forth in the paperwork. The completed material must be turned in as required.

Some counties will not schedule your hearing until they have made sure that your ex has been personally served. What they are waiting for and looking for is either the Affidavit of Service from the sheriff or the private process server, or the Acknowledgment of Service from your ex. Once received, a date will be set. Be sure once you get the date in the mail, you send a copy of the paper setting the date to your ex with a letter saying "here is our court date." Keep a copy of this letter as proof of your mailing it to your ex.

Court Scheduling

Court dates are usually set by a person called the calendar coordinator or courtroom clerk. Do not harass this person! You are not an attorney, so you basically do not have anything going on in your life that requires your court date to be any day other than the date the court wants it to be. Noteworthy exceptions are surgeries, funerals, out of town business meetings, graduations, and vacations that were set well in advance. If you know of any of these serious conflicts within two months of the day you are filing, you should mention them in a note attached to the blank Notice of Hearing form. Write something like this:

Dear Calendar Coordinator,

I wanted to advise the court that I will be out of town for a graduation May 23–27, 20XX. When possible, please do not set my case during this time. Thank you for your attention. If you should need to reach me please call me at xxx-xxx-xxxx.

Sincerely,
Your Name
Your Phone Number
Your Address

The coordinator may or may not agree to your dates. Understand that if an emergency arises (colds don't count, for any illness you'd better have a doctor or hospital letter) just before your court date, you must ask the court's permission to continue the hearing by resetting it; not showing up will get your case thrown out. While you can request a continuance on the phone, it is more proper to do so in writing either by motion or by letter to the court. See template 19.2 in the Appendix. If you do not show up on a case you filed and the court has not excused you, it will most likely dismiss your case, and, even worse, your ex's attorney can request money for your failure to show up.

Your Day in Court

Always plan to arrive at court no less than thirty minutes before your court time. Wear conservative and professional clothes.

Do not wear the following to court:

➤ Jeans of any kind

➤ Denim pants, jackets, or shirts

➤ T-shirts

➤ Logo wear

➤ Fashion jackets

➤ Puffy jackets

➤ Short skirts (more than four fingers above the knee)

➤ Anything tight

Handy Tip

If money is an issue, you can get the type of clothes you need for court at places like Goodwill. Men can usually find a white collared shirt for $3, a tie for $2, and a jacket for $10. Women can find a plain black skirt for $5 and a simple blouse for $3.

➤ Sexy high heels

➤ Sandals

➤ Athletic shoes

➤ Open-toed shoes

➤ Sweat clothes

➤ Super baggy clothing

➤ Hats of any kind

➤ Excessive jewelry (men and women)

➤ Anything noisy

➤ Anything that draws attention to your body

➤ Any shirt that exposes cleavage

➤ Any clothing that permits tattoos to be visible

➤ In rural areas women should avoid wearing pants

The judge will not rule in your favor because you are dressed respectfully; however, if your clothing looks disrespectful, a judge may think less of you and doubt you on points that you can't back up with proof, especially if your ex looks nicer than you do.

Do not bring the following to court:

➤ Babies or children: Babies and children are not usually allowed in courtrooms, especially when the dispute is between their parents. Either do not bring them or bring someone who can sit in the hall with them the entire time.

➤ Cell phones that are turned on (they shouldn't be on vibrate either): There are counties that will fine you between $50 and $100 for a cell phone ringing and/or put you in jail. Always double-check that your phone is turned off.

➤ Friends and family: Do not bring your entire support group. No one should be with you who cannot control themselves. Judges hate snickering, laughing, glaring, chatting, gum popping, outrage, head rolling, eye rolling, noises, threats, and interruptions from spectators. If you bring such an entourage, the judge may take his annoyance out on you and your case. Do not give your ex this edge.

➤ Messy piles of unsorted, crumpled papers: Organization of your documents is key to hearing going smoothly. If it is important enough to bring, then it should be organized.

➤ Attitude

Necessities for Court

The following are items you need to have with you at court:

> ➤ The prior order your ex is not following, your contempt motion, and proof of service

> ➤ The evidence that your ex is not doing what he should be doing: If your ex wrote you a check and it bounced, bring a copy of the bounced check or the bank statement showing it was returned, for example. If your ex was supposed to transfer a car title to you and hasn't, bring the unsigned title if you can. If your child support goes through an agency, bring the agency's records of your account showing the arrearage and nonpayment. If your ex was supposed to make mortgage payments and hasn't, bring letters from the mortgage holder or your credit report showing nonpayment. Bring the original, if possible, plus two copies. The original is evidence for the judge to see, one copy is for your ex and/or his counsel, and one is for you to keep. It makes your hearing more difficult if you do not come with copies for everyone! As soon as you are called forward, give your ex his set of copies or place them on his table.

It is best for you to write a list of your evidence exhibits and use it to keep track of what you have brought, whether you used it, and whether the judge accepted, or admitted it (see "Exhibits and Evidence Admission" below).

> ➤ A calculator, pen, and notepad: You should have totaled your expenses and placed this number in your contempt and your Monies Sought for Reimbursement form. Your expenses should include the service fee, if any, cost of this package as legal assistance/counsel, and parking. Usually expenses like photocopies or time away from work are not included, even though they are a valid loss to you. Depending on how much money you are seeking to be awarded, adding them in may look like you are nickel and diming the court. If the lost work time is a serious issue, claim for it conservatively.

> ➤ Your proof of money spent and/or lost to try to get your ex to follow the order: Make sure you bring your proposed order that includes blanks for the judge to write in what the contempt order will be. This will encourage the judge to rule on your matter on the spot and give you an order you can leave the courthouse with instead of waiting for the court staff to draft it. Usually attorneys are given the task of drafting the order, but the court has the burden of doing it in pro se matters. This will also help you if you are pro se and your ex has an attorney. The judge may choose to fill in your order on the spot instead of assigning the drafting to your ex's counsel, who you may not trust to write up what the judge said.

> ➤ Your requested order with blanks

Exhibits and Evidence Admission

Don't go overboard, here. Select a few very important pieces of proof before court. Make two copies of each page you want to use, one for you, one for your ex, and original for the judge. Mark your documents with numbers behind a P (for plaintiff) like P-1 and P-2 on the bottom of the page in middle, if it will fit there. In general you should tell the judge that the document is the original and is accurate. The judge will take care of the rest. You should have as few exhibits as possible. When you are testifying, wherever a document fits into your story, you say, "I have that letter or that bill here today judge, I marked it Exhibit P-1."

What to Expect on Court Day

Court procedures follow a pretty basic format. Here is a general rundown of what you can expect:

Calendar Call

Divorce Vocab

A calendar call is when a judge in a courtroom calls out the names of cases on the calendar, determines when the attorneys on both sides of a case are ready to proceed to trial, and then schedules the date.

Make sure you have the correct courtroom information for your calendar call. Ask a bailiff or officer in the court where your judge will be, if you're in doubt. Often a calendar that contains the judge's schedule for the day is posted outside the courtroom door or inside on a table. It would confirm that your case is to be heard and give you your case's position number.

Say the calendar says there are thirty-four cases on the 9 a.m. calendar and yours is #17. This does not necessarily mean you will be the 17th case heard. Judges often rearrange the order in which they will take cases depending on the length of time of the case and whether they are pro se or not. They often take the lawyers' cases first to save their clients' legal fees before taking the pro se cases.

After your court date has been scheduled, be sure to check if your court day is just one day or on a multiday calendar. For those on a multiday calendar, the court calls in a number of cases on Monday morning and plans to take two, three, or five days—even two weeks—to go through them all! If you're scheduled on a multiday calendar, your case is not on Monday at 9 a,m,; you are to report on Monday at 9 a,m, to find out when it will be set.

For example, you appear at court on Monday at 9 a.m. You find out you're on a three-day calendar, which means your case may be heard on Monday, Tuesday, or Wednesday. You won't know until the last minute, so be sure your boss is aware of this and that you have made appropriate child care arrangements, if necessary. The court may tell you to come back for your case on Tuesday after lunch at 1 p.m. You must do so. Or it may tell you to leave a number and you will be called and given two hours' notice to appear. Be prepared for whatever the court tells you to do.

Your Case is Finally Called

The judge may just start calling cases one at a time, or he may announce which cases will be heard in what order. The court may say you are third or it may say you can come back after lunch or that you won't even be heard that day. Listen carefully.

If for some reason the judge does not call your case, you should move to the front and stand where the judge can see you after he's done calling the calendar and respectfully, trying not to interrupt anything, say, "Excuse me, your Honor (pause and wait for the judge to notice you), I didn't hear my case called and I got notice it was on the calendar for you today." If that is not possible, try to get the attention of a bailiff or officer in the courtroom to assist you.

When the judge calls your name or case, you are to stand up and say the following:

"Good morning, Judge. My name is _____. I am the pro se plaintiff in this case. It is a contempt for_____. I am ready to proceed. I do/do not want the case recorded. I estimate the case will take about _____ minutes. I have no/one witness other than myself."

The judge may ask if you want to speak to the other side to see if you can resolve any or all of the matter. Always say yes, unless there is an issue of domestic violence. You lose nothing, might reach an agreement, and it looks cooperative to the judge. If you are saying no because of domestic violence or out of fear, say, "Judge, there have been issues of domestic violence, so I would rather not speak directly to the defendant."

If your ex has an attorney, he may stand up and make an announcement to counter your time estimate, for example. You may then reply, stating whether you agree with the opposing attorney, and say the following:

"Good morning, Judge. My name is _____. I am the pro se plaintiff in this case. I am ready to proceed. I do/do not want the case recorded. I agree/disagree with the time estimate for the whole case. The case will take about _____ minutes. I have no/one witness other than myself."

Time estimates are tricky, even for lawyers. If your ex has an attorney, it's best to agree with his estimate unless it is absolutely silly. Two pro se parties and a one-issue contempt might take fifteen to twenty minutes; multiple issues may take thirty to over forty-five minutes.

Making your estimate in a range is usually safer than just saying a set number. The judges will be worried or even aggravated if you give an estimate longer than forty-five minutes, unless one side has a lawyer and agrees with that estimate. Don't be surprised if the other side makes fun of your time estimate! This is common even with lawyers.

Court Reporting

My law firm never skips having a case recorded by the court reporter. The reporter either types or repeats in shorthand everything said into a mask (called a take down) for a fee. In pro se contempt cases, recording is much less common. If you think your ex will lie, you will have to go back to court with him on this same issue, or the judge will do something crazy, then you should consider having the proceedings recorded so have proof of this in case you need it later.

The take down fee is a price paid just for the recording. Having the record transcribed, or typed out, is an additional fee and is usually pretty expensive. The longer your hearing, the higher the fees. If you are concerned, ask the court reporter what it would cost for a thirty-minute hearing. To give you an idea, at the writing of this book, a take down cost $1 a minute. Be prepared to pay for this in cash, as many court reporters require immediate cash payment from pro se parties.

If you get a take down, get the court reporter's card or name and keep it, so if you need the proof from the record you know who to call. Also, be aware that if one side orders and pays for the take down, and the other side does not participate, the side paying owns the record, and the side that didn't pay for it has no access to it.

You should alert the judge in your opening announcement as to whether you want the proceedings recorded.

When your case is called forward to be heard, proceed to a table in front of the judge. Technically, the plaintiff sits at the table closest to the jury box, but it really doesn't matter. You may spread out your papers on the table so that they are easy to get to. Place the defendant's copies on his table.

Opening Statement

Cases usually begin with an opening statement, but the judge may want to skip it because you are not a lawyer. If your judge lets you or asks if you would like to make one, say yes and give a brief opening, such as the following:

"Good morning, Judge. My name is _____. I am the plaintiff and will show the court that the defendant is in willful contempt of court for his failure to _____. The defendant was aware of the order and was asked to comply and has refused. I am asking the court to award the monies on my reimbursement list. May I approach the judge?"

Ask this question first, get approval, and hand the judge or bailiff or whoever sticks out a hand your reimbursement list and proposed order, and say the following:

"Judge, this is a summary for the court of the money requested and a proposed order that the court can fill in with its rulings. The defendant has a copy. I will provide evidence to support the $------ I am requesting."

If the judge doesn't mention the opening statement and just asks you to call your first witness, which by the way is you, ask permission to make a brief opening and present the judge with your documents by saying the following:

"Judge, if I may, my brief opening will assist the court. I will show the court that the defendant is in willful contempt of court for his failure to _____. The defendant was aware of the order and was asked to comply and has refused. I am asking the court to award the monies on my reimbursement list. May I approach the judge?"

Ask this question first, get approval, and hand the judge or bailiff or whoever sticks out a hand your reimbursement list and proposed order, and say the following:

"Judge, this is a summary for the court of the money requested and a proposed order that the court can fill in with its rulings. The defendant has a copy. I will provide evidence to support the $------ I am requesting."

If the judge says you may not make an opening statement, then just start with the following:

"I am asking the court to award the monies on my reimbursement list. May I approach the judge?"

Ask this question first, get approval, and hand the judge or bailiff or whoever sticks out a hand your reimbursement list and proposed order, and say the following:

"Judge, this is a summary for the court of the money requested and a proposed order that the court can fill in with its rulings. The defendant has a copy. I will provide evidence to support the $------ I am requesting."

If the judge won't let you hand him anything, don't panic and don't insist. You will simply use your list once you are testifying on the stand. You should put your case information on the top of the blank proposed contempt order, but do not fill in anything else, that is for the judge!

From here, the judge can vary the order of events greatly, but what follows illustrates the common pro se order.

First Witness—You

You are your first and most likely only witness. Go to the witness stand bringing your evidence documents with you, including your reimbursement list. Do not have to fumble to gather these items! A folder or labeling system will help. (See how to create a trial book in Chapter 15.) Remain standing and look around to see who will swear you in. You will raise your right hand and respond "I do" or "I affirm" to the oath given to you if you cannot swear because of religious reasons. You can then be seated. You should turn to face the judge and say, "Judge, I would like to testify by narrative." This means that you will simply tell your story. You can make notes ahead of time and use them to read your statement to the court so you don't forget anything. It should be structured basically as follows.

"My name is _____ and I live at _____. I work for _____ as a _____. On ___DATE____, this court entered an order for the defendant to do/not do _____. The defendant has not followed the order. He failed to do/did _____ on ___DATES___. I asked the defendant to follow the order by PHONE, LETTER, E-MAIL. Here is my letter to the defendant of __DATE__, asking him to comply with the order. The defendant never responded/told me to_____. This letter is plaintiff's Exhibit 1. The letter is an accurate copy of the letter I sent to the defendant and is signed by me. I move to admit P-1."

The judge will then ask the defendant if he has any objection. Do not speak unless the judge asks you a question. Most likely the judge will admit the exhibit, and you will hand it to the judge or to someone next to the judge. (Note: some judges wait to get or read all the exhibits at the end of the proceedings.) Continue to testify as follows:

"The defendant kept refusing to follow the order. It cost me a lot of money. The defendant owes me a total of $----. That number is made up of $---- for ____ORDER NOT FOLLLOWED___; $---- for ____ORDER NOT FOLLLOWED___; $---- for service of the contempt on the defendant; $---- for the fees I paid for legal instruction on how to prepare and try my contempt. My receipts are plaintiff's Exhibit 2. (Receipts can be a copy of your paid checks.) The receipts are true and accurate copies of the money I spent and am owed by the defendant. I move to admit P-2."

Again, the judge will ask the defendant if he has any objection. Do not speak unless the judge asks you a question. Most likely the judge will admit the exhibit, and you will hand it to the judge or to someone next to the judge. Continue to testify as follows:

"Not having this money is causing problems for me. I have been unable to _____. The money I am requesting is on my reimbursement list."

If the judge did not let you submit it earlier, identify it as P-3 and testify that it accurately sums up the monies you seek and the receipts you've submitted, and move to admit P-3. If the judge accepted it earlier, you don't have to hand it to him again, just refer to the document.

If the defendant will still continue to owe you money in the future, like for child support or alimony, ask the court that you be paid by the defendant's employer through an Income Deduction Order by saying, "I would like to be paid in the future by Income Deduction Order so that the payments are on time."

That basically concludes your testimony. Remember that you can say what the defendant said to you, but you cannot quote people who are not present to testify, as that is hearsay. Now, as a practical matter, if you slip up, don't worry, the judge is expecting it. The judges are often a lot more relaxed with the hearsay rules when there are just one or no lawyers.

Once you are done, the defendant can ask you questions, a cross-examination of your testimony.

Cross-Examination of You

First, you will be nice. You will not be nasty. You will not sound angry. You will not sound aggravated. You will not snap. You will not yell or raise your voice. You will speak to your ex as you would a loan officer in a bank when you need money. He has the right to ask you questions, and in almost all cases you must answer truthfully and without drama.

If your ex has an attorney, you are not to try and outsmart him; it will make you look bad. You must answer his questions one at a time without trying to figure out if he is laying a trap. The judge may or may not protect you. Do not worry about this. Listen carefully to each question so you don't answer the wrong information.

Answer each question first by saying yes, no, I don't know, or I don't remember, then explain if necessary in three sentences, with all the important information at the beginning. Do not ask to explain and do not pause for a long time. Do not give speeches!

Here are some examples of answers to a question:

Q: Isn't it true that you make more money that he does now?

BAD A #1: I don't see what that has to do with him paying his child support like he is supposed to … .

Reason it's bad: Didn't answer the question and sounds aggravated

BAD A #2: I had to get a second job and work because he won't pay me … .

Reason it's bad: Didn't answer the question and sounds aggravated

BAD A #3: Did he tell you about his live-in girlfriend and her money?

Reason it's bad: Didn't answer the question and asked a question. You may not question the attorney or your ex if they are questioning you.

GREAT A: Yes, but I still have a hard time keeping up with my bills without his help. My car note is two months behind and all my utilities are late.

If you are asked a damaging question, just answer it. Do not avoid answering it. The court hates that. Tell the truth, apologize if you need to, and say why it won't happen again and how you've changed. You look worse if you don't admit it. This does not apply if you are asked to admit to the commission of a criminal offense because you may endanger your freedom. Consult an attorney if your case has criminal elements in it, especially if the issues are against you. Admitting to a crime waives your Fifth Amendment right to remain silent and can be used against you.

When Your Ex Cross-Examines You

It can feel pretty uncomfortable to have your ex cross-examine you, so you should put some thought into how you're going to answer his questions. This is what you won't do:

➤ Ask him questions.

➤ Accuse him of anything.

➤ Yell or raise your voice.

➤ Glare at him.

➤ Cry.

➤ Call him a liar or any other name.

Answer the reasonable questions as best you can. If you don't understand a question, say so. If he keeps making statements and not asking questions, say, "I'm sorry, I didn't hear your question, only a statement." The judge should help keep his questions in line. You are to be patient and not get flustered. Your ex wants you flustered; it will support his case. Take slow, deep breaths.

If you are nervous or frightened, squeeze your hands together in your lap—no one can see that. Try not to rock, bounce your leg, tap your feet, etc. If you have a nervous stomach, do not eat heavily before your hearing. If you absolutely have to, you can ask the judge to be excused to the restroom, but not unless you would otherwise have an accident. There is usually water and tissues in the courtroom. If you know you will cry, bring your own.

Pro se questioning usually contains a lot of interruptions. You must be very polite, but do finish your answers! Judges can't read your mind and know what else you were going to say, so they might not ask you to finish. Say, "I'm sorry; I need to finish my last answer." You don't need to ask permission to finish an answer; it is your right.

When a question sheds light on some past bad behavior, it is easier to accept the responsibility and move on. Your ex can linger on it if you play around and sound like you are trying to hide that you were involved in something bad. Saying "I don't know" is a valid answer; so is "I don't remember." State your answers firmly, and don't sound overly apologetic.

Your Redirect or Clarification

The judge may not allow you to clarify your statements. If you are permitted, be quick. You shouldn't need much more than several sentences to clarify, as long as you did a good job answering the other side's questions on cross-examination. Hit the major points that you messed up, and then be quiet!

Pro se parties talk too much and about too many different things. Remember that people can usually retain concepts in groups of three. So you might make three points and stop. Don't forget that you still have a chance to ask your ex questions. If something came out that you did that was bad or wrong, you may want to explain it briefly, apologize, and then leave it alone.

The next witness you can call is the defendant. The judge may not want you to or let you cross-examine him. The judge may want him to just get up and tell his side of the story. You should assume you can ask questions, unless you are told you cannot. It is also common for the judge to do part or all of the cross-examination himself.

Defendant's First Witness—Him

Just as you did, your ex will testify in a narrative, unless he has an attorney to question him. You are not to interrupt no matter what is said, no matter how wrong it is; make notes, but do not interrupt. Do not head roll, eye roll, snort, giggle, laugh, or slam things around at your table; the judge should forget you are there, or if he looks at you, he should see you respectfully paying attention and/or taking notes.

Cross-Examining Your Ex

When it's time for you to cross-examine your ex, ask the following questions:

> ➤ Please state your name and current address for the court. (Write it down if you don't have it)

> ➤ What do you do for a living?

> ➤ How many jobs do you have?

> ➤ What is the name and address of your employer? (Write it down if you don't have it)

> ➤ What is your gross yearly or monthly income?

> ➤ Do you have a tax return here with you?

(If yes) Can you please show it to me and the court?

> ➤ Do you have your pay stub/s here with you?

(If yes) Can you please show it to me and the court?

> ➤ You knew that the __NAME OF ORDER__ required you to __WHAT IT REQUIRED___, correct?

> ➤ Isn't it true that you have not ___WHAT HASN'T BEEN DONE___?

> ➤ Isn't true that I asked you and finally wrote you to ___WHAT HASN'T BEEN DONE___?

➤ Do you know how much money you owe under the order?

(If yes) How much?

(If no or if his amount is different from yours) Do you disagree with the $---- that I say you owe?

(If yes) Based on what proof do you disagree?

➤ If the court awards me $----, how do you plan to pay that money?

You are not trying to ask your ex a great number of questions for several reasons:

➤ He will most likely lie.

➤ He will confuse the issue and try to get pity.

➤ The case must be short and to the point.

You are only seeking to establish where he lives, what he does or used to do for work, that he knew about the order, that you asked him to follow the order, that he could have followed the order, and that he did not follow the order. If your ex ignored the order on purpose and you have some proof, you can ask about this also and maybe get him to admit he didn't comply.

If you can't get answers to all of your questions, don't worry about it; that's what your proof is for. In a good contempt case, the case is proved by the plaintiff's testimony and evidence before the defendant ever says a word. Thus, do not feel you need to keep talking to get your ex to admit something.

Handy Tip

Good lawyers do not keep defendants on the stand for a long time unless they are harming their own cases. And we avoid open-ended questions and usually do not ask questions we do not know the answers to. A closed-ended question is answered yes or no. Avoid ones that ask for a long explanation; your ex is likely to make something up and confuse the judge.

The judge may interrupt your questioning with his own questions—that's normal. If your ex has a lawyer and his lawyer objects to something you ask, stop talking, face the judge, and wait. The lawyer should have a reason for his objection. He will give his reason. The judge will either agree, sustaining it, or disagree, overruling it.

Technically, lawyers respond to objections, but you aren't a lawyer so remain silent unless asked a question by the judge. Worst case, you will be told you cannot ask your question the same way or at all.

The witness cannot ask you questions. If he does, very politely say, "I cannot answer your questions from the stand."

Closing Arguments

The judge may or may not allow closing arguments after everyone rests their case. If he doesn't and you want to make closing arguments, you can ask permission to do so. You would say something like this:

"Judge, the defendant knew about the order, knew about my requests that he follow the order, and he refused. The defendant has not shown this court any/sufficient reason for his failure to follow the order. I ask that the monies listed on my reimbursement list be awarded in full, and that the defendant be found in willful contempt of court and made to start repayment immediately."

Can you add stuff? Yes, but take it easy. The judge has probably known what he was going to rule for the last fifteen minutes and may just be waiting to shut everyone up so the ruling can be announced. If you have a specific repayment structure in mind, then this would be the time to mention it, or you could include it at the end of your testimony.

The judge may rule immediately or he may reserve his ruling and put the order in the mail later.

Sometimes you can get a judge to rule on the spot if you have a motion for contempt form. You can ask the judge if he will accept your form, which has blanks where he will fill in the ruling. Some judges will fill it in immediately to save time and future effort. See template 19.1 in the Appendix for a sample motion for contempt form and other supporting forms you can personalize.

Jail

Offenders very rarely go to jail on their first contempt. It is more common when they are brought in for a second or third contempt that the court really begins to lose patience. The judge may ask you if you want the person to go to jail. Have your answer ready in advance. Here are some good answers to that question:

> ➤ I just don't know what it will take to get him to follow the order. I leave that decision to you, Judge.

> ➤ Maybe if the jail time was just on weekends so he won't lose his job.

➤ Can he be given seventy-two hours to come up with the/some money, and only go to jail if he doesn't?

➤ Yes, Judge. I think it would help keep us out of court in the future.

Golden Rules

Here are some rules that will help you in the courtroom:

➤ Never interrupt anyone, especially the judge. You will be given a chance to speak your side of the issue and/or reply to the other side's statements.

➤ Don't raise your hand in court to be heard.

➤ Unless you are testifying, stand up whenever you speak to the judge.

➤ Try to avoid asking if you can ask a question. Usually you cannot. The court is not there to answer your questions. You can't ask one from the stand nor can you ask opposing counsel.

➤ Stick very closely to the subject at hand. If you are discussing nonpayment of child support, what his sister says about you when the kids come home has no place in court. If you are there for money, confine yourself to the finances.

➤ Don't go backward several years into events of the past, especially if the events were before the issuance of your divorce decree or other order.

➤ Write out your cross-examination questions in advance—don't try to wing it.

➤ Do not object. You are not a lawyer and are likely to do this incorrectly. Trust the court to take care of objectionable issues. Also, the court is usually lenient with the rules of evidence and hearsay for pro se litigation; it'll ignore what it needs to ignore.

➤ Do not argue with your ex. A courtroom is not for debates or arguments; it is for asking and answering questions, presenting evidence, and asking the court for relief.

➤ Do not stare at, glare at, mumble at, swear at, or talk to your ex while your hearing is going on. Do not respond physically to anything your ex says or does.

➤ Take notes so that you remember what points you need to correct when it is your turn to speak.

PART SIX

Moving On

 Financial Emergencies After the Divorce

In This Chapter

➤ What to do if your ex disappears or dies

➤ How your ex's bankruptcy may or may not affect you

➤ Losing a house and job loss

➤ What to do when there's been an arrest

Life is unpredictable and sometimes just downright mean! Any number of things can go wrong and turn your life upside down. We'll take a look here at five of the most common post-divorce emergencies I hear about from clients.

Your Ex Dies or Disappears

If your ex dies, the first practical question would be if he was insured or supposed to be insured. If the divorce decree required him to carry a policy, hopefully you were getting annual proof of the policy being in force. Go directly to the insurance company and inquire. You will also need a proof of death, usually a death certificate.

If the order required him to carry a policy and you have no idea whether he did, things can get messy. If you don't want to seem crass, you may want to have an attorney inquire of the estate (your ex's family) for you.

Depending on how your decree was written, you may be able to pursue action against your ex's assets if he didn't carry a policy. These types of cases usually need to be dealt with quickly before those assets are liquidated without the knowledge of your existing claim. In this case, you would need to talk to a trust and estate lawyer to understand the rules of intestate inheritance in your state.

Divorce Vocab

A person who dies without having a valid will is said to have died intestate.

Since you are the ex, you probably won't inherit anything. Your children, however, should have standing. How children stand against an ex's parents depends on the state you're in. Usually the stronger claim is with the closest generation.

The main problem you face if your ex has died without insurance is that you are truly out of child support. You may try approaching sympathetic family members (especially if the death was sudden) and see if they will bring your plight to the family and request some financial or property assistance.

If your ex disappears it is almost as though he has died without a will, except your child support order stays in force. You can't find your ex to serve them papers, so suing him for back child support is almost impossible.

Keep a log of any contact you do have with your ex or any tidbits of information you hear. One upside to a disappearing ex is that many states allow for stepparent adoptions of children who have been "financially and emotionally" abandoned by their other parent. The time frames and requirements differ, but if your ex has been out of contact with no support paid for at least a year, that is sufficient in many places.

You can try online resource services like Intellius and www.USA-People-Search.com to find your ex. You pay a fee to search the database for a document trail on your ex. If that doesn't work, you can employ a skip tracer. Skip tracing is just like it sounds and is usually done by private investigators and process servers. The fees for skip tracing can vary widely from $75 to $2,000. It depends on what is needed to find the person and how serious you are about your results. If a person isn't really hiding, you can usually find him for $100 or less using just computer research. If your ex is actively covering his trail, it will be more difficult and thus more expensive.

To give your ex notice pursuant to your decree after he's disappeared, a letter sent first class mail to his last known address is usually sufficient. Be careful not to send registered or certified mail, as it won't get picked up, and that tends to prove he didn't get the notice you wanted him to get.

Handy Tip

When you're planning a trip and need to get a US passport for your children, you'll need to get the application signed by your ex because it requires the signature of both parents. Try to get this done well in advance of planning a trip when your ex is in a good mood and around to sign the documents, just in case he decides to leave one day. It would save you the hassle applying for an exception and explaining to the government why you can't get the father's signature.

If your ex reappears after a long stint of being out of contact, you may want to be aggressive and serve him as quickly as possible with your arrearages contempt and possibly a request to modify (reduce) his visitation. You may want to try to get the court to allow for a reintroduction period so your children can get reacquainted with their father and used to him being back in their lives.

Your Ex Files Bankruptcy

Child support and alimony have always been protected from bankruptcy. The Bankruptcy Abuse Prevention and Consumer Protection Act (BAPCPA) of 2005 added some additional protections for divorce. You are now protected if your ex tries to use bankruptcy to get out of paying debts your divorce decree deemed his responsibly, so you can't be left on the hook with creditors.

For example, you are both on a Home Depot credit card, and the divorce decree requires your ex to make payments, pay off, and then close the account. In the past, if your ex didn't pay off this debt, Home Depot could legally pursue you to pay the debt. You would have to take your ex to court, sue him for violating the decree, and demand he protect, indemnify, you. The latest changes close that loophole by not allowing divorce decree obligations to be included in a bankruptcy filing.

In fact, your ex filing for bankruptcy isn't an emergency for you. It will either wipe out or greatly reduce your ex's debt payments, so in theory it should become easier for him to manage your support payments.

Do not be alarmed if or when you receive papers from the bankruptcy court listing your child support. This is not an attempt to get rid of it! On the contrary, the court likes to make sure you know it is there, and the trustee on the case will likely be friendly to you. You may contact the trustee if you need something or have a question. Remember to be prepared and polite. Often trustees prefer being contacted by e-mail, so you may try communicating in that fashion.

Check over the paperwork and make sure your current support amount and any stated arrearage is correct. If it isn't, alert the trustee as soon as you notice the error. Remember, when in doubt, write it out.

Bankruptcy court is a federal court and should be taken very serious. Never lie or fudge on anything to a federal court. Also, don't be on time—be early for any appearance you must make.

The common meeting for a Chapter 7 (liquidation of all debts) is called the creditors meeting. You are a creditor so you can go. While it is true that very few creditors go to these meetings, it's better to be safe than sorry, especially if you see any inaccuracy (or lies) in the Chapter 7 petition your ex filed. So if you know your ex had a $10,000 paid-off antique car and it's not listed or he just gave it to his brother, you might need to report this knowledge to the trustee, who will check it out.

Take Heed

Police reports are not admissible as evidence in court without someone from the police department to verify them as accurate business records. That means you will need to subpoena the officer who wrote the report.

It can be some time before your court date comes up. The officer could easily forget details. If you know you will need to have the officer in court, it's a good idea to notify him and ask him to make or keep notes so that he will have an easier time testifying. Do not attempt to subpoena an officer at the last minute before your court date. It's best to do it a month or so in advance, and then send him reminders.

Generally, creditors attend creditors meetings only if they have an objection or want to question the creditor about his petition. It may also be a factor that federal buildings require a driver's license or other formal ID for admission, and most will not let you go past security with a cell phone that takes pictures. It's easier to just leave anything electronic or with a battery in the car.

Getting Arrested

Your ex getting arrested can cause any number of problems. If the children were with him, hopefully the police called you and asked you to get them. They do not always do this. They can place the children temporarily with a children's agency, which then has to find you. If you get a call to pick up your children—get them! Your children will have questions. Tell them that you don't know very much right now, but when you figure out what is going on, you will tell them as much as they can know.

Get a copy of the police report. Ask when it will be available, how much it will cost, if you will need to pick it up in person (usually you do), and when during the day you can retrieve it. If you have a lawyer, he will want this document. Ask if there is any special certification process done on police reports and what the cost is to do this.

Depending on why your ex was arrested, you may need or want to protect your children. If your ex is given bail, find out the bail conditions—they usually prohibit violence or weapons access. Check to see if there are any child or person restrictions.

If your ex has been arrested for something the common person would view as dangerous to children (drugs, DUI, physical violence), you may need to give your ex notice that you wish to alter the visitation based on the arrest and ask his consent. If he does not agree, you will have to go to court, otherwise you risk changing a court order unilaterally, which is illegal and can subject you to contempt of court charges.

You will want to do a criminal records check on your ex if you think he has been arrested but you cannot be sure. There are many online sources that will help you do this inexpensively.

Keep in mind that there is a difference between an arrest and a conviction. A person may have been arrested three times but never convicted for various reasons. If you are questioning your ex in court or seeking discovery, be sure to ask about how many arrests, and when and what were the charges.

If you're the one who gets arrested, make sure your children are taken care of! If you are going to be gone indefinitely, you may as well be the one to call your ex, since he'll find out eventually. It can make you look worse if you spend four days in jail and your ex finds out you've been "hiding" the kids with your mother. Next thing you know, you will have a custody case on your hands. So focus on minimizing the impact on your children, then protecting your job, and finally worry about your pride and your ex finding out.

Losing a Job

This is one of the most common emergencies, so don't panic if you lose your job. First, figure out if you are getting any type of future salary, severance, or continuing benefits package. Sit down with your bills. Most people have heard that we should all have six months' living expenses set aside for an emergency; that seems hard to come by for divorced folks. Look at what you do have and figure out how long it will be until you cannot pay for a critical living expense such as your home, utilities, car, or car insurance. If your support is pretty reliable, factor it in. If your support is iffy, count only 50 percent of a month's payment. This will give you a pretty good idea of when you may need to start panicking. Now do some or all of the following in no particular order:

> ➤ Write and call your ex. Tell him you lost your job and that his support payments will be especially important until you are able to replace your income. At this early juncture you don't have to have a huge conversation, but you need to let him know so he has no excuses later for not helping however he can.

> ➤ Look at your children's fixed expenses for the next six months. Figure out if any of these are shared with your ex and which ones are to be paid solely by you. Can you cancel or delay payment to any of them? As soon as possible, ask the organizations and companies for a grace period or payment plan. Do not wait until the night before Little League starts to seek assistance.

> ➤ Tell your older children that you lost your job. Take care not to panic them or let them see the depth of your fear. You are their rock, and you don't want to look like gravel. I have found it's better to tell children what will and will not be impacted, and when you will have a second update meeting with them. Kids feel much better when they know what is going on and how it affects them. If you need their help, ask. Children are often eager to make some kind of contribution to help you out.

> ➤ Get outside assistance. Many, many people before the recession had never even considered the idea of getting food stamps—they are for people who are truly poor. If you qualify for government assistance, don't let your pride get in your way.

There are so many different programs for government assistance, including a nutrition program for women, infants, and children (WIC), and temporary assistance for needy families (TANF). If ever you cannot figure out how or where to go for social services, seek out a domestic violence shelter in your area and ask if someone there can point you in the right direction.

Do not overlook the faith communities around you. You don't necessarily have to be a member of a church to seek its assistance.

Check out websites like Craigslist.org that facilitate the barter of goods and services (you may have some items you can trade or sell) and have a free section where you may be able to get some items you need at no cost. You can also use the Internet to help you find local ministries and charities.

Above all do not give up and stay as positive as you can. There is a depressed and defeated air to some people who have been unemployed for a long time that is a turnoff to people who would otherwise assist them. Don't miss an opportunity because you seem broken—keep your chin up.

If your ex loses his job and you will be in a bind without his support, I recommend you go through the same exercises as you did above. Tighten the belt immediately and assume your ex will be unemployed for six months to a year. You have to begin to restructure your finances so that you are not dependent on his support.

The fact that he is amassing an arrearage is usually not a great help. Even when he eventually gets a job, he will not be able to write a check and pay back all that money at once. Be prepared for your ex to file a lawsuit to reduce his child support responsibilities. If you think there is something not quite right with the job loss, you need to hire an experienced family lawyer who is good at imputation of income cases, where it's proved that the ex should be making more than he does. These cases are difficult.

Your ex may ask you to agree to reduced support verbally or in an agreement you both sign. These agreements are not legally binding in court, as you two cannot change a court order without a judge. However, the court can decide to take evidence of an agreement and honor it. What does this mean? It means the support receiver doesn't have much to lose, but the support payer does. The court could ignore the agreement and charge your ex the full amount for each month.

Long story short, these types of kitchen table child support modifications are not the best idea. If you must do them, execute them with a notarized signature for both parties and don't lose the agreement. You can even file this agreement so long as you don't call it an order, which requires a judge's signature. Most clerk's offices will simply take the document, stamp it, and file it. Filing it doesn't make it anyh more legal, but it helps avoid the "I didn't make a deal" argument.

You Lose Your House

I have to remind people that we are not turtles; if we lose our homes, we are not going to languish in the street and freeze to death. No matter what people think of our country, it is pretty much impossible to starve to death here or to truly be homeless with children as long as you are willing to be open to change and to work.

There has to be some point at which you switch from trying to save the house to resigning yourself to starting over. Get to that point, because things are easier after you accept that you have to start over. Many rich and powerful people from Abraham Lincoln to Zsa Zsa Gabor had to start over or declare bankruptcy.

If you have primary custody and lose your home, that doesn't mean you'll lose your children. Remember, you have your custody by court order, and it can only be changed by court order. It is important that you go over your options and pay attention to selecting one that is not only good for the children, but financially sustainable as well. If you are moving,

Take Heed

Too many people jump from the frying pan into the fire. Don't rent a home or apartment you can barely afford just to stay in the "it" school district.

this might be the best time to make the break from an area that you cannot reasonably afford to live in on one salary. The bright side of losing a home is that it usually means you're removing a major overhead expense that you otherwise wouldn't be able to reduce.

After you select a reasonable option, you must discuss it with your ex. Do not wait until your home is sold on the courthouse steps to tell your ex that it's in jeopardy. In fact, it is usually far better to tell an ex much earlier, while nothing much is happening than to call frantically asking to borrow his truck to help you move.

The biggest fear is that your ex will try to take the kids because you've lost your home and he hasn't. If you are otherwise doing a good job with the children and have made efforts to minimize the move as much as possible, courts aren't switching custody these days just for a home loss. That doesn't mean your ex won't threaten it or file it.

Pay attention to the side effects of your move, which can include the following:

➤ Will the new location be temporary, requiring another move and more moving expense?

➤ Will the new location shorten or lengthen your ex's commute?

➤ Will the new location be in a different school district?

➤ Are there any safety issues in the new neighborhood?

➤ Are there any new roommates and interpersonal dynamics to deal with?

It is just easier if you consider all the changes and deal with them.

Be very wary of moving in with your boyfriend. Your ex may see this as a perfect excuse to take you back to court for custody, depending on the ages of the children, how long you've been divorced, whether the boyfriend was involved in the breakup of the marriage, whether he has children of his own, and past history between your ex and your new love.

CHAPTER 21

Child Emergencies After Your Divorce

In This Chapter

➤ What to do if your ex takes the children

➤ How to handle an ex who's stalking you

➤ Your children's behavioral and medical crises

It seems when children are involved, people feel more vulnerable. There is no better way to hurt you than by keeping your children away from you. Your ex knows this. And then there is overseeing the health and safety of your children. This is amplified further by not having the other parent around to help in an emergency. Let's find out how we can turn our responses to child emergencies into actions that matter.

Your Ex Takes the Children

One of the most common emergencies having to do with children is when an ex refuses to return the children until he feels like it. Worst and most dangerous is when you believe he will take the children away.

The easiest step you can take to prevent this from happening is to follow your decree to the letter. When you are dealing with someone who will hold your children hostage and terrorize you, you can't afford to have him use the defense that you "agreed" to something other than what is in the decree. If you have been agreeing to do things outside the clear terms of your decree, you need to stop. You also have to send your ex a letter or e-mail similar to this one:

"In the past you have failed to return the children according to agreements we made. I have experienced problems with our visitations and child transfers being done outside of our decree. This letter is formal notice that I will no longer agree to visitation changes and wish to go strictly by the final decree of divorce. Further, should you fail or refuse to return the children in accordance with the decree, I will move the court to hold you in contempt and to comply."

The most common outcome to such a letter is that you will lose whatever leeway you in exchange for not enforcing that part of the decree. Your ex will scrutinize the decree to see where you can possibly be in violation. You must be comfortable with the terms of your decree and their inflexibility, and be able to adhere to those terms. You should also be prepared to take your ex to court either on your own or with your attorney.

Once you have sent the letter (and kept a copy for your files, your attorney's files, and future court, if need be), you must insist the decree be followed. This will likely result in a fight with your ex. Be prepared. Document to the extent that the law in your area allows (recordings, video, witnesses, etc.).

When your ex defies the decree, you need to decide what to do. If the defiance is minor, you may wish to send a notice of violation with a request for future compliance. If it is major, file the contempt. What is major? Everyone has a different opinion, but I think any time children are kept out of school or away from home for twenty-four hours or more past their return time is a major defiance. If your ex is particularly angry, four hours may be considered major and constitute a dangerous red flag.

Once your ex is at least thirty minutes late returning from a visitation, try to contact him. After three hours, if there is no word from your ex despite your messages and the ex's family has no information, call the nonemergency number for the police and report your concern. All jurisdictions handle these matters differently.

Make sure you have your divorce decree, your letter establishing you're following the decree to the word, and any violations letters readily available to give to the officers. At this point, you will need to follow the advice of your local police department. However, reports should be made and action taken once the children have been gone for more than twenty-four hours.

If after he picked them up, your ex told you that he is not going to return the children at the required time, you may wish to call the nonemergency number for the police. Advise them of the threat and seek advice on how to proceed if your children are in fact not returned on time. That way you will know what steps to take.

If the police will not act, your lawyer will. I have filed emergency motions to suspend visitation and return children to the jurisdiction of the court within thirty-six hours of the children being overdue.

Take Heed

Be aware that filing an emergency case is usually more costly than filing a nonemergency case that doesn't need to be rushed. This is why it's important for you to have your documentation together. If you need to file, it has to be done quickly.

Thankfully, the majority of these cases have more to do with an egotistical ex than someone actually trying to kidnap a child. Usually, once the ex has received a scary enough consequence, he gets the idea that he cannot do this. You can also use these kinds of events and any court order that comes out of them to seek reduction or alteration to your ex's visitation on the grounds that he is acting against the best interests of the children.

Crossing Borders

What happens when you believe your ex will leave with the children and not return? If he might take the children out of the United States, your first concern is citizenship, especially if your ex is a citizen of another country. In that case, you must find out if that country is part of the Hague Convention, a multinational treaty that ensures the return of a child taken illegally from one member country to another.

Divorce Vocab

The Hague Convention is a contract among participating countries that the legal systems, although different, will honor the custody rights as stated by the child's home country. The participating countries will require the return of children to their home country, where custody will be determined or enforced.

You have cause to be worried if your ex has taken your children to a country that is not part of the Hague Convention. If you can, record your ex stating he plans to take your children to his country and that you will never see them again. Get witnesses, it will be critical for you convince a judge to take the impossibility of recovering the children into account.

The good, basic precaution is to have the court or attorneys hold your children's passports, if they have been issued. You may need a court order for this. Investigate your ex's home country to find out if a child of one of its citizens even needs a passport for admittance into that country. Again, if your ex can get your children into his country without United States documentation, that is another red flag to be raised and shaken vigorously.

Handy Tip

International custody disputes and kidnapping are highly specialized. Hire an attorney who has experience with this type of case.

The best defense here is to be watchful and alert to the threat, and document it as best you can. Determine if the likely countries or family members would cooperate with your ex, and then obtain the best help you can before something happens.

Teach your children age-appropriate ways to protect them from parental abduction. You should be certain they know that you would never willingly leave them and that if you are not around it is because something is wrong. The children should know who to go to for help getting back to you. Teaching them a safe word so that they know your ex has permission to take them on a long trip is also easily done.

Be careful that you do not get yourself in trouble by exaggerating the need for this kind of preparation and end up being charged with contempt for alienating the children against your ex. The help of a licensed professional is the best way to avoid this problem.

Your Ex Turns Your Children Against You

The buzz phrase is *parental alienation* and is most commonly alleged by fathers of custodial mothers. It doesn't matter to you what it's called or whether or not it is recognized by the American Psychological Association; it means the other parent is out to destroy your relationship with your children.

When Your Children Are With Your Ex

Counseling is the gold standard for dealing with this problem, but there are many reasons that counseling is not possible such as lack of time, finances, and insurance; or refusal by custodial parent or by the children. When counseling is not an option, you have to choose ways to keep in contact with your children and demonstrate your willingness to be there for them. Here are some ideas:

➤ Phone calls at set times, like every second and fourth Sunday in a month you will call at 10 a.m.

➤ Video calls (kids like technology)

➤ Communication via a cell phone (be careful, you will need to discuss providing a cell phone and all the many challenges it entails)

➤ Communication via first class and priority mailed letters with delivery confirmation

➤ Communication via e-mails

➤ Continued requests for visitation so that the interfering parent cannot correctly say you have not sought visitation for months or years (he won't mention that is because he wore you down)

➤ Ask other family members (where legally possible) to check on your children for you and tell the children that you want to see them

➤ Communication via Facebook, Twitter, and other social media

The second gold standard for these situations is a very experienced family lawyer with at least seven years' experience. This kind of case is messy and difficult and that translates into more time, which is more money. Even if you don't have the money now, put it aside little by little so at least at some certain date in the future, you will have the assistance you need to bring the interference to light.

If you are still unable to see your children, be careful that you aren't the one making the situation worse by doing any of the following:

➤ Asking your children about your ex

➤ Complaining about how little time you have

➤ Complaining about how the children don't like you or don't like you enough

➤ Complaining how the children used to like you more

While the Children are With You

One way you can counteract the poison your ex is using to turn your children against you is to improve yourself so your children will want to spend time with you. Have you read new books or seen recent movies you can discuss with them? Do you keep up with their school and its events? Do you know who their best friends are? Are you following their extracurricular events? Do you watch the professional teams they like so you can talk about that?

Even better is for you and your children to undertake a new activity together. Sadly, many people are so focused on the unfairness of their ex that they don't do what they could to make their children more likely to want to see them.

If your bond with your children has been broken, perhaps you can reforge it as a cool adult who listens to them and thinks what they say and do are important. Do not complain with them or to them! It is so much harder for one parent to alienate a child who wants to see you, than a child who is lukewarm about you.

If you have more than one child, do your best to make a strong bond as quickly as you can with the youngest children. They are the most susceptible to the pressure to "give you up" and least able to defend themselves for the crime of loving you. An older child may intervene to protect your access to the younger ones (which is sad, but necessary). However, once the older sibling leaves, the youngest ones lose their protector.

If you have a situation like this, it would help for the older children to talk to someone and tell the truth about what is going on at home. Often they will refuse to step back into the middle of a situation they feel like they just escaped. This is doubly true when the financial support of the interfering parent is needed by the oldest children for school or living expenses.

It is critical that you get yourself counseling, because losing your children is horrible. Losing your children by inches is almost unbearable and can tempt you to do things that your rational self would never do. Also, whatever reason is being alleged for keeping you at bay can usually be addressed by counseling. Getting a clean bill of mental health can go a long way with showing the court that the interference is more about personal vendettas than safety of the children.

Your Ex Stalks You or Your Family

Stalking is to be taken very seriously and needs to be handled with direct and specific professional legal advice and the assistance of the authorities. It is most often considered to be a felony criminal offense (see Chapter 5).

Handy Tip

The key to almost any stalking case, is to document the behavior of the stalker and seek a restraining order or order of protection, and then enforce it. To get you started, you must detect if a stalking pattern is emerging.

The very best thing you can do, male or female, is to contact your local domestic violence shelter and ask for resources and someone to talk to. You also want to sit down and do some worst case scenario planning. You will have to ask and answer some tough questions such as the following:

➤ Has my ex ever threatened me before?

➤ Has my ex ever threatened to harm or kill me?

➤ When did my ex make those threats?

➤ Did my ex follow through with his threats?

➤ Am I aware of anyone else my ex has threatened?

➤ What was the outcome in that case?

➤ Have I sought a criminal and civil background check to see if my ex has other charges or stalking situations?

➤ What is it that my ex says I have or haven't done—what is his "excuse?"

➤ What steps can I take to secure my job?

➤ What steps can I take to secure my home?

➤ What steps can I take to secure my car?

➤ If I wanted to attack me, what are the best three times and places to attack and get away with it?

➤ What can I do to make it harder to get to me at those weak points?

➤ What steps can I take to protect myself?

➤ What steps can I take to protect my children at home and at school?

➤ Who needs to know about the danger I may be in to help protect me?

➤ What does my family need to do and not do to help protect me?

➤ Is my family a target?

➤ Is my job a target?

➤ If I had to leave home without advance warning, where could I go and how long could I stay?

➤ If I needed someone to hide me and/or the children, who would it be?

➤ Do I have the money to get an attorney to obtain protection?

➤ If I had to leave without returning home, do I have clothes and items stored in a safe place that I could retrieve?

➤ What can I do to alter my routine to make it harder for someone watching me to predict where I will be?

➤ In my opinion, what will this stalker give up or risk to harm me?

➤ Have I kept clear documentation of all incidents and given it to the police?

➤ Have I talked to the children about safety and abductions?

➤ Do I have current photos and fingerprints of my children?

➤ Do I carry my certified order of protection with me at all times?

➤ Do I have multiple copies of my certified order of protection everywhere?

➤ Have I provided copies of my order to the school, daycare center, and my employer?

➤ Do I understand that the order is merely a piece of paper and I must do what is necessary to stay safe if my ex appears?

➤ Am I taking my own protection seriously and following the advice of professionals without deviation?

➤ Will I invest in self-defense classes and other items (like pepper spray) to improve my safety?

Take advantage of technology and use it to help protect you. Installing surveillance cameras is a great idea. If you can't afford it, even installing fake cameras can have some effect. Get a security system and use it.

Always have your cell phone and have it charged for emergency calls. Also carry a small video camera if your phone doesn't have one built in. You can use the camera to quickly document someone following you, to identify the car and license plate parked right by yours, and even to record verbal confrontations.

If you have the funds, engaging a private investigator to document your stalker's criminal activity toward you is a good investment in your piece of mind. Investigators are credible witnesses, and most can potentially offer an expert opinion on the stalker and his actions and threat level.

Above all else, be the squeaky wheel. If you have to call 911 every other night for two months, so be it. Obtain copies of every 911 call and every police report. Do not let an officer skip documenting any event you report. Tell him that you have to have it documented for a stalking case. If he will not comply, get his badge number, contact his supervisor, and ask for the report to be done.

Child Behavior Crises

It seems when you are least able to handle it, your child will have a behavior crisis. By crisis I mean one of the following:

➤ Runs away

➤ Is arrested

➤ Beats up another child

➤ Is in danger of being expelled from school

➤ Has become a physical danger to himself or others in your household

Regardless of what has happened, the general response steps are the same

➤ Ensure the child's current safety

➤ Obtain the facts to determine objectively what happened

➤ Notify your ex

➤ Determine if anything immediate needs to be done to address harm or damage caused by your child

➤ Consider and possibly consult with other adults to determine what options are available for your child's situation

➤ Make a decision, live with it, prepare to receive criticism about it

If you need to, begin the process of locating your child and use any and all resources you have. If he is running away because he is in trouble, his judgment will be impaired and he will make more foolish decisions. Once he's with you, resist the urge to deal with him immediately. This will keep you from losing your temper and possibly making a bad situation worse.

Do not challenge or judge your child. It is important to give him this one moment of neutrality. He may be and likely is guilty of whatever rash thing you were told he did, but how you handle this now can make a difference in years to come.

It can be better to contact a difficult ex before you have the details, since you can't stay on the phone and talk about what you don't know. The more dangerous, urgent, and critical the situation, the quicker you should notify your ex. I recommend a phone call (voice mail message a must) followed by a text or e-mail sent to a different location. The e-mail or text is provable that you attempted to reach your ex. You should state in the written attempt that you phoned first, which number you called, and at what time and that you left a message.

If you know that your ex is the kind of person who will start calling around screaming and threatening everyone in sight to get information, it would be best for all if you obtained as much information as possible to feed to him to keep from being artificially aggravating the situation.

There may be personal liability or a lawsuit involved if your child has caused damage or harm to another person. In this situation it is best to find a local attorney to give you at least a preliminary opinion on how to proceed before you show up with wood and nails to start patching the destroyed fence or a credit card to pay for a vet bill.

When appropriate, assure the injured party that you take this very seriously and as soon as you get in touch with the other parent, you'll be back to address everything. Here, you will be using your ex as a means to buy you time to figure out what to do and to talk to an attorney if you need one.

You will probably end up talking to teachers, police officers, and others about your child's behavior. Remember that your child, presumably, is at fault and did something wrong. Keep your tone humble and apologetic. The options available to your child will always be greater if others believe that he is remorseful and you can get him back under control.

Take Heed

Stay cool when your child acts up. If you can't control your own behavior, the odds that you can control your child's are much lower.

Whether you make a decision on your own and tell your ex about it or hash it out with him, prepare for complaints. Your family, your child, your ex, the school, someone will not like your decision and will tell you so. This is where the thick skin you had to grow to go through your stressful divorce has some use. You made the best call you could at the time, and it can be aggravating if after the fact someone comes to you with more information and under less stress to tell you differently. Let it go. I'm sure I could pick better lottery ticket numbers for last year's drawings if they'd let me do it now!

Child Health Crises

An emergency medical crisis follows the same path, except you should not wait for the facts before you reach out to your ex. He should be notified using all means at your disposal, and messages should be left everywhere. If it is a true emergency, many people will ask how they can help you. Give one of them all of your ex's contact information and ask him to find your ex and get him to the hospital so that you can stay with your child and focus on any ongoing medical decisions that need to be made.

Also, if you believe your ex will cause problems at the medical facility, ask someone to get a copy of your divorce decree and bring it to you. Hopefully, it addresses how and by whom emergency medical decisions are to be made. It would be wise to get this document into the hands of the hospital staff and explain your concerns about the impending arrival of your ex. If the hospital is already in possession of your court order stating you have full medical authority, it can be ready in advance. Alert hospital security before your ex's arrival if you have any concern about physical misbehavior. Make sure security has a copy of the decree and all questions are answered before a scene is made in ER.

Make sure that heated conversations are held outside of your child's hospital room for two reasons:

1. You want witnesses

2. Your child should not have to endure seeing his parents fight at such a time

You can and should keep the hospital door open if you are concerned about your ex starting a disturbance, but it's even better not to be alone with him. Keep in mind that his normal crazy is even more aggravated by the stress of your child's condition.

If your ex insists on blaming you for whatever went wrong with your child, try to surround yourself with medical staff. Hopefully, this will deter the blaming, but if it doesn't, at least you have witnesses.

Your goal is to make sure your child is attended to and your ex's drama is minimized. Good luck!

 Your Marriage Failed—You Didn't!

> ## In This Chapter
>
> ➤ Dealing with shame
> ➤ Letting go of hate
> ➤ Making changes in yourself
> ➤ Gaining peace

Most people who have gone through a divorce is scared or hesitant to talk about it. That's how it used to be with certain diseases like cancer. It wasn't until people felt they could speak up about cancer and not feel ashamed that progress was made in the treatment of the disease.

The same can be said of divorce. Just as there are nonsmoking people living a healthy lifestyle who get cancer, there are good people who worked to keep their marriage together getting divorced. But just because your marriage failed doesn't mean that you have failed. In this chapter, we take a look at how you can overcome the sense of failure and other negative feelings you may have as a result of your divorce.

When You're Ashamed of Your Divorce

Let's take a look at just some of the depressing and negative thoughts you may be entertaining:

➤ I gave up
➤ I choose poorly to start

➤ I didn't listen

➤ I betrayed a religious vow

➤ I'm lazy

➤ I'm not strong enough

➤ I didn't try hard enough

➤ I didn't forgive enough

➤ I'm impatient

➤ I'm weak

➤ I'm jealous

➤ I failed my children, my family, my religion, and myself

➤ I'm not a good parent

➤ I'm setting a bad example for the kids

➤ Mine was supposed to be the marriage that ended the divorce trend in my family

➤ I'm too demanding

➤ I've been living in a fairy tale

➤ My life wasn't so bad; I could have stuck it out

➤ I lost my kids for no reason

➤ I've destroyed my kids

➤ I broke my kids' hearts

➤ I drove away my spouse

➤ I still want to be married

➤ I can't do this on my own

➤ No one wants me, and no one ever will

➤ I'm used up, too old, and my body is gone forever

➤ I don't want to be alone any more

Whew. That hurt to write, so I hope it hurt to read. When you look at all that misery, it seems pretty clear that you need to go easier on yourself. Yet, many of you have a lot of that kind of venom circulating in your head. Depending on how often you take a dip into this pool of despair, you might actually be depressed.

Depression and a difficult divorce are almost like chocolate chip cookies and milk. You can find one without the other, but when you see them together they seem to just fit. The depression question comes down to whether you can choose to move your mind away from those dark thoughts or whether they take over.

Divorce Vocab

Depression is a chronic medical illness with symptoms that include ongoing sadness, feelings of hopelessness, lack of energy, and a loss in interest of life. Many people suffering from depression have difficulty maintaining everyday activities. Depression isn't a weakness or an emotion that you can control. It usually requires medical treatment.

Feeling shame for being divorced is pretty natural. While I was writing this book, I entered and completed my own divorce. A divorce lawyer divorced. It seems cliché. I didn't want to be that person. I didn't want to be single and so close to forty. When the feelings of shame crept in, I remembered that it took a lot of self-esteem (love of self) to raise my hand and say, "I do not want this." That is something to be proud of.

I noticed that most of my shameful feelings were not really mine. They came from my fear of what other people would say or think. What would my family say? What would all the family members whose shaky marriages I'd shaken my head at say to see my own marriage has failed? A woman who helps people overcome obstacles couldn't keep her own marriage together. It's like a personal trainer being unable to lose weight.

Once I figured out that my feelings came from the worry of other people judging me—judging my reasons, my timing, my efforts, my choice of husband in the first place, my dedication to my spiritual beliefs, my lack of children—I was able to start letting go of my negative thoughts.

To feel less ashamed of my divorce, I had to let go of my expectations of other people's reactions. Most people were supportive. Some people tried to tell me what they would have done in my place.

If you have been divorced for more than six months still feel ashamed about it, there are some mental exercises you can do to help you get back on the right path.

One exercise that I like is to sit still and imagine the most horrible day you could possibly have on a guilt and shame scale. Really push the boundaries of your imagination and reality.

A Catholic might imagine the Pope being in town and banning her, specifically, from going to church because of her divorce. An animal lover may imagine her cat turning on her and refusing to love her anymore because she's divorced. Really pour it on thick.

Now let yourself feel the shame. Feel the guilt. Focus as hard as you can on how wrong you are and how you deserve the horrible day that you've just imagined. Do this for at least ten minutes. Then think about what currently makes you feel ashamed—living in an apartment instead of your house, driving an old car on the edge of breaking down, being unable to give your kids new toys and clothes, being single and feeling too worn out to try to attract someone to date. You shouldn't have to try very hard to feel the difference. Most of what you are feeling comes from your state of mind, not from reality or from people condemning you.

For the most part, getting divorced doesn't automatically make people happy. If someone put a heavy weight on your chest so you could barely breathe, you would wish and wish for it to be gone. When it was lifted, you'd be so happy for just a moment. But soon you would go back to breathing normally. You see, removing a negative condition does not create a positive condition. You have to create your new happy life.

Moving Past Blame and Hate

The problem with negative thoughts is that most people don't keep them to themselves. They get out the biggest "everything is awful" paintbrush they can find and start on themselves. Once they are coated, they tend to paint the people nearby. It's really easy for them to blame others because it turns down the pressure on them; it gives them a breather.

In a lot of my cases, there was a spouse who was crazy, mean, or evil, and sometimes all three. I know that a lot of the bad things that happened where, in fact, their fault. I saw clients who were so emotionally flattened that I prayed they would get up enough emotion to be angry and blame their ex! But the other extreme is the person who cannot see how she contributed to the situation.

I tell some of my angry clients that they chose to marry their exes. If they can't see how their choices (or lack of choices) contributed to the wrecked marriage, then, yes, they are probably doomed to repeat it. There usually comes a time when they recover from the initial rawness of a new divorce and take a peek into the responsibility box.

So many divorcees stay angry. And I mean really angry. They burn with hate. The level of focus they have on the wrongs they suffered is incredible. They can tell you exactly what their ex cost them. They stop living their life in the present and instead live their life as a continuous loop in the past.

If you have ever heard (or been) a teenage girl with a "boy did me wrong" story, you've seen this firsthand. The girl suffers trauma at the hands of boy. She comes home and tells her best friend (that takes about four hours, give or take), her brother, the dog, her mother, the neighbor, her aunt— and this is just day one. Wait until the weekend arrives and she really has some time. She can tell everyone how awful this boy is with the kind of running monolog that would make sportscasters envious. Fast forward two months. Are we done? Not by a long shot. She meets another guy, but instead of being present and smiling, she tells *him* the story. She carries the story with her like Linus carries his security blanket.

Take Heed

Focusing on the past and blaming others for your situation keep you from moving ahead in your life. Don't be stuck like a hamster running on a wheel reliving the pain and anger from your past.

Does this girl sound familiar to you? Are you wrapped up in the security of your tale of woe, unable to face the scary prospect of growth and new experiences that won't always work out? Do you chose the safety of your "saga?"

Here's the hard news: You helped your marriage go south, at least on some level. When you hide from that truth, you can't forgive yourself for it and move on. You can't look at it and figure out how to stop it from happening again. When you can look at what you did to contribute to your divorce, you can crank down the blame-o-meter on yourself. As you learn to be fair with yourself, you can be more fair with your ex.

I have a case I've been involved in off and on for ten years. The husband is evil—child abuse, domestic violence, threats, addictions, sociopath, etc. But still, my client greased some wheels. She was as fragile as a tissue when I met her, and she grew a spine. Since she was so lost, she chose to make herself anew. She turned the corner in that process when she was able to look at her contributions to her failed marriage: hiding bruises, hiding evidence of his addiction, propping up the kids when he crushed them, teaching them to hold their head down, looking the other way. Her biggest monster was not him; it was what she had let herself become. Once she was able to face that demon, she rose from the ashes like a phoenix.

Changing Yourself

The only person you can change is you. There is a saying: life if 10 percent what happens to you and 90 percent your opinion of it. Think about that. How much more of your time are you going to use in the opinion box instead of the happening box?

One thing you gain as you age is perspective. Think back to a time when something happened to break your heart and you didn't think you could get through another day, but you did. And later, as time passed, you realized that you were a wreck then, but you made it through. What if you choose to think in those terms about your divorce?

If you live long enough, there will be a time in the future when you will feel okay, and then feel better, and finally feel good again. You will have made to the other side of your heartache. You know for certain that this has happened in your life with every other difficult experience. Why not choose to get to that point a bit faster?

Handy Tip

When you are filled with anger and hate toward another person, you still care about that person. The strong negative feelings come from hurt. You wouldn't feel these strong emotions if you didn't care.

The opposite of love is not hate; it's indifference. People who are angry at their ex and filled with hate for him are showing that they still care for him, and they will continue being hurt by him. The trick is to choose not to feel hurt. When you don't care that your ex is dating a nineteen-year-old life guard, you are over it. When you see your ex-wife spending money from your years of hard work like a drunken sailor at a convention and you don't become furious, you have moved on. Passing time can help you move on, but it is better if you make a choice to let go of your outrage.

Forcing the Balance, Fighting for Peace

When people talk about the law of balance in the universe, they are usually talking about it on a massive scale. When it comes to any individual's life, post-divorce, balance seems curiously absent. Part of this is the erroneous notion that balance just happens. But peacefulness is a choice. Most of us who choose to have a peaceful life, have to give something up. To regain peace in your life, you might have to limit your kids to just one extracurricular activity. There is a price to be paid for everything. That is the balance.

If you want peace in your life you need to make room for it, and then you need to feed and maintain it. Peace thrives when life is organized and structured. Figure out what in your life interferes with your home's organization? What is preventing you from having a structured day each day? As mentioned earlier, it is not enough simply to remove an agent of unrest (your ex, for instance). It must be replaced with a good habit. If you stop taking up your time fighting and stressing, you will have to fill that time with activities that make you feel at peace.

CHAPTER 23

Create the Life You Want

In This Chapter

➤ Getting clues from your past

➤ Making plans for your future

➤ Putting plans for your future in action

You've just been through a divorce. Your life has been turned upside down, but you've finally come up for air. It's time to take stock and create the life you've been waiting for.

Looking at Your Past for Clues

So many divorcees want to put their past behind them and never look back. But this doesn't work. Your past is part of your life. Although you don't want dwell in your past, you need to use it as a tool to help you learn from your mistakes.

You don't have to have a degree in counseling, you don't need to read a bunch of self-help books (except this one, of course), you don't need to poll your friends and family; you know what happened. Maybe you never spoke up to ask for what you wanted. Maybe you were always speaking up and could never let anything go. Maybe you are a laid-back homebody who married a 24/7 ladder climber. Take a moment to determine how and why your marriage went south, and what your role was in creating its demise. Your past can tell you where you made your mistakes.

If you genuinely do not know what went wrong, you will need to get help from someone. You can start with a close friend or family member, but you should seriously consider seeing a counselor. Either you have aggressively repressed your memories to protect yourself, or you lack the social skills necessary for reading clues.

Take Heed

Don't put off determining what went wrong in your marriage or asking for professional help if you need it. The best way to build a better life for yourself is to understand what went wrong with your marriage and what you need to do to keep that from happening in the future. Your newfound skills will improve all aspects of your life.

Even though being in a future relationship may be far from your mind right now, that won't always be the case. The sooner you understand what went wrong, the sooner you will be able to take action on bettering yourself for a more fulfilling life. Start this process now, and you may be lucky enough to be standing firmly on two feet, knowing what you want in life, and ready and open for a new relationship when a kind, decent, loving person comes along.

Mental Exercises to Get You on Your Way

Identify three to five major decisions you made in your past that had clear options. Can you see what the consequences were of your choices? What do you think may have happened if you had chosen differently?

Now identify three to five decisions you made when the choices were not so clear. Can you still see how the consequences flowed from your decisions? Can you now see, in hindsight, that there were more choices available to you than you saw at the time?

Once you've pinpointed some of the decisions you've made and understood their consequences, you need to take some time to figure out how you would choose differently in the future. Do not take this exercise too lightly. Many of life's challenges are very similar, and if you can manage to make the right choices for a certain type of problem, you can feel confident that you will make good choices in the future.

A common problem that many women have is putting everything and everyone ahead of their own personal well-being. You will see this when you agree to chair committees you don't have time to head, when you continue to give money and time to a spouse who began to show obvious signs of cheating on you, when you work hard to cook for other people but don't eat well yourself.

This is such a universal problem among the divorced that I will remind you that how you take care of yourself teaches your children, more than your words do, about self-esteem, self-love, and how much they should value you. If you don't treat yourself very well, you are extending an open invitation to your family, coworkers, and especially your ex to do the same.

Planning for Progress

You can find a lot of people who will happily give you advice on what you need to do now. Most of that advice is so complicated that it is paralyzing. Keeping things simple works best.

Let's use a flooded kitchen as a metaphor. Your best plan will accomplish three things:

1. Stop the leak

2. Clean up the mess

3. Redecorate

Handy Tip

Show the world how to treat you by treating yourself well.

Stopping the Leak

A leak is whatever makes you lose energy. It is when your ex calls. It is the sleep you are not getting. It is the fun you are not having. Your leaks are going to be personal to you, but you know what they are. Use the sample chart below to help you make a list of your top ten leaks, the top ten ways that you are beat up, held back, and generally made to feel miserable. The chart has two important facts—the identity of who can stop the leak and how quickly the leak could be repaired if it were deemed critical. I encourage you to attack your leaks the way you would if water were rising in your kitchen. Here is a chart that can help:

My Top Ten Leaks	Who Can Stop the Leak	When

Your ability to have a great life is totally dependent on how much energy you have to live that life. Are you always exhausted, unhappy, depressed, unable to see the point in just being silly or in daydreaming? Your life force is being siphoned; it is leaking and dribbling away. Here are some common leaks:

➤ Gossiping over the same old bad stories

➤ Lacking sleep

➤ Overcommitting your time

➤ Biting your tongue, not sharing your real feelings

➤ Procrastinating

➤ Complaining ex

➤ Ignoring yourself, not allowing yourself time for just you

It's important you take steps to plug those leaks. Stop gossiping, get more sleep, give yourself some down time, kindly make your feelings clear, move forward with your plans, don't put much importance on your ex's complaints, and do something nice just for you.

Clean Up the Mess

The mess a leak leaves in a kitchen can destroy the floor and leave a nasty smell behind. Most everything that got soaked is ruined, so you toss it out. As with a flooded kitchen, you need to clean up and clear out what was damaged by your marriage and divorce. Trust your instincts here. There was a big mess in your life, and right now you need to clean it up and toss out everything that was damaged.

You may have a particularly toxic friend who was great during the divorce when you were angry and hurt all the time. Now that you want to move on, will that friend be able to switch gears with you, or will she stay comfortable just where she is with all things dark, rotten, and mildewy?

When you are cleaning, you don't clean half of the floor and one cabinet. You look everywhere the water went—you follow the path of destruction and get it all. If you don't, your half-clean kitchen will still smell.

Examine all of your associations and see if you need to do some cleaning. Remember, you have only a finite amount of time each day and in this life. Spend it only where it is valuable and where you receive good things in return.

Take Heed

Many believe that we are each most like the five people we spend the most time with. Think about the five people you spend most of your time with. Are they great, average, mean, kind? Even your income is most like those five people, who on average all earn about the same. Is this what you want? It is time to choose and clean accordingly!

Undertake the cleaning process happily! Attack it with vigor and an attitude of once it's done you won't have to deal with floods again.

You probably need to clean your thoughts and attitudes as well. The ones that allowed your ex in your life in the first place. The ones that had you stay with him in the second place. The ones that trapped you in the murky waters you called life in the third place. You especially want to throw out all the thoughts your ex handed you about not being good enough, attractive enough, smart enough, parent enough, strong enough. And from here on out don't allow anyone to tell you that you are lacking in anything.

One great way to attack these thoughts is to place a rubber band around your wrist and wear it every day. Every time you notice yourself thinking a thought that needs to be cleaned out of your head, gently snap your rubber band and think, "out it goes" while imagining a dustpan emptying into a trash can, a big boot kicking something out a door, a bucket of dirty water being dumped down a drain.

Do not, by the way, underestimate the symbolic power of real physical cleaning. This is especially important if you are in the same home or space that you were in during your marriage and divorce. It doesn't matter if you are reading this book in November, you should immediately schedule a spring cleaning party and donation. It is necessary to go through and scrub your new environment to prepare it to be yours and yours alone. As you clean, find the courage to donate whatever you can. Someone who is in need will be so grateful for your goodwill. You get to be a secret angel for another in need and get rid of something that is just going to sit there and constantly remind you of worse times—like that lingering bad smell. You can't get completely comfortable in a place that has a bad feel or smell to it.

Finally, tackle the messes you're responsible for because you were so preoccupied with your failing marriage and divorce. There will be relationships that need to be scrubbed clean and started anew. Do not neglect this! Look around you and see who you have gotten dirty with your anger, drama, unavailability, and constant turmoil. Tell these people that you appreciated them sticking by you and that you are going to honor the sacrifices they made, which you never noticed because you were so preoccupied with your issues, by cleaning up your life right now, in the present, in time for everyone to enjoy the bright and shiny new you!

Forging Your Future

The easiest way to get yourself on track to a better future based on the new you is to make plans. Do it right now! Use the monthly boxes below and write in at least one activity you will do each month. Just one. Can you commit to doing just one thing a month with the new life you are making?

Planning for the future is good for children, especially if their lives have been turned upside down. They get so excited knowing there is something to look forward to. They experience joy just thinking of what's ahead; they improve their behavior to earn it.

Use the list of new you plans below to spark your imagination. Make sure you plan something big for your twelfth month that feels just a tiny bit impossible or unlikely to you right now. Make yourself work for it. I planned to run a half marathon—13.1 miles; a perfectly good distance to drive. I have to push and stretch myself (literally!) to stay on track with this plan. But every time I see improvement, I see myself coming nearer to being able to accomplish this huge, scary thing, my self-esteem shoots up!

Here is a list of new you plans to consider:

> ➤ Running/walking a 5K
> ➤ Personal retreat weekend
> ➤ Monthly girls/boys night in
> ➤ Join a book club
> ➤ Go to a concert
> ➤ Take a day trip to a park
> ➤ Visit a nursing home to cheer up someone
> ➤ Go on a $20 frivolous shopping spree in a dollar store
> ➤ Give your car a full-detail cleaning
> ➤ Have lunch by yourself, with a book, at a nice restaurant
> ➤ Go to a matinee with a friend
> ➤ Have a garage sale shopping Saturday—no kids
> ➤ Window shop at your favorite store

➤ Listen to audiobooks in the morning

➤ Join that new gym

➤ Find an exercise buddy

➤ Clear the clutter in the closet

➤ Return to your old hobby

➤ Go to a big conference about something interesting

➤ Take dance lessons (yes, singles are welcome)

➤ Do a huge favor for friend—help with a move, clean a basement

➤ Have a used bookstore Sunday

➤ Buy and use one expensive hygiene product (fancy razor or spa nail polish)

➤ Volunteer to walk dogs at the humane society

➤ Read/finish a book that you've always wanted to

➤ Get up early and spend quiet time meditating

➤ Stretch

Your new you plan can be tiny or huge, but it's critical that you have one. You are doing only one new activity for yourself each month. You can choose the frequency, but it should be done at least one time in the assigned month. You should also set it down on an actual day of the month to increase the odds you'll do it. Make sure it is not the last day of the month. That way if you miss, you have some buffer time to make it up! This a great exercise in using your imagination for something positive.

Jan	Feb	Mar	Apr
May	Jun	July	Aug
Sep	Oct	Nov	Dec

 Creating Support for Your New Future

Now that your divorce is over, you need to gather together a strong support group to help you move forward and continue to deal with challenges from your ex.

Your main network is likely composed of family, friends, and members of your faith group or church. In each of these groups, people fall into three main categories: the

1. Well-wishers

2. Active supporters

3. Disapprovers

The domestic violence cases are a little different, so we'll look at those separately.

The Well-Wishers

Well-wishers are people who agree with the idea or concept of your divorce but choose not to contribute any resources to assist you with the process or the aftermath. They may be relieved for you, they may tell you that you made the right decision, and they may reinforce that your divorce was a long time coming. But it stops there.

What separates a well-wisher from an active supporter is that well-wishers are not active. They do not want to get involved or their life is such that they can't get involved. So although you may feel that the well-wishers in your life are not doing enough, don't bad-mouth them; they may be doing the most they can for you.

For instance, a well-wisher's reluctance to get more involved may be because divorce goes against her beliefs, or she may not have known how bad your marriage was because you hid that from everyone; she wants to stand by you, but she doesn't know enough to throw some muscle behind that sentiment.

Airing out one's dirty laundry, so to speak, is not necessarily accepted at work either by coworkers or by the administration. When coworkers learn of your divorce, they're likely to fall into the category of well-wishers.

Some well-wishers don't take the step to actively support you because they want to avoid negativity. Most divorces are abysses of negativity, seasoned with evil, nastiness, and fear—all the awful emotions that a lot of people actively avoid.

A good example of a well-wisher is the neighbor who knew both you and your ex. You tell him the divorce has been finalized, and he doesn't know what to say. He gauges the expression on your face and confirms you must be glad it's all over. He says kind words to you, but he doesn't want to come into your kitchen and pore over documents and court orders with you.

Be Careful

Well-wishers tend to be eager to share your victories, but they don't want to hear about the struggles that you endured. You may tell a well-wisher that you went to court, things came out ok, custody is fine, and support has started. That's pretty much all well-wishers want to know. They do not want to hear the gritty details—that you stayed up all night, what your attorney said and what his attorney said, and what the judge said.

Take Heed

Avoid using well-wishers to lean on in a time of crisis. They've offered surface-level support, and that's it. So, when the judge slaughtered you and your attorney failed you and everything has gone to hell in a hand basket—that is not the time to call a well-wisher and try to drag her into your case. She's not going to like it; she will probably resent it.

Honor your well-wishers' right to make decisions that best align with their emotional needs. Save your energy and complaining if you know that a well-wisher could do more but chooses not to. So even if your rich sister could pay for your next attorney, she has the right to stay out of it. It's important that you stay away from adding more negativity and stress to your life. This wasn't your sister's divorce and this isn't her problem.

Keep things light with well-wishers. Don't drag them further in than they want to go! You don't want to lose your well-wishers by making them uncomfortable around you. Think of them as your cheerleaders; they're not going to go into the field and assist the play, but they'll be by your side, cheering you on.

The Active Supporters

This is a really important group of people. These people want in! They are people who are going to help. They are your active supporters.

Active supporters are people who not only listen to you vent (some well-wishers do a little of this also), but also try to come up with solutions to your problems. When your child support leaves you $200 short each month, active supporters brainstorm to figure out how you can cut another $200 off your budget and still make it. If need be, they will lend you the $200, or help you get an extension on a credit card or a loan. When your child care becomes a problem, active supporters will watch your kids while you go on job interviews. These are people who will help you out in any way they can.

Family members often play the role of active supporters. Many parents have spent years watching their child in an unhappy marriage and finally have a chance to do something to help. They may offer a temporary place to stay in their home, to loan a car or cosign a car payment.

Diehard friends are active supporters. These are the friends who listened to you when your ex was doing you wrong. They know when you're getting ready to freak out and do something stupid, and they talk you through it. They interrupt their family dinners to take your stress-filled phone calls. They're always available when you need them.

You can have active supporters at work. These are the bosses who allow you to take off yet another day to go back to court without writing you up or giving you a bad review. They know your court documents are being faxed to the office, and you're reviewing them on company time. When you show up at work an emotional wreck, your coworkers pull together to funnel the work around you.

Active supporters at work can be a very powerful resource. They will help you keep your job, which is critical at this time in your life. If you were to lose your job because of your post-divorce emotions, you would be creating an infinite number of new problems. So if you have a sympathetic and helpful workplace, protect it at all costs, and don't take undue advantage of it.

Active supporters from places of worship abound. It's difficult to show up at a place where you've been seen weekly as part of a couple. You've been sitting with your spouse in the same spot for years, and now showing up alone seems overwhelming. You don't want to explain, defend, or be pitied. You don't want to wonder what everyone is thinking. More likely than not, when you finally get the courage to go back, everybody will welcome you and give you a hug. They may offer a special prayer for your new journey.

Be grateful if you have a church that's rallying around you. While you can't address every single religion, you can safely say across the board that most religions aren't giant fans of divorce, especially the more conservative religions. If they're pulling for you, it's because they believe in you. They don't believe that you just decided to give up and not work on your marriage. They believe you've done everything you could. That is definitely a good example of a church being one of your active supporters.

Handy Tip

Do you actively support yourself, or are you in the well-wisher category and just watch life go by, hoping everything will work out? Are you making a commitment to improve your life? Are you paying attention to how your divorce is affecting your children? Are you following instructions from your attorney? Your commitment to creating the life you've always wanted is the biggest determinant of your success.

How to Treat Your Active Supporters

Treat your active supporters like they are made of gold and dipped in angel dust. Be careful you don't rely on your active supporters too heavily; you don't want to wear them out. Constantly tell them how important they are to you. Tell them upfront how grateful you are, and say this often. Make a note to yourself, if you must, to thank your active supporters every ten days, for instance. Just write it on your calendar.

It's important that your active supporters feel like they're making a difference and that you're noticing and appreciating what they do so they don't feel like their good deeds are being done in vain. Don't let your active supporters burn out on you.

For instance, if your boss let you miss work to go to court, send a thank-you note the next day with a positive tidbit of how the day went. Don't feel like you need to tell your boss everything in this note. Just a brief note saying, "Thanks; court went well," will suffice. This will make your boss feel good about helping you, and will encourage goodwill in the future. You can't praise and thank your active supporters too much.

Be Grateful for the Truth

Active supporters don't just do what you want them to do or tell you what you want to hear; they also tell you what you need to hear. This is a tough thing to do. It takes a certain amount of bravery to risk the wrath of a friend so that you can open her eyes to the reality of a situation.

Although you may not like it at first, you're likely to come to realize that your active supporters are doing you an immense favor by being upfront and honest with you. Be sure to let them know how much you appreciate what they do for you. The positive reinforcement will encourage their behavior, and then you'll have a trusted circle of supporters who you know have only your best interests at heart.

Handy Tip

Whether you're in the middle of your divorce or done with it, give your active supporters permission to tell you the tough stuff, the stuff you don't want to hear. Promise that you will keep quiet and listen. You need to know the truth, no matter how hard it is to hear, and your active supporters are the best and safest people to trust to tell you what you'd rather not know.

You can ask your active supporters for this type of input. At work, you can encourage a supportive boss to let you know if you're in danger of getting a bad performance review so you can work on improving yourself. Tell your supportive coworkers that you're having a tough time at home and are somewhat preoccupied. Then ask them to warn you if they notice your performance slipping.

Lifting Yourself Up

A wonderful way to show gratitude to your supporters is to focus on becoming a person who deserves such extraordinary support. The best way to do that is to pull yourself up so you don't need that type of support any more. Don't be that person who is in constant need of being bailed out. Even your most ardent supporters will become weary of coming to your rescue if you're not making an effort to get a better grip on your life.

Easier said than done, you moan. Well, not really. You have great role models right in front of you. Learn by example how your supporters deal with life—its obstacles, trials, and normalcies. Yes, normalcies. You've been living in drama for so long that you may not know how to keep your life on a normal, even keel. Ask your supporters for advice—and then take it.

When you start sending out signals that you're ready to grow and change, to get out of the quagmire of the post-divorce doldrums, life will start to change for you. With the help and encouragement of your active supporters, it won't take you long to be in a position to be an active supporter for someone else!

Imitation is the best form of flattery, they say. Your supporters will feel so gratified to know that you aspire to help someone the way that they helped you—that you want to be the home with the extra bedroom, or the car to lend, or the cushion of money.

The Disapprovers

The disapprovers are the people who criticize your decision to divorce. They begin with, "I can't believe that you …" and the lecture goes from there. Family members, unfortunately, make up a large portion of disapprovers. Here are some examples:

➤ Your parents who are still married: "We can't believe you filed for divorce. How could you? Your father and I are still married. You need to go back and make it work."

➤ A divorced parent: "I can't believe that you would file for a divorce knowing how horrible it was for me, and how I don't have anything and my life has been such a misery."

➤ Your happily married sister in another state who you haven't confided in: "I can't believe you've left him. Why didn't you try harder to make your marriage work?"

Friends can disapprove also. Often they don't know all the facts, or they're really wedded to their particular religious view of divorce. It is more common for coworkers to disapprove because you will be skipping out of work and slacking off and piling your stuff on them.

Take Heed

Your place of worship may strongly disapprove of your divorce on religious grounds. You will have to address this attitude if you plan to stay with that congregation. It's not unusual for people to change their place of worship because of attitudes and beliefs surrounding divorce.

The most dangerous disapprovers are those who doubt themselves. They second-guess their decision to divorce. They don't want to go forward with their life. They can't change or move forward because of the mantra that keeps running through their head, "I can't believe I did this. I never wanted to do this. I can't believe that it's come to this. I told myself I would never do this."

One of the biggest culprits are those who have been divorced before and have sworn they would never get divorced again—and here they are, going through their second divorce.

If you're a self-doubter, you have to stop what you're doing immediately and get on your own team.

There are two subgroups of disapprovers: covert disapprovers and overt disapprovers.

Overt vs Covert Disapprovers

Overt disapprovers are at least up front with their feelings. You know what you're up against when dealing with overt disapprovers. They tell you outright that they disapprove of divorce in general or your divorce in particular. They speak their mind.

Covert disapprovers, on the other hand, are the saboteurs, the people who will secretly undermine you. You never know what they're thinking or what they'll do behind your back. They have their belief system but aren't willing to be up front about it. Instead, they act out their disapproval in sneaky, passive-aggressive ways.

The people in the disapprover category, mostly the covert ones, are pretty negative people. You just simply can't afford to be around them. You certainly can't afford to count these people as part of your support group, because the idea of having a support network is to keep your stress level down, keep you on the right path, keep you energized, reinforce your good behaviors, and reduce and decrease your bad behaviors.

Being involved with such negative people will keep your feelings of shame, guilt, fear, and censure alive. You'll be less likely to move forward and grow. Growing and changing is how you're going to pry yourself away from the divorce doldrums.

So, keep your distance from those who seem to undermine your recovery. When you walk away from someone and feel worse than you did at the start of your conversation, don't seek out that person again.

Take Control of Your Happiness

Happiness is a choice. If you're unhappy, you've got to do something different to get yourself to a better place. It won't happen overnight, though. It doesn't happen in leaps and bounds, either. So don't expect to go from miserable to joyous in one grand swoop. But even moving from miserable to coping is a big improvement.

Your happiness is not dependent on your situation. Rather, it is a state of thought that you can control. It's normal to feel disappointed when a judge rules against you, for instance. You can't change the reality of the ruling, but you can change the way you think about it. You can change how you react to the order, how you feel about the order, and how you process the order.

Divorce Vocab

The phrase *"look on the bright side"* epitomizes the conscious decision one needs to make to be happy. Monitor your thoughts and make a conscious decision to think positively when you find yourself mired in negativity. It may be difficult to do at first, but after a while, you may actually find yourself living on the bright side.

Nobody can tell you how to feel about something. That's your choice. You might as well decide to feel good and have a positive outlook on life. Making the choice to feel better can bring your head up high enough to be able to see a way to change your situation.

Here are some ways you can help yourself out of the negative and into the positive:

➤ Exercise

➤ Take part in your favorite activity

➤ Listen to upbeat music

➤ Think about your favorite pet, book, friend, experience

➤ Call or get together with a happy-go-lucky friend

➤ Work on a hobby

Domestic Violence

This is just a brief discussion about domestic violence cases because you need professionals as your support group. Your friends, family, church, coworkers, and everybody you know try to be helpful, but you really need a professional who specializes in these issues to help you recover from domestic violence. So many people who don't get the professional support they need end up back in abusive relationships. They rationalize it. They are used to it and don't notice when they are falling back into their old patterns.

If you've been in an abusive relationship for more than a couple of years, you've become warped. You've been twisted and bent under the pressure of your abusive marriage. This is not a bad statement about you; it's just what happens when people are constantly put under pressure. You've become warped, and you'll become even more warped unless you get help. Your support groups are therefore very important.

You need to determine the damage or the amount of warping that's been done to you. Your best bet is to hire a counselor to help you assess how much you've changed since before you were in an abusive relationship. You can ask this question of a friend, but you need to be prepared to hear things about yourself that you won't like. Wait at least twenty-four hours before allowing yourself to reply to your friend.

Self-reflection works also. Most people know they aren't the same any more after they have been in an abusive relationship for a while. They wake up one day and realize that they don't like who they've become. You got yourself where you are today; only you can truly get yourself out of your situation. Take responsibility for your choices, realize your need to change, and take the steps to get the real you back.

Support comes in many flavors. A counselor, psychologist, or psychiatrist is a necessary form of support for someone recovering from an abusive relationship. Friends, of course, are important forms of support, as are books and your place of worship. But you also need to have some fun again. Join an activity, get some exercise, volunteer for a good cause. Helping others goes a long way toward making you feel happy and worthwhile.

 Divorced, Single, and Successful

---

In This Chapter

➤ Keeping your life under control

➤ Replacing bad habits with good habits

➤ Letting go of worries

Your life for the last few months has been hijacked by your divorce. Your mind and time have been consumed by positioning yourself strategically for the best outcome. When your divorce is finalized, you may be left with time to fill and hours of purposelessness. You may feel you've forgotten how to live life without a bad marriage or a divorce filling your days. In this chapter, you'll see ways to rebuild your life, making your days better for your children and for yourself.

Controlling What You Can

You are divorced. The single most important point about that statement is that you can improve your life simply because you are the one in control. When you were married, your spouse was involved in your choices, opportunities, and decisions. That's changed now. You're at the helm, guiding and controlling the path of your life.

When you were married, you were involved in your spouse's every crisis, heartache, disappointment, failed plan, and emergency. If your spouse lacked discipline, drive, responsibility, and self-esteem, you got an extra dose of problems created by all his personal issues. If he had depression, anxiety, or anger issues, you were always being called to his rescue. All of that is out of your life. You now have to account for, fix, and resolve only what you generate.

In the course of implementing your newfound control, you'll need to change the bad habits you acquired during your marriage. Unfortunately, many of your bad habits will be hard to notice. One bad habit many newly divorced people seem to be unwittingly mired in is continuing to be involved with their ex's life. There are several reasons for this:

1. It is a well-settled habit

2. It gives you something to do other than deal with your own issues

3. You haven't forced yourself to notice that it's not your job anymore

Habits

Let's take a moment to discuss habits. A habit is a learned behavior that you have ingrained in yourself so deeply that you do not have to consciously think about it. Habits, like a sharp knife, can either be incredibly useful tools or very dangerous. As you step into your life after divorce, you'll need to notice, address, and overcome some of your habits before you can regain control over your life.

Start to Notice Your Habits

The first step to recognizing your habits and whether they are considered to be good or bad by most people is to ask those closest to you to fill out the My Good and Bad Habits form found in the appendix.

Make a number of copies of the table and hand them out to your friends. Keep one copy to fill out for yourself. It will be interesting to compare your thoughts with your friends' observations. No matter what you admit or hear from others, do not be discouraged.

Identify Your Good and Bad Habits

No habit is neutral; it either adds or detracts from your life. Use template 25.1 in the Appendix to help you determine if the majority or just a serious few of your habits are causing problems. Choose one big habit that you may have a hard time changing and one little habit that you feel more confident about fixing. On the sheet, fill out how the habit benefits you or costs you.

Don't skip your good habits. Identifying good habits can be tricky. They are important to list so you can see what great things in your life come from your good habits. Too often we don't pay attention to our good habits because they make life easier, so we don't notice them and start taking them for granted.

For example, it's a good habit to hold your car keys in your hand when you close your car door or trunk. I started this habit because I had to wait two hours for my father to get off work and drive to high school, where I'd locked my keys in my car, thinking they were in my purse. For over twenty years, I've kept my car keys in my hand until I was out of the car. This habit belongs on my good habits list.

Handy Tip

Your success at breaking a bad habit may require a no exceptions rule. That means you stop the bad habit no matter what—no excuses, no promises to break your habit starting tomorrow, no thoughts of doing it just one more time. Break the habit and don't look back.

Stop a Bad Habit—Motivate Yourself to Change

Most bad habits produce some sort of instant gratification. The only way to motivate yourself to change your habits is to believe that changing, as difficult as it will be, is worth more than holding on to the bad habits. The long-term benefit of eliminating a bad habit has to overwhelm the satisfaction you instantly get from the bad habit.

Many people can't change a bad habit until it is clearly and undeniably what must be done. For instance, an overweight person may not be able to give up eating whenever, whatever, and how much he wants until he's faced with a serious health issue or even the probability of death. Similarly, staying in a bad marriage may have become a habit that won't be changed until your happiness or safety is so much at stake that it overwhelms the trouble and cost (financially and emotionally) of a divorce.

Some of you didn't initiate your divorce; you weren't the one in the marriage who was motivated to change. All that means is that you hadn't reached that point where a divorce was a better option than staying in the marriage. The same is true for the person who decides to remain overweight; the health benefits of losing weight aren't enough to motivate him to diet and exercise.

So how do you speed up the process of motivating yourself to change a bad habit? You can focus on the benefits of a future without the bad habit, or you can focus on the ways the bad habit negatively affect your life; or, even better, supercharge your motivation by doing both. You can focus on how good it would feel to have a peaceful home every night and how much you hate the constant fights yo have with your spouse. Once you start drilling that in—whammo—you make the paradigm shift to wanting, needing, and demanding the more peaceful life. You're on your way to breaking the bad habit of living in a bad marriage.

Here's a real-life example:

One of my clients determined that the big habit she had to fix was worrying excessively about her kids when they were with her ex. The little habit she wanted to change was leaving the kitchen messy after cooking.

She wanted to break the habit of worrying because it drove her kids nuts, made them anxious about their visitations, and made her ex call her names for worrying "for no reason," and not take any of her other worries seriously. She was making it hard for her kids to be with their father. This excessive worrying also led her ex to ignore her valid concerns.

She wanted to break the habit of leaving her kitchen messy because it depressed her to see a messy kitchen in the morning, and made her not want to cook, so they ate out too much, which was something she couldn't afford and wasn't particularly healthy for the kids.

When my client began to imagine how much better her kids would be, how much calmer she would be, and how much less grief her ex would give her, she got motivated to stop worrying so much. Then the thought of how much she would love cooking in a clean kitchen and how she hated wasting money on junk food full of chemicals, she became motivated to change her messy kitchen habit.

Forcing New Habits

Those old habits won't go easily. You have to consciously make yourself change or replace old bad habits. Here are some actions you can take to help you implement new habits:

> ➤ Tell people about your efforts so they can support you and keep you accountable.

> ➤ Determine what triggers the bad habit so you will be better equipped to head it off or at least know when to be on guard for it. If it's a big bad habit, don't try to change it right away. Getting a sense of its patterns can make you feel more empowered to tackle it. The client with the messy kitchen found that she was worse at cleaning when she cooked in a hurry because dinner was late. A small change in dinner time helped her fix most of that issue.

> ➤ Set a goal to hit a conservative number of successes in your first week. It is important not to pay attention to the number of times you repeat the bad habit. Instead, note the times you replace the bad habit with your new habit. Using the kitchen example, my client intended to cook six nights a week, but she started changing her messy habit by expecting herself to clean the kitchen right after cooking one of the six nights. By purposefully setting this number low, she was more likely to attain it.

➤ Congratulate yourself every time you successfully replace a bad habit with a good one. The momentum you gain from instituting a small change can be harnessed to create much larger changes in the future.

➤ Have a day and time planned to start changing your habit, and then just get going.

Reward Your Results

Rewards are the biggest tools you have. Many people skip this step—don't. Set rewards for yourself at certain milestones and when you meet your goal of implementing an improved habit. Your journey to improvement will feel more like fun and less like work.

If you are at all worried about your ability to tackle your big bad ugly habit, tackle one or two smaller ones first to put some habit-busting experience in your tool chest.

A Habit Change Scenario

A great way to practice changing a habit is to start drinking more water. Very few people drink enough water. There are many ways to figure out how much water you should be drinking each day based on your weight. But the tried and true advice to drink eight glasses of water a day will suffice for this example.

Take Heed

Don't expect to switch from a bad habit to a good habit in one fell swoop. You'll experience many relapses, but in time, the good habit will become prevalent, and the bad habit will begin to disappear altogether.

Take Heed

It's important to notice when you've successfully eliminated a bad habit and to reward yourself and your newfound ability to have control of your life.

Here are some steps you can take to begin making it a habit to drink eight glasses of water a day:

➤ Tell your children, coworkers, and family that you want to drink eight glasses of water a day. Ask them to remind you of this at meals if you reach for a soda.

➤ Track what you drink for three days in a row. Carry a notepad and pen, and every time you drink something, water or not, write it down. At the end of three days, look at your list. Did you drink eight glasses a day of anything? Did you drink any water at all or did you drink some water but need to increase the amount?

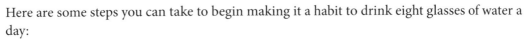

➤ Set your water-drinking goal depending on your three-day survey. If you didn't drink any water for three days, start by drinking one glass of water a day. Then add one additional glass of water each week. In eight weeks, you'll be drinking eight glasses of water—you'll have reached your goal and have a new good habit. Of course, you can take a faster or slower schedule to reach your goal.

➤ After you've reached your goal of drinking eight glasses of water a day, cement your habit by allocating certain times of the day to drink a glass of water.

Time and continuous practice is important when changing a habit. Keep in mind that it's much more difficult to develop a new good habit than it is to break one. For example, if you have the habit of exercising three days a week on Monday, Wednesday, and Friday, it may take as little as skipping one week of exercise to throw that fitness routine off kilter. After that, you'll have to work again to turn an exercise routine into a habit.

Letting Go

We all spend time feeling trapped in the decisions we've made or yearning for the opportunities we've missed. We can wallow in what might have been, but that just keeps us stuck where we are and miserable. Those happiest and most content in their lives let go of thoughts of what might have been. But that isn't easy for everyone to do. Over years of giving my clients the advice to let it go and seeing how difficult it was for many of them to follow, I have found a few tips to help the divorcée let things go:

➤ Write down the worst that could result from your worry or fear

➤ Write down the best that could happen without you worrying

➤ Write down every single thing you can do to actually change the results of your worries

➤ Decide if you can do any of those things to change the results of your worries

➤ Make a plan and do what you can do

➤ Decide that your worries are beyond your control and influence

Hopefully, you are able to recognize those things that are outside your influence. Weather is outside your influence. Ocean currents and hungry bears are outside your influence. The actions of a third world despot bent on destruction are outside your influence. The actions of your ex are definitely outside your influence.

Recognize what you can and cannot influence, and let go of those things that you cannot control. Worrying about a mountain halfway around the world will not influence the mountain, but it will drain and depress you.

Train yourself to spend your energy on what you can influence. This will take practice but can eventually become a good habit. And as with other habits, it is important to practice on a small issue that is not as scary as your big worry.

There is no prescribed way of letting go. But you first must believe that you can let things go. And don't expect to stop doing something without starting something else. Focus on something positive. Replace your worry by thinking about something you enjoy, get involved in plans for Friday night, read a magazine.

To start, let go of a worry for five minutes. Every couple of days increase the amount of time you keep your worries at bay. Soon, you'll be able to let go of most any niggling or gargantuan worry by letting it go, deliberately refocusing your attention on something within your control. Your faith may offer prayers, meditations, and interventions that can help you release the burdens you are carrying.

Above all, give yourself permission to believe you can change your habits and let go of what no longer serves you!

AFTERWORD

Be proud of yourself. You've taken a huge step toward the life you've always wanted by investing in and reading *The Smart Guide to Life After Divorce*. If you make use of some of the suggestions in this book, you will ease that weighty feeling you've had on your chest for so long.

To be most successful after your divorce, you need to look at your past choices, make peace with your old outcomes, and begin to choose to consciously craft the life that you really want. Getting to a new place emotionally, financially, and physically will involve change, and any change brings the discomfort of the new and unknown.

The trick is learning to become comfortable with the discomfort of growth. I have investigated and received an Advanced Certification in Hypnotherapy while writing this book. I believe hypnotherapy is the future of showing people how to recover quickly from divorce trauma and accomplish business and personal goals easily. I truly hope this book has and continues to be a resource to you. Make sure you grab a copy for a friend at the start of their divorce!

If you are looking for divorce advice, divorce-specific hypnotherapy, or private coaching through a difficult divorce, look me up at www.CompleteFamilyLaw.com.

My FREE Thank-You Gifts for Reading

If you write to me at LawyerTanya@SmartGuidetoLifeAfterDivorce.com and tell me your thoughts about the book, I will send you a free copy of my e-book *How to Feel Better in Just 7 Days After a Bad Divorce* and my free hypnotherapy CD *Deep Sleep* to help you rest.

Remember, you can't change anyone else but you—so start there!

All the best,

Tanya Stewart, Esq.

APPENDIX

Chapter 1

Resources for Learning to Manage Money

Books

Miller, Steve J. *Enjoy Your Money!: How to Make It, Save It, Invest It and Give It*. Acworth, Georgia: Wisdom Creek Press, 2009.

Ramsey, Dave. *The Total Money Makeover: A Proven Plan for Financial Fitness*. Nashville, Tennessee: Thomas Nelson, 2009.

Richards, Charles. *The Psychology of Wealth: Understand Your Relationship with Money and Achieve Prosperity*. New York: McGraw-Hill, 2012.

Websites

Online Courses

"Financial Peace University." Dave Ramsey, accessed January 16, 2013, www.daveramsey. com/fpu.

"Manage Your Money." Ohio State University, accessed January 16, 2013, http://ohioline.osu. edu/mym/.

Websites

"Money 101: A Step by Step Guide to Gaining Control of Your Financial Life." CNN Money, accessed January 16, 2013, http://money.cnn.com/magazines/moneymag/money101/ lesson2/index.htm.

"Money Matters 101," accessed January 16, 2013, www.moneymatters101.com.

"Money Wise: Helping Children Learn to Manage Money." Doris K. Walker, Cooperative Extension Service, Kansas State University, Manhattan. Posted February 1993, accessed January 16, 2013, www.douglas.ksu.edu/DesktopModules/ViewDocument.aspx?...1736.

Chapter 3

Resources for Ridding Your Life of Clutter

Books

Bohn, Marilyn. *Go Organize: Conquer Clutter in 3 Simple Steps*. Cincinnati, OH: Betterway Home Books, 2009.

Glovinsky, Cindy. *One Thing At a Time: 100 Simple Ways to Live Clutter-Free Every Day*. New York: St. Martin's Griffin, 2004.

Palmer, Brooks. *Clutter Busting: Letting Go of What's Holding You Back* . Novato, CA: New World Library, 2009.

Wittmann, Laura. *Clutter Rehab: 101 Tips and Tricks to Become an Organization Junkie and Love It!*. Berkeley, CA: Ulysses Press, 2011.

Websites

"Clutterless." Mike Nelson, accessed January 12, 2013, www.clutterless.org.

"FlyLady.net." Marla Cilley, accessed January 12, 2013, www.flylady.net.

"Get Organized Now." Maria Garcia, accessed January 12, 2013, www.getorganizednow.com.

National Association of Professional Organizers, accessed January 12, 2013, www.napo.net.

"The Clutter Diet." Lorie Marrero, accessed January 12, 2013, www.clutterdiet.com.

Chapter 9

Always keep copies of the letters you send.

Template 9.1 Demand Letter for Unpaid Child Support

Your Name
Your Mailing Address or PO Box Number
Date of Letter

Dear **(most common to use first name)**,

I am writing to you about the child support payments. The court order from _**(date of court order)**_ states that I am to receive $**(amount) (frequency)** per month on the **(date or dates the monies are due to be paid)**.

Currently, I have not received a total of ___ payments and am therefore owed a total of $_____.

The payments that are missing are: **(list the due dates of the payments here)**.

Optional if the your ex made partial payments:

You paid the following partial payments: $_____ on **(dates of partial payments; list as many as have occurred)**.

I need the overdue child support as it is an important part of my budget and how I provide for our child/ren.

Optional if the situation is extreme:

I have been unable to pay the following bills on time without the support: **(list those that apply; good examples are utilities, car payments, insurance payments, medical bills, rental and housing payments—items that directly impact a child's welfare)**.

Please send payment for the overdue support as soon as possible but no later than ten days from the date of this letter, which is **(put deadline date here)**.

Please respond to my letter in writing (e-mail is acceptable) and provide me with your proposal for how you plan to repay these monies and how much you can provide to reduce the balance in the next ten days. (Use this provision if you have already sent a lump sum payment request as above or if the amount is such that you know your ex cannot come up with it within ten days.)

Optional:

I have researched getting legal assistance with the collection this child support and found that the fees to handle this matter in Court will be no less than $1,500 and usually much more. I do not want to go that route. Please consider this a demand for the payment of the overdue child support and that you begin to pay support on time so that lawyers and the Court do not have to become involved. If I have to retain a lawyer, I will ask them to recover their fees from you.

If you do not respond to this letter, I will take it that you admit to the amount that you owe and that you are refusing to pay, and I will seek legal remedies immediately.

I would really like to work this out with you. Please write and reply.

Sincerely,
Your name

Optional:

Cc: The _____Law Firm

(If you have or previously had a lawyer, it is often nice to let the other side know that you are copying the lawyer on this demand; it may make him more willing to pay. If you send a copy to a former lawyer, just include a note explaining that it is a copy for the lawyer's files and that you are not ready to proceed yet.)

Template 9.2 Thank-You Letter for Back Payment

Always keep copies of the letters you send.

Your Name
Your Mailing Address or PO Box Number
Date of Letter

Dear **(most common to use first name)**,

I am writing to thank you for the payment you just made toward the overdue child support.

The court order from **(date of court order)** states that I am to receive $**(amount)** **(frequency of payment, for example: twice per month on the (date or dates the monies are due to be paid)**.

I did not receive a total of **(number of payments)** and am therefore owed a total of $**(amount)**.

You paid $**(amount)** on **(date)**. That clears up all the arrearages of child support owed through (date).

Thank you for getting this taken care of. We really appreciate it. Let me know if you'd like **(Offer something small and nice to your ex, something child related would be good. You want your ex to get a good feeling from paying you money owed. Reinforce good behavior!)**.

Optional, if your ex still has a balance:

This leaves a remaining balance of $**(amount)**, covering support due through the month of **(last month that was unpaid in the balance)**. You've told me that you plan to resolve the balance by making the following payments: **(list dates and payment amounts if known, or the date it is to be paid off)**.

Or: Please write to me by **(date ten days away)** and let me know when you will finish paying off the balance of $**(amount)** still owed.

Sincerely,
Your Name

Template 9.3 Letter Accepting a Payment Plan

Always keep copies of the letters you send.

Your Name
Your Mailing Address or PO Box Number
Date of Letter

Dear **(most common to use first name)**,

I wrote you on **(date)** regarding the overdue child support payments. Thank you for replying and giving me a great idea to consider for the repayment.

You told me on **(date)** on the phone/in person that you would **(spell out his proposed deal clearly without any emotion—be sure to include dates and amount proposed)**.

I think that plan is workable for us.

Optional:

There was one part that wasn't totally clear to me: **(list the unclear part or missing date or amount)**. Can you explain that further?

I accept your offer to resolve the overdue child support. I will look for your first payment of $**(amount)** on the **(date)**.

I know you feel better getting this under control, and managing the financial stress will certainly help us parent better.

Thank you so much for working this out with me.

Sincerely,
Your Name

Template 9.4 Letter Declining Approval of Payment Plan

Always keep copies of the letters you send.

Your Name
Your Mailing Address or PO Box Number
Date of Letter

Dear **(most common to use first name)**,

I wrote you on **(date)** regarding the overdue child support payments. Thank you for replying and giving me an idea to consider regarding the repayment.

You told me you could **(spell out his deal clearly without any emotion)**.

I know that you gave this some thought, but I don't think this plan is workable for us.

(Use any of these reasons that apply, more than one if necessary, or write your own—but stay unemotional:

> ➤ I have some pretty serious bills to pay because of the late child support, and your plan won't get them paid quickly enough.

> ➤ I'm going to lose the good daycare arrangements I've found unless I make a big payment sooner than your plan allows for.

> ➤ The car/house/utilities are in danger, and I need the funds sooner than your plan will get them here.

> ➤ I had to borrow money when the support didn't arrive on time, and I have to pay it back right away.)

It would work for me if you could **(detail the necessary change you want to see in the plan—remember that asking for everything often results in nothing, so focus on the most important pieces)**.

Please let me know if you can do that before (date—can be less than ten days).

I would really like to work this out with you. Please write and reply.

Sincerely,
Your Name

Template 9.5 Letter Requesting Voluntary Increase of Child Support

Always keep copies of the letters you send.

Your Name
Your Mailing Address or PO Box Number

Date of Letter

Dear **(most common to use first name)**,

I am writing to you about the child support payments. The court order from **(date of court order)** states that I am to receive $ **(amount) (frequency of payment, for example: twice per month on the (date or dates the monies are due to be paid)**.

It has been **(amount of elapsed time)** since the order was entered. Since then, you know that I have **(briefly list relevant financial changes in your life, such as job loss, salary reduction, health concern)**. Also, **(name of child)** has **(briefly list factors that increase**

expense, for example: started driving, started high school, is playing a team sport, got braces, has a health condition, is preparing for college, has tutoring needs).

Note: If it has been more than five years since the support was last changed (many jurisdictions consider two years acceptable), even if your ex doesn't like it, an increase will likely be in order.

Best Option:

I checked with the state's child support calculation software to see what new support might be. It looks like it would go from $**(current amount)** to $**(increased amount)**. I know that might be a big jump, so I am asking if you would agree to increasing support to $**(an amount less than the estimate above so your ex has incentive to agree)**.

Once you and I agree to an increased amount, we don't have to go through a fight in the courts, drag in all sorts of financial paperwork, and take lots of time off work. We just send our agreement to one lawyer who can write a draft. (**Technically, the lawyer will have to file a case, act as one side's attorney, and draft a settlement agreement.**) This will cost so much less than going through the courts.

Note: It may be a good idea to find out how much it would cost to make these arrangements through a lawyer and offer to pay for it.)

I am asking you to agree to a higher support amount. Please let me know your thoughts in writing by **(date)**?

Note: Since this option is vague and doesn't have you asking for a particular amount, you are likely to receive less or no answer.

I know this is tough, but I needed to ask and I wanted to come to you first and not turn it into anything messier or more stressful than it has to be. Thank you for reading this.

Let me know your reply.

Sincerely,
Your Name

Note: It can be a good idea to attach a particular bill or need for the increase, such as an estimate for the cost of braces or documentation of your salary cut. Your ex would be entitled to see these kinds of documents if you fought in court anyway.)

Chapter 10

Template 10.1 Cease and Desist Harassment Letter

Always keep copies of the letters you send.

Your Name
Your Mailing Address or PO Box
Date of Letter

Dear **(most common to use first name)**,

I am writing to you to advise you about a problem I am having when you **(general description of the problem, for example: text me repeatedly, call and hang up, come to my home and work unannounced, remove things from the home without agreement, curse at me in public, etc.).**

If you have a court order, use the following section:

The court order from **(date of court order)** states that you are not to **(general description of unwanted activity).**

You have **(state what he has done) (number of times he's done it)** since **(date it began or list the specific dates the offenses occurred).**

Your behavior is unwelcome and constitutes harassment (in violation of our court order—if appropriate). By this letter I demand that you cease and desist immediately. I will not give any further warnings on this issue. Hereafter, I will pursue my legal remedies to the fullest extent of the law. Should it become necessary for me to retain a lawyer hereinafter, I will ask that you be required to pay any legal fees and court costs.

I do not wish to dispute or discuss this matter with you in person or by telephone and will respond only to writing. No response to this letter is required, only that you cease and desist immediately.

PLEASE GOVERN YOURSELF ACCORDINGLY.

Sincerely,
Your Name

Note: I highly recommended that you avoid confrontations that can escalate. Always become more careful if you find it necessary to send a cease and desist letter.

Optional:

Cc: The ____Law Firm

Chapter 11

Template 11.1 Request to Pay the Mortgage on Time

Always keep copies of the letters you send.

Your Name
Your Mailing Address or PO Box Number
Date of Letter

Dear **(most common to use first name)**,

I am writing to you about the mortgage payments. The court order from **(date of court order)** states that you are to pay the mortgage amount of $**(amount)** on or before the due date, which is the **(date of each month the mortgage is due by)** of each month.

Historically, you have not paid the mortgage on time. In the last **(number of months)**, you have been late a total of **(number of times late)**.

Optional:

Late fees in the amount of $**(amount)** are charged each time the mortgage is late.

It is important that the mortgage be paid on time because **(select all that apply: my credit is impacted, your credit is impacted, our credit is impacted, it is stressful to deal with late payment notices, it is stressful to wonder if the house will enter foreclosure, securing our place to live is important)**.

If this issue is a temporary one, coming from an unexpected expense that got you off track, let me know. If the issue is connected to the dates you receive your pay, we may be able to figure out a way for it to work for everyone.

Please take this letter as a request that you pay the mortgage on time beginning with the next payment due on **(date)**.

If you need to contact me about this, please contact me in writing.

Sincerely,
Your Name

Template 11.2 Request to Bring a Mortgage Current

Always keep copies of the letters you send.

Your Name
Your Mailing Address or PO Box Number
Date of Letter

Dear **(most common to use first name)**,

I am writing to you about the mortgage payments. The court order from **(date of court order)** states that you are to pay the mortgage amount of $**(amount)** on or before the due date, which is the **(date of each month the mortgage is due by)** of each month.

Historically, you have not paid the mortgage on time. In the last **(number of months)** it has been late a total of **(number of times late)**.

Optional:

Late fees in the amount of $**(amount)** are charged each time the mortgage is late.

Currently, the mortgage company has not received a total of **(number of missing payments)** payments and is therefore owed a total of $**(amount)**.

Note: It is a good idea to attach a recent statement from the mortgage company to this letter.

The payments that are missing are: **(list the due dates of the payments here)**.

Optional if your ex made partial payments:

You paid the following partial payments: $**(amount)** on **(date of partial payment —list all that has occurred)**.

It is important that the mortgage be brought current because **(select all that apply: my credit is impacted negatively, your credit is impacted negatively, our credit is impacted negatively, it is stressful to deal with late payment notices, it is stressful to wonder if the house will enter foreclosure, securing our place to live is important, etc.)**.

The mortgage company has threatened to escalate the late payments and send the home into **(pre-foreclosure, foreclosure)** if $**(amount)** is not paid on or before **(date)**.

Please respond to my letter in writing (e-mail is acceptable) and advise me of when you plan to bring the mortgage current as soon as possible but no later than ten days from the date of this letter, which is **(date of deadline)**. (If you are fairly sure your ex does not have the financial ability to pay the amount necessary, ask him to provide a plan to prevent the home from foreclosing.)

Optional:

I have researched getting legal assistance to enforce your obligation to pay the mortgage on time and found that the fees to handle this matter in court will be no less than $1,500 and is usually much more for a contempt case. I do not want to go that route. Please consider this a demand for the payment needed so that the mortgage be brought current, and that you begin to pay the mortgage on time so that lawyers and the court do not have to become involved. If I have to retain a lawyer, I will ask him to recover his fees from you.

If you do not respond to this letter, I will take it that you admit to the amount that you are behind and that you refuse to pay, and I will seek legal remedies immediately to try and protect the home. Should the home foreclose and the equity I am entitled to is lost, I will pursue you for that amount also.

I would really like to work this out with you. Please write and reply.

Sincerely,
Your Name

Optional:

Cc: The _____Law Firm

(If you have or previously had a lawyer, it is often nice to let the other side know that you are copying the lawyer on this demand; it may make him more willing to pay. If you send a copy to a former lawyer, just include a note explaining that it is a copy for the lawyer's files and that you are not ready to proceed yet.)

Chapter 12

Template 12.1 Communications Log

Communications Log with _____											
Date	Notes	I Called, Texted, or Emailed			They Called, Texted, or Emailed			Message Left		Ok or Problem		Type of Problem
		C	T	E	C	T	E	Y	N	OK	NOT	
		C	T	E	C	T	E	Y	N	OK	NOT	
		C	T	E	C	T	E	Y	N	OK	NOT	
		C	T	E	C	T	E	Y	N	OK	NOT	
		C	T	E	C	T	E	Y	N	OK	NOT	
		C	T	E	C	T	E	Y	N	OK	NOT	
		C	T	E	C	T	E	Y	N	OK	NOT	
		C	T	E	C	T	E	Y	N	OK	NOT	
		C	T	E	C	T	E	Y	N	OK	NOT	
		C	T	E	C	T	E	Y	N	OK	NOT	
		C	T	E	C	T	E	Y	N	OK	NOT	
		C	T	E	C	T	E	Y	N	OK	NOT	
		C	T	E	C	T	E	Y	N	OK	NOT	
		C	T	E	C	T	E	Y	N	OK	NOT	
		C	T	E	C	T	E	Y	N	OK	NOT	
		C	T	E	C	T	E	Y	N	OK	NOT	
		C	T	E	C	T	E	Y	N	OK	NOT	
		C	T	E	C	T	E	Y	N	OK	NOT	
		C	T	E	C	T	E	Y	N	OK	NOT	
		C	T	E	C	T	E	Y	N	OK	NOT	
		C	T	E	C	T	E	Y	N	OK	NOT	
		C	T	E	C	T	E	Y	N	OK	NOT	
		C	T	E	C	T	E	Y	N	OK	NOT	
		C	T	E	C	T	E	Y	N	OK	NOT	
		C	T	E	C	T	E	Y	N	OK	NOT	
		C	T	E	C	T	E	Y	N	OK	NOT	

Communications Log with _____												
Date	Notes	I Called, Texted, or Emailed			They Called, Texted, or Emailed			Message Left		Ok or Problem		Type of Problem
		C	T	E	C	T	E	Y	N	OK	NOT	
		C	T	E	C	T	E	Y	N	OK	NOT	
		C	T	E	C	T	E	Y	N	OK	NOT	
		C	T	E	C	T	E	Y	N	OK	NOT	
		C	T	E	C	T	E	Y	N	OK	NOT	
		C	T	E	C	T	E	Y	N	OK	NOT	

Chapter 13

Resources on Parallel Parenting

Books

Lyster, Mimi. *Building a Parenting Agreement That Works: Child Custody Agreements Step by Step*. Berkeley, California: Nolo Press, 2010.

Ross, Julie and Judith Corcoran. *Joint Custody with a Jerk: Raising a Child with an Uncooperative Ex: A Hands-on, Practical Guide to Communicating with a Difficult Ex-Spouse*. New York: St. Martin's Griffin, 2011.

Stahl, Philip Michael. *Parenting after Divorce: Resolving Conflicts and Meeting Your Children's Needs*. Atascadero, California: Impact Publishers, 2007.

Websites

"Parallel Parenting Takes Your Children Out of the Middle of Conflict (Part 1)." Deena Stacer, PhD, Parents in Conflict. Posted January 2, 2013, accessed January 16, 2013, http://parentsinconflict.info/parallel-parenting-takes-your-children-out-of-the-middle-of-conflict/.

"Model Parallel Parenting Plan Order." State of Indiana, accessed January 16, 2013, www.in.gov/judiciary/files/rules-prop-ptg-2012-appendixb.pdf.

Chapter 15

Template 15.1 Evidence Chart

Evidence Chart							
#	Name	Description	Admitted	Denied	Not Offered	Ruled Inadmissable	Plaintiff or Defendant

Chapter 19

Template 19.1 Motion for Contempt Form

IN THE SUPERIOR COURT OF _____ COUNTY

STATE OF GEORGIA

_____,   *

Plaintiff   *   CIVIL ACTION

v.   *   FILE NO. _____

_____,   *

Defendant   *

PLAINTIFF/DEFENDANT'S MOTION FOR CONTEMPT

COMES NOW,_____**(your name)**_____, Plaintiff/Defendant in the above styled case and moves this Court to hold **(offender's name)**, in contempt for her/his flagrant failure to comply with this Court's Order by **(nature of offense)** and shows this Court as follows:

1.

This Court issued the Order offended and has proper jurisdiction and venue to enforce its Orders. The Plaintiff/Defendant resides at **(address that is within the county filed in)** and has been personally served.

2.

Pursuant to the **(your order name)**, the Plaintiff/Defendant was awarded _____ _____ _____. The Order specifically provides:

" **(quotation of the language in the Order telling the offender what they had to do)** ."

3.

The Plaintiff/Defendant (Offender) has refused to follow this Court's Order. He/She has __ _____ _____ _____. Their actions have resulted in injury to the Plaintiff/Defendant from delay and cost the Plaintiff/Defendant $____ out of pocket monies, damages from their failure like late fees on rent payments, bad marks on credit. See Exhibit "A" (If you have a piece of evidence to attach to prove your claim).

4.

The Plaintiff/Defendant has repeatedly asked the Plaintiff/Defendant (Offender) to comply with the Order and they are fully aware that they are in violation of this Court's Order. See Exhibit "____". (This exhibit is a copy of the demand letter sent to the Offender).

5.

Accordingly, the Plaintiff/Defendant was forced to pay $_____ to file and serve this case and seek the Court's intervention. The Plaintiff cannot afford to bear this cost without reimbursement. The Plaintiff/Defendant (Offender) must stand financially accountable for their actions.

WHEREFORE, the Plaintiff/Defendant requests the Court Order the following to purge the Contempt:

(1) That the Court order the payment of $_____ to the Plaintiff/Defendant;

(2) Set a Contempt hearing for the Plaintiff/Defendant (Offender) to show cause why the relief requested should not be given; and

(3) The Plaintiff/Defendant be awarded any such other and further relief as is appropriate in the circumstances.

Respectfully submitted this _____ day of _____, 201__.

_____

Your Name here, Pro Se Plaintiff/Defendant

(your mailing address here)

(your phone number)

Here is sample wording you can use for varying scenarios:

➤ Failure to pay child support

2. Pursuant to **(your Order name)**, the Plaintiff/Defendant was awarded child support in the amount of $_____ per month/week. The Order specifically provides:

" **(quotation of the language in the Order telling the offender what they had to do)** ."

3.... . paid only $____ as of **(date)**. Thus, the Plaintiff/Defendant owes the sum of $_____ as of date the arrearage is calculated to, **(the day of or before the filing date of the papers.**

> ➤ Failure to pay health insurance payments

2. Pursuant to the **(your Order name)**, the Plaintiff/Defendant was awarded health insurance payments in the amount of $_____ per month/week. The Order specifically provides:

3.… . paid only $____ as of **(date)**. Thus, the Plaintiff/Defendant owes the sum of $_____ as of date the arrearage is calculated to, (the day of or before the filing date of the papers.

> ➤ Failure to provide life insurance proof

2. Pursuant to the **(your Order name)**, the Plaintiff/Defendant **(the Offender)** was Ordered to provide life insurance coverage for the benefit of the minor children in the amount of $_____. The Order specifically provides:

3.… . not provided written proof from the insurance company showing the required coverage is in place with the proper beneficiary as of **(date)**.

> ➤ Failure to pay alimony payments

2. Pursuant to the **(your Order name)**, the Plaintiff/Defendant was awarded alimony payments in the amount of $_____ per month/week. The Order specifically provides:

3.… . paid only $____ as of **(date)**. Thus, the Plaintiff/Defendant owes the sum of $_____ as of **(date the arrearage is calculated to; must be the same day or before the filing date of the papers)**.

> ➤ Failure to pay property settlement payments

2. Pursuant to the **(your Order name)**, the Plaintiff/Defendant was awarded property settlement payments in the amount of $_____ per month/week. The Order specifically provides:

3.… . paid only $____ as of **(date)** . Thus, the Plaintiff/Defendant owes the sum of $_____ as of **(date the arrearage is calculated to; must be the same day or before the filing date of the papers)**.

> ➤ Failure to make marital debt payments

2. Pursuant to the **(your Order name)**, the Plaintiff/Defendant (Offender) was Ordered to make payments towards marital debt in the amount of $_____ per month/week. The Order specifically provides:

3.… . paid only $____ as of **(date)** . Thus, the Plaintiff/Defendant owes the sum of $_____ as of **(date the arrearage is calculated to; must be the same day or before the filing date of the papers)** payable directly to Plaintiff/Defendant or (name of creditor) .

Possible Exhibit "A"

Do not provide too many papers. I recommend one, maximum three, exhibits that directly demonstrate the willfulness of your ex's failure or the damages caused to you. Some good examples are as follows:

➤ A copy of NSF check

➤ A letter/note written to you telling you he'll never pay

➤ Late statements from your mortgage company

➤ Eviction/late notices from your apartment

➤ Overdue daycare bill

➤ Outstanding medical bill your ex was supposed to pay or assist with

➤ Credit reports with bad marks due to your ex's failures

➤ Child support agency payment summaries

Each document should be labeled by writing Exhibit "___" on the bottom, using capital letters for *A*, *B*, and *C*. One good reason to use an exhibit is that it gets the court to see documents before you have to try to introduce them into evidence at trial.

Notice of Contempt Hearing Form

IN THE SUPERIOR COURT OF _____ COUNTY

STATE OF _____

_____

Plaintiff,   *

                                              *

vs.   CIVIL ACTION FILE NO. _____

                                              *

                                              *

_____   *

Defendant

NOTICE OF CONTEMPT HEARING

The _____(insert Plaintiff or Defendant, whichever the Offender is) is hereby ORDERED to appear and show cause before the Honorable _____ _____, Judge of the Superior Court of _____ County, State of _____, on the _____ day of _____, 20__, at_____ o'clock ___.m., in Room _____ as to why the prayers for relief in the _____ (insert Plaintiff's or Defendant's, whichever you are) Motion for Contempt should not be granted.

This ___ day of _____, 201___.

_____

JUDGE

_____ COUNTY SUPERIOR COURT

Prepared By:

_____

(Your full name), Pro Se Plaintiff or Defendant, whichever you are
Your Full Address
Your Telephone number

(The Court will fill in the date, time, room number and "This day" line. All the rest you fill in.)

➤ Cover Letter that Accompanies Your Motion for Contempt to the Court for Filing

Date_____

Clerk of Court
Superior Court of _____ County
_____, GA _____

RE: You vs. Other side
Superior Court of _____ County
Civil Action File No_____(the case number assigned when you filed the Contempt)

Dear Clerk:

Enclosed please find an original and one copy of Motion for Contempt. Please file the original and return the copies to me in the enclosed self-addressed stamped envelope.

Thank you.

_____

Your signature
Your address

Letter to Request the Court's Staff Set a Court Date for your Motion to be Heard

Date_____

Clerk of Court

Superior Court of _____ County

_____, GA _____

RE: You vs. Other side

Superior Court of _____ County

Civil Action File No_____(the case number assigned when you filed the Contempt)

Dear Clerk:

Enclosed please find an original and two copies of a blank Notice of Hearing. Please set a hearing on the Motion for Contempt. Once set, please file the original and return the copies to me in the enclosed self-addressed stamped envelope.

Thank you.

_____

Your signature

Your Address

Evidence Exhibits

Item	Admitted	Not Admitted
P or D-1		
P or D-2		
P or D-3		
P or D-4		
P or D-5		
P or D-6		
P or D-7		

Letter to Request a Copy of Your Court Order Already in Existence

Always keep copies of the letters you send.

Date_____

Clerk of Court
Superior Court of _____ County
_____, GA _____

RE: You vs. Other side

Superior Court of _____ County
Civil Action File No_____(the case number of your Order)

Dear Clerk:

I am requesting a copy of my _____Order in case number _____
which was filed on or about _____(date). I am enclosing (call clerk's office to
find out cost) $_____ to cover the cost of the copies and postage or use the self-addressed
stamped envelope I have enclosed for your convenience. I do/do not require a certified copy.
(If certified: I have enclosed an additional $_____ to cover the cost of the certification.

Thank you.

_____
Your signature
Your Address

Monies Sought for Reimbursement

Amount	Why	Proof
$		
Total:		

Summons

SUPERIOR COURT OF _____ COUNTY

STATE OF _____

_____   CASE NO.: _____

PLAINTIFF

VS.

_____

DEFENDANT

TO THE ABOVE NAMED DEFENDANT:

You are hereby summoned and required to file with the Clerk of said Court and serve upon the Plaintiff's whose name and address is:

Your Full Name
Your Full Address
City, State, Zip

an answer to the compliant which is herewith served upon you, within 30 days after service of this summons, upon you, exclusive of the day of service. If you fail to do so, judgment by default will be taken against you for the relief demanded in the complaint.

_____County Superior Court

By_____
Deputy Clerk

Order on Contempt

You should be able to easily obtain this document for free from your local courthouse—this is a good model of what it generally looks like this:

IN THE SUPERIOR COURT OF _____ COUNTY

STATE OF _____

_____,	*
Plaintiff	* CIVIL ACTION
v.	* FILE NO. _____
_____,	*
Defendant	*

ORDER ON CONTEMPT

The Court held a duly noticed hearing on the Plaintiff's Motion for Contempt and finds as follows:

1.

The Defendant is/is not found in willful contempt of Court for failing to/doing:

_____

_____

_____

_____

The Defendant shall purge themselves of contempt by following this Order and paying the Ordered monies.

2.

The Plaintiff has requested monetary relief totaling $_____. The Court awards the Plaintiff a total of $_____ . This amount is to be paid by the Defendant directly to the Plaintiff in cash or negotiable funds on or before the close of business on_____ or by:_____

_____

_____

_____

3.

The Court finds as follows on the remaining issues:

_____

_____

_____

_____

SO ORDERED THIS _____ day of _____, 201__.

_____

JUDGE, SUPERIOR COURT

Verification Form

This is a general order full of blanks that the judge can fill in with his ruling on your matter. Sometimes it speeds your receipt of a ruling because a judge may just complete it on the spot so you can leave the courthouse with a final order on your contempt the same day that it was heard.

STATE OF _____

COUNTY OF _____

VERIFICATION

Personally appeared before me, the undersigned Notary Public, duly authorized by the laws of the State of _____ to administer oaths, _____(print your name)_____ _____, who, being first duly sworn, deposes and states on oath that the facts contained in the foregoing Motion for Contempt are true and correct.

_____

TYPE YOUR FULL NAME

Sworn to and subscribed before me this _____ day of _____, 201__.

_____

Notary Public

Template 19.2 Motion for Continuance

COMES NOW, (your name), Plaintiff/Defendant in the above styled case and moves this Court to grant a continuance of the (name of hearing) hearing currently scheduled for _____(date scheduled)_____.

I request the Court reset the above hearing to a later date to permit me time to _____

_____

_____.

See attached Exhibit "A" (If you have a piece of evidence to attach to prove the seriousness of your request-such as an already purchased airline ticket, surgery or other serious document. Remember, in general a court does not accommodate personal schedules. Seeking time to obtain a lawyer is the most common reason a continuance is sought and granted).

If the Court grants my requested continuance it will not harm the other side. (Note, if the delay will harm or affect the other side, it is best to be upfront about it and ask for your continuance with awareness of that fact.)

WHEREFORE, the Plaintiff/Defendant requests the Court grant their Motion for Continuance by resetting the Court Date to a future date. And that the Court permit the Plaintiff/Defendant be heard prior to (the scheduled court date) on their continuance as soon as possible under the circumstances.

Respectfully submitted this _____ day of _____, 201__.

_____

Your Name here, Pro Se Plaintiff/Defendant
Your mailing address here
Your phone number here

Chapter 25

Template 25.1 My Good and Bad Habits

My Good and Bad Habits

Please circle any of the habits you think I have and whether you think they help (Good Habit) or hold me back (Bad Habit). Do it quickly and go with your first thought. You can mark as many as you think I have. I am asking several people I trust to help me with this. You will be filling this out anonymously, so please be truthful.

	Good Habit	Bad Habit
Anxious		
Argumentative		
Bad listener		
Belching		
Borrowing money		
Bragging		
Caffeine addiction		
Chemical abuse		
Chewing tobacco		
Chewing with mouth open		
Chronic lateness		
Clutter		
Complaining		
Compulsive shopping		
Cracking knuckles		
Critical		
Cursing		
Dependency on sleeping pills		
Desiring something for nothing		
Drinking alcohol		
Drinking too many soft drinks		
Eating disorder		
Eating junk foods		
Eating too much chocolate		
Eating too much meat		
Eating too much sugar		

	Good Habit	Bad Habit
Eavesdropping		
Exaggerating		
Excess use of over-the-counter medicines		
Excessive throat clearing		
Fidgeting		
Fighting		
Flaking out		
Flatulence		
Freeloading		
Gambling		
Getting angry easily		
Gossiping		
Grinding teeth		
Hair pulling/twirling		
Interrupting		
Jealous		
Know-it-all		
Laziness		
Letting mail stack up		
Lip biting		
Littering		
Lying		
Monopolizing the conversation		
Nail biting		
Name dropping		
Nose picking		
Not cleaning		
Not putting things back		
Overeating		
Overspending		
Overworking		
Panicking		
Poor sleep habits		
Popping gum		
Porn addiction		
Procrastination		

	Good Habit	Bad Habit
Shoplifting		
Shyness		
Smoking		
Snoring		
Speeding		
Spitting		
Tailgating		
Talking during a movie		
Talking inappropriately on a cell phone		
Tapping pencil, fingers, etc.		
Thumb sucking		
Too much television		
Using illegal drugs		
Whining		
Worrying		

INDEX

The Smart Guide Series

Making Smart People Smarter

THE **SMART** GUIDE TO

GREEN LIVING

The most complete guide to green living ever published

How green living benefits your health as well as the Earth's

How green living can save you lots of money

Why the green economy and job market is an attractive, new, lucrative frontier

Julie Kerr **Gines**

Titles

Smart Guide To Bachelorette Parties
Smart Guide To Biology - Second Edition
Smart Guide To Bridge - Second Edition
Smart Guide To Chemistry - Second Edition
Smart Guide To Classical Music - Second Edition
Smart Guide To eBay
Smart Guide To Fighting Infection - Second Editions
Smart Guide To Freshwater Fishing - Second Edition
Smart Guide To Getting Published
Smart Guide To Green Living - Second Edition
Smart Guide To Healthy Grilling - Second Edition
Smart Guide To Hiking and Backpacking
Smarat Guide To The History of Science
Smart Guide To Horses and Riding - Second Edition
Smart Guide To Life After Divorce - Second Edition
Smart Guide To Managing Stress - Second Edition
Smart Guide To Nutrition - Second Edition
Smart Guide To Patents
Smart Guide To Practical Math - Second Edition
Smart Guide To Single Malt Scotch Whiskey - Second Edition
Smart Guide To Starting Your Own Business - Second Edition
Smart Guide To The Perfect Job Interview - Second Edition
Smart Guide To The Solar System - Second Edition
Smart Guide To Understanding Your Cat - Second Edition
Smart Guide To US Visas
Smart Guide To Wedding Weekend Events
Smart Guide To Wine - Second Edition

THE SMART GUIDE TO

BACHELORETTE PARTIES

Planning your dream
bachelorette party

Planning non-racy bashes,
spa parties, dinners and
Girls' Getaways

How to hire a hot male
dancer

The most complete guide
to bachelorette parties
ever published

Sharon **Naylor**

THE SMART GUIDE TO

BIOLOGY

A must-have book for
anyone who wants learn
the about world of living
things

Understand the workings
of plants and animals

Take the first step to
understanding the
biosphere

Anne **Maczulak**

THE SMART GUIDE TO

FRESHWATER FISHING

A complete guide to
everything you need to
know to catch freshwater
fish

Practical advice for the
novice and seasoned
angler alike

Detailed information on
more than 50 popular
freshwater species

Mike **Seymour**

THE SMART GUIDE TO

HEALTHY GRILLING

Low fat, low calorie grilling
tips and techniques

Make succulent heart
healthy burgers on your grill

Convert fish avoiders into
seafood lovers

Grill fresh veggies so tasty
even your kids will crave
them

Barry **Fast**

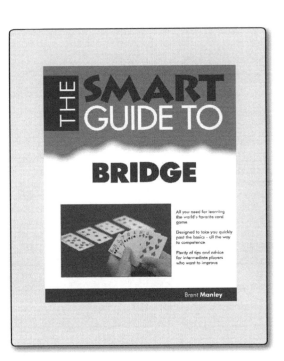

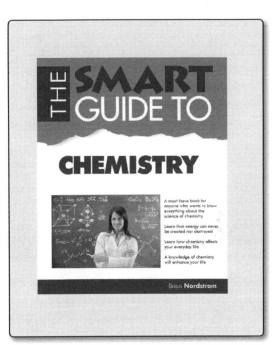

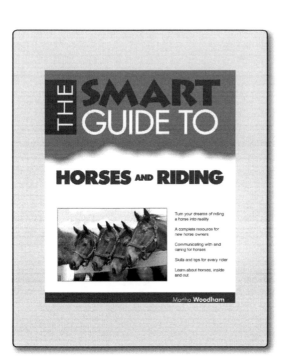

THE SMART GUIDE TO

HORSES AND RIDING

Turn your dreams of riding a horse into reality

A complete resource for new horse owners

Communicating with and caring for horses

Skills and tips for every rider

Learn about horses, inside and out

Martha **Woodham**

THE SMART GUIDE TO

SINGLE MALT SCOTCH WHISKY

A must-have book for anyone who wants to know anything about single malt Scotch whisky

Information about all the distilleries and the whisky they make

Learn how to taste and appreciate single malt Scotch Whisky

Elizabeth Riley **Bell**

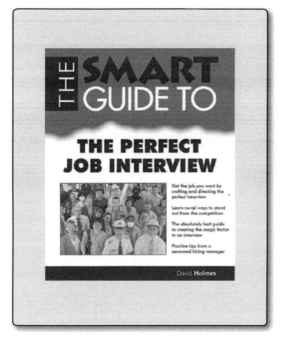

THE SMART GUIDE TO

THE PERFECT JOB INTERVIEW

Get the job you want by crafting and directing the perfect interview

Learn novel ways to stand out from the competition

The absolutely best guide to creating the magic factor in an interview

Practice tips from a seasoned hiring manager

David **Holmes**

THE SMART GUIDE TO

UNDERSTANDING YOUR CAT

If only cats could talk, they'd tell us almost everything in this book

How to connect with your cat

Everything you need to know to make your cat feel at home in your home

Take a closer look at your lovable feline friend

Carolyn **Janik**

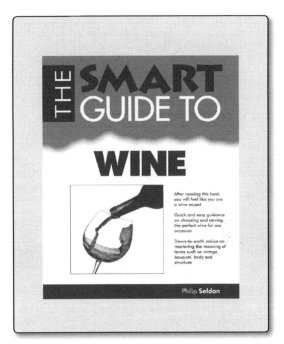

ABOUT THE AUTHOR

Tanya Stewart was a full-time divorce attorney with over fifteen years' experience and is not retired from practice. She founded her firm, The Stewart Law Firm, in 2001. She specialized exclusively in the practice of family law, including high-conflict divorce, multi-year litigation, child support, custody, and domestic violence. She has been featured as a family law expert on the radio, on local television, and in *Atlanta Parent* magazine. She has been a workshop leader and regularly featured speaker at the Alive! Expo at the Georgia Convention Center, which attracts close to 20,000 visitors annually.

She hosted the radio show *The Stress-Free Divorce* on HolisticGloberadio.com. In 2009, her show *How to Select Your Attorney* was the most downloaded of the year. She began her second business, The Work Well, providing stress coaching and business solutions to women in 2008. The Work Well "Gives Success a DeadlineTM."

Ms. Stewart is also a member of the American Association for Justice, Cobb Bar Association, and local family law bars. She has served as the chairman of the board of Georgia Rainbows, an international child grief organization. She is an ordained minister and chaplain at a local hospital. She has won National Moot Court competitions. She is a certified mediator. As a practicing Guardian Ad Litem, she is a court-appointed custody investigator, providing her recommendations to judges. She has been inducted into The Mensa Society, an organization for individuals scoring in the top 2 percent of the country's intelligence exams. She is currently finishing her PhD in metaphysics and is certified as an advanced clinical hypnotherapist, providing help to divorcées and those needing life changes.

She personally experienced a stress-free divorce and is an avid tennis player and runner. She is happy post-divorce, and her boundless energy is a source of inspiration for all of her clients, providing a tangible example of how applied choice and effort improves life.

Made in the USA
San Bernardino, CA
16 February 2015